PERSPECTIVES

A COMPANION READER TO THE INTRODUCTION TO ACADEMIC WRITING

THE FRESHMAN WRITING PROGRAM
DEPARTMENT OF ENGLISH
UNIVERSITY OF MARYLAND, COLLEGE PARK

General Editor: Adrianne Johnston DiMarco

Associate Editors:
Unit One and Appendix: Tricia Slusser
Unit Two: Dina L. Longhitano
Unit Three: Matthew Elliot
Unit Four: Patricia A. Lissner
Unit Five: Nancy O. M. Dickson
Unit Six: Adrianne Johnston DiMarco

PEARSON CUSTO

D1378169

Cover art "Reader," by Christian Stolte.

Printed in the United States of America

10 9 8 7 6 5 4 3 2 1

Please visit our website at www.pearsoncustom.com

ISBN 0–536–02650–5

BA 990322

PEARSON CUSTOM PUBLISHING
160 Gould Street/Needham Heights, MA 02494
A Pearson Education Company

Copyright Acknowledgments

"Spielberg's War is Hell," by Stephen Hunter, reprinted by permission from *The Washington Post*, July 24, 1998. Copyright 1998 The Washington Post.

"Now Arriving," by Paul Goldberger, reprinted from *The New Yorker*, September 28, 1998, The New Yorker.

"Give Children the Vote," by Vita Wallace, reprinted by permission from *The Nation*, October 14, 1991, The Nation.

"Who Shot Johnny?" by Debra Dickerson, reprinted by permission from *The New Republic*, January 1, 1996. Copyright 1996 The New Republic, Inc.

"Play Doctors on the Hill," by Charles Krauthammer, reprinted from *The Washington Post*, by permission of the Washington Post Writer's Group. Copyright 1999 The Washington Post Writer's Group.

"Henry V," by William Shakespeare, reprinted from *The Complete Pelican Shakespeare*, 1969 edited by Alfred Harbaye, Penguin Books, Ltd.

"Letter From a Birmingham Jail," by Martin Luther King, Jr., Copyright 1963 by Martin Luther King, Jr. Copyright renewed 1991 by Coretta Scott King. Reprinted by arrangement with The Heirs to the Estate of Martin Luther King, Jr., c/o Writer's House, Inc. as the agent for the proprietor. reprinted by permission from Writer's House, Inc.

"They Can Be a Couple, But Not Married," by Jeff Jacoby, reprinted from *Baltimore Sun*, July 17, 1996, by permission of the Boston Globe.

"Gay 'Marriage' Obfuscation," by Thomas Sowell, reprinted from *The Washington Times*, July 1996, by permission of Creators Syndicate.

"Should Same-Sex Couples Be Permitted to Marry?: Evan's Two Moms," by Anna Quindlen, reprinted from *Thinking Out Loud: On the Personal, the Political, the Public, and the Private*, 1997, by permission of the New York Times. Copyright 1997 The New York Times.

"Why I Changed My Mind," by Sidney Callahan, reprinted by permission from *Commonweal*, April 1994. Copyright 1994 Commonweal Foundation.

"Ice-T: Is the Issue Social Responsibility" by Michael Kinsley, reprinted by permission from *Time*, July 20, 1992.

"Or Is It Creative Freedom?" by Barbara Ehrenreich, reprinted by permission from *Time*, July 20, 1992.

"Making the Grade," by Kurt Wiesenfeld, reprinted by permission from *Newsweek*, June 17, 1996. All rights reserved.

"A Liberating Curriculum," by Roberta F. Borkat, reprinted by permission from *Newsweek*, April 12, 1993. All rights reserved.

"Imagebusters," by Todd Gitlin, reprinted by permission from *The American Prospect*, 16 Winter 1994. Copyright 1994 The American Prospect. All rights reserved.

Contents

An Introduction
to Perspectives

Many students enter the Freshman Writing classroom thinking, "Yuck. Another required writing class." And, indeed, English 101 will help you to become a better writer by providing you with a toolbox full of rhetorical, grammatical, and compositional skills. It will also help you learn the conventions of a particular genre of writing: Academic Writing. But there is much more to learn in English 101. This course will ask you to become a better, more critical reader, and a more complex thinker. You will be asked to examine the ways in which skilled writers present their perspectives, and others', on a variety of issues. And, because writing is the focal point of the course, you will be asked to present your own perspectives, and others', in writing.

Perspective is a fascinating thing to think about. As you are no doubt aware, sometimes there is no one "right" answer. Rather, there are a variety of viable, defensible points of view, each of which *looks* like the "right" answer when considered from the proper perspective. For example, take a look at the figure on the front cover of this book. Is the figure male or female? What is she or he reading? What is her or his cultural background? In which direction is the figure's head inclined? What is she or he looking at? I might argue that the figure is a woman, that her multi-colored eyes, hands, and feet represent the variety of cultures and experiences that make up her sense of identity, and that she is at once looking down into the book and out at the world, imagining the ways in which the text she is reading can help her make better sense of the world in which she lives. You might have a different "reading" of that figure. We could get together and debate our ideas, perhaps convincing one another on this point or that. At the very least, we would become aware of each other's point of view.

The readings in this text come from a wide variety of perspectives, and we expect that you, the readers, will read them from an equally wide variety of perspectives. Thinking critically about your own perspectives, and those of others, will be a large part of your work in this course. Learning to write about these thoughts will help you to have a voice in your classroom, in your university, and in your society. When you look at it from this perspective, English 101 becomes more than just a required class. It becomes an opportunity for you to learn more about who you are, what you think, and, perhaps most importantly, to put that knowledge to work for you.

The compilation of this reader has been a group effort, and, as such, it provides you and your teacher with the opportunity to draw on the experience and expertise of the many people who have taught and are currently teaching this course. You, too, have the chance to influence the content of future editions of this text. Tell your teacher what you think of the readings, suggest new articles that you read during your research — you might even consider submitting your own writing! As you read, think about your own perspectives on the issues about which you are reading, and imagine what it would mean if your own perspectives were represented here.

I would like to thank the teachers of English 101 — past, present, and future — for their assistance in conceiving of and developing this project. Many thanks, too, to the editorial staff who found time in their busy schedules to plan, read and edit submissions, write original material, and design this reader: Nancy O. M. Dickson, Matthew Elliott, Patricia A. Lissner, Dina L. Longhitano, and Tricia Slusser. Thanks to Linda Coleman, the Director of Freshman Writing, and the 1998–1999 team of Freshman Writing Coordinators — Allison Brovey, Matthew Elliott, Jaime Osterman, and Tricia Slusser — for their moral and logistical support. Thanks to John O'Brien of Pearson Custom Publishing for his input, patience, and high standards. Finally, thank you to our audience — you, the students of the University of Maryland College Park — without whom this project would have no exigence.

Adrianne Johnston DiMarco
May 1999

UNIT ONE

Introduction to Rhetoric

INTRODUCTION

If you are like most people, you probably consider "rhetoric" to be primarily a negative word. Like others, you may find yourself bombarded by communication—everything from letters to the editor to "dialogues" with telephone solicitors—that seems passionate and persuasive on the surface, but which, after a bit more thought, seems unconvincing, or maybe even thoughtless. A typical reaction is to dismiss such communication as "a bunch of rhetoric."

Have you ever stopped to consider, however, that the very same arguments you find lacking may be precisely the type of arguments that persuade other people? Further, did you know that any communication that seeks to persuade—whether not it is successful—qualifies as "rhetoric," and that rhetoric does not, in fact, always carry the negative connotation with which so many of us invest it? Simply stated, rhetoric is a word used to describe that communication which seeks to persuade, using the available means of influence.

Of course, the "available means of influence" vary, depending upon the audience the author seeks to sway. Information that will convince a parent to allow her teenager to attend a party is not the same as the information that will convince friends of the teen that they should attend. While a parent might be swayed after hearing that the party will be well-supervised, friends might be persuaded by hearing that their favorite local band will be playing, or that their latest "crush" will be there.

What should become clear, with the above example, is that not all discourse can effectively persuade every person. When you find yourself dismissing shoddy arguments, you should realize that the author probably did not have a certain sense of the audience he was addressing. The readings in the following chapter are designed to give you a clearer picture of rhetoric as writing that seeks to persuade. Additionally, you will have ample opportunity to work with issues of audience, and the schemas that audiences carry with them. Finally, you'll look at several pieces meant to persuade their readers that the subject at hand—everything from Hillary Clinton to New York's Grand Central Station—are praiseworthy. By that point, you should have a better idea how to determine the effectiveness of an argument, as well as how to construct your own persuasive rhetoric.

Tricia Slusser

I

What Is Rhetoric?

GENIUS AT WORK: HOW TO ARGUE

Diane Cyr

> *In this profile of prominent attorney Alan Dershowitz, Diane Cyr reveals some of Dershowitz's key thoughts on constructing and carrying out a successful argument. Readers will likely be surprised to discover what, in Dershowitz's estimation, constitutes a "victory." As it turns out, for this highly successful and often controversial lawyer, winning isn't everything.*

On the one hand, lawyer, professor, and professional provocateur Alan Dershowitz likes to find bones to pick. He has defended Claus von Bulow, Mike Tyson, O. J., and flag-burning. He has given his books such titles as *Contrary to Popular Opinion*, *Chutzpah*, and *Taking Liberties*. He does sound-byte battle with just about anyone on cable, network, or syndication.

On the other hand, his favorite joke goes like this: This man orders a bowl of soup at the same deli from the same waiter every day. One day the soup comes and the man doesn't eat it. So the waiter comes by and says, "You don't like the soup? Maybe it's too hot? Maybe it's too cold? What's the matter with it?"

The man looks at him and says, "Why don't you taste it?"

"All right, I'll taste it," says the waiter. Pause. "There's no spoon!"

"Aha!" says the man.

"AHA! AHA!" says Dershowitz, cracking up. Because his point is this: In-your-face opinions are one thing. In-your-face arguments are another. The best arguments aren't won by bullies who make you scream "Uncle!" They're won by the guys who make you go "Aha!"—who lead you subtly down the garden path of your own undoing.

In this, Dershowitz has had much practice. In 35 years of law (he's 59), he has consulted on or argued approximately 250 cases. He argues before judges, trial juries, grand juries, television audiences, classrooms, and assorted paying listeners and readers. He also argues with just about anyone, from his Harvard criminal-law students (student: "The policed invited them to headquarters . . ." Dershowitz: "They invited? What, like a little engraved card?") to crackpot Holocaust revisionists.

Throughout, he argues that argument—whether with one's spouse, boss, or chief justice—is best achieved "with a scalpel, not a hatchet." In other words, if you want to get your way, first you have to get your opponent invested in *wanting* things your way. Like the man in the deli, you have to go for the "Aha!"

The bad news: This methodology ain't easy. The good news: It's got a terrific track record.

"Look, this is not my invention," Dershowitz says of his argument style. "Socrates invented it. Rabbi Hillel invented it in the Talmud. It's a technique as old as recorded history, and the best philosophers, the best arguers, have always been those who led their students to come to their [own] conclusions." Take Jesus. "Did he say 'Don't cast the first stone?' He said, cast it! 'Let he who is without sin cast the first stone.' Socratic teaching at its best."

Of course, emulating Dershowitz is likely more doable (if less noble) than emulating Jesus or Hillel. For those who choose to wield the scalpel in their encounters with the Other, consider the following:

1 Don't fight just to win.

If you're arguing simply to best your opponent, you just might do it. But it won't make anyone happy. The object, remember, is to get the person on your side. "Why should anybody else want you to win?" Dershowitz reasons. "You have to have a motive beyond winning." So if you're fighting with your boss about more vacation time, or with your spouse about whose family to visit for Christmas, fight for the larger picture: the health of the relationship, or the ability to do a better job at work.

"Advocacy is not overpowering your opponent," says Dershowitz. "It's *persuading* your opponent that your ideas are his." Hence:

2 Know your opponent.

Injustice, ill will, shoddy treatment, and plain idiocy are all perfectly clear from one's own side. The harder part is placing yourself in the purported idiots' shoes to determine what accounts for their point of view. "You have to think like they do," he says. "You have to put yourself in their position." Which further means:

3 Don't assume the opponent's an idiot.

Go in swinging, and your opponents will swing back. Go in humble, shaking hands and making eye contact, and your opponent just might soften to hear your side. "Don't believe you're going to make yourself seem smarter than they are, or better then they are," says Dershowitz. "Assume they're smarter than you are, they're righter than you are, they believe in their position as much as you do or more, they're as nice as you are."

And by the way: Mean it. "Never underestimate your opponent," Dershowitz says. "I learned that from a friend of mine, a lawyer from Atlanta. She spoke with some kind of rural Alabama accent, and people thought they could run all over her. And she was one of the most brilliant lawyers and the best poker players I ever met."

4 Do your homework.

It's one thing to tell your boss that Project X is stupid. It's another to line up pages of market research, focus-group studies, customer call reports, budget projections, and profitability estimates. It's even better to bring it up in the context of the boss's top ten Favorite Things about Project X—and then show why Project Y (your baby) just might be what your boss really wanted all along.

Doing homework is more than merely lining up evidence for your side. It is also key to defusing intimidation. It's letting your opponent know that, yes, while she might be brighter, tougher, or better-paid than you, she can't slip you up on the facts. "I work my head off in preparation," says Dershowitz. "I have to know more than anyone in the room. I have to know the record cold. Know all the cases. Once I know everything, then I feel comfortable shifting to the psychological strategies of winning."

5 Then make your case.

The first serve in tennis tends to set the rhythm of the game. Same in arguing: Keep the serve, and you can keep things in your court.

The way to do it is to pick the framework for the argument. You want to go bowling with your buddies on Monday nights? Then set out a road-map you know your spouse will follow. Talk about your need for quality time with him, your crabbiness after a long day at work, your mutual need to make more time for fun. "Start the logical argument," says Dershowitz, "and let the other person be able to finish it for you. If you can frame the question knowing what the answer is going to lead to, then you don't have to hammer away."

Warning: Make your case real, or else prepare yourself for major resentment (perhaps accompanied by flying dishes) over your passive-aggressive shenanigans. "You must truly believe it," says Dershowitz. "It can't be an act. People see through acting."

6 Listen.

"This is key, key, key," says Dershowitz, who won't let his law students take notes for the first two weeks of class. Listening not only establishes respect for your opponent's point of view, it also clues you to information for your own case. Since people love the sounds of their own arguments, "take advantage of the last thing said," he says. "I always start my argument, in almost every case, with 'My opponent said . . .' And I turn their argument into my argument."

7 Avoid the following:

- EGO, the desire to be right at any cost (usually your own);
- EMOTION, the desire to engage in fights with bank tellers or rotten drivers, or to call your opponent a big, fat jerk; and
- ELOQUENCE, the desire to bowl over the opponent with craft and vocabulary (see "ego"). Advice: Stories and analogy work best. When defending, for instance, flag-burning (controversial), Dershowitz compared it to dumping tea in Boston Harbor (noncontroversial). "Let your opponent make the leap," he says.

8 And when you win, don't hog the credit.

If you've done a great job on your argument, your opponent just might end up thinking he has won—which is fine, if you've gotten your way. After all, the true object isn't winning, but getting on the same side. Once you're there, who cares who gets the credit?

Besides, credit usually backfires. "Claiming credit is a way of distancing people from your point of view," Dershowitz says. "I learned this early on when I clerked for a justice of the Supreme Court. When I would shove my ideas down his throat, he would always say to me, 'I'm the Justice, you're the law clerk.' So I learned the technique of subtly conveying information. In the end, it works. People will notice that when you're there, more is done."

In other words, strong arguments, by extrapolation, can actually lead to a chain reaction of "Ahas!" Rather than buckle under the sledge-hammer of your self-righteousness, your opponents and observers might simply observe, by your humble example, that yes, thank you, you were right all along.

Of course, that's assuming you're facing reasonable opponents. Mention one particular TV host to Dershowitz, for instance, and he grimaces. "I can't argue with someone like him," he says. "He's smug, he's self-righteous, he thinks he knows it all." Then he grins, momentarily emulating the dozens of Dershowitz faces on the book jackets stacked on the shelves behind his desk. "He could benefit," he says, "from coming to a class on the philosophy of law."

Questions:

1. What does Dershowitz find to be the best way to "win" an argument?
2. Imagine yourself as a high-profile lawyer like Dershowitz. What ways might his method of "arguing" be of benefit to you? In what (if any) ways might it harm your effectiveness?
3. Why does Dershowitz insist on the importance of knowing one's opponent? Think of a few instances where you've found yourself in an argument with someone you knew well. (How) were you able to use that knowledge of the other person to your advantage?

AIN'T I A WOMAN?

Sojourner Truth

Sojourner Truth, born into slavery around 1797 and sold numerous times, fled at approximately age thirty following a rape by one of her masters. After her escape, she dedicated much of the remaining fifty-six years of her life to speaking on spirituality as well as racial and gender inequalities. Though consistently a supporter of measures to gain racial equality, she refused to subordinate women's rights to issues of race. The selection that follows is believed to be an extemporaneous speech she gave at a religious meeting in 1851, recorded in the diary of an eyewitness. It is said that the people to whom she was speaking believed her to be less intellectually developed than they, and were not in favor of her being allowed to speak.

Well, children, where there is so much racket there must be something out of kilter. I think that 'twixt the negroes of the South and the women of the North, all talking about rights, the white men will be in a fix pretty soon. But what's all this here talking about?

That man over there says that women need to be helped into carriages, and lifted over ditches, and to have the best place everywhere. Nobody ever helps me into carriages, or over mud-puddles, or gives me any best place! And ain't I a woman? Look at me! Look at my arm! I have ploughed and planted, and gathered into barns, and no man could head me! And ain't I a woman? I could work as much and eat as much as a man—when I could get it—and bear the lash as well! And ain't I a woman? I have borne thirteen children, and seen them most all sold off to slavery, and when I cried out with my mother's grief, none but Jesus heard me! And ain't I a woman?

Then they talk about this thing in the head; what's this they call it? [Intellect, someone whispers.] That's it, honey. What's that got to do with women's rights or negro's rights? If my cup won't hold but a pint, and yours holds a quart, wouldn't you be mean not to let me have my little half-measure full?

Then that little man in black there, he says women can't have as much rights as men, 'cause Christ wasn't a woman! Where did your Christ come from? Where did your Christ come from? From God and a woman! Man had nothing to do with Him.

If the first woman God ever made was strong enough to turn the world upside down all alone, these women together ought to be able to turn it back, and get it right side up again! And now they is asking to do it, the men better let them.

Obliged to you for hearing on me, and now old Sojourner ain't got nothing more to say.

Questions:

1. Sojourner Truth's audience for the impromptu speech was composed largely of intellectuals who dealt mainly in abstract philosophies. In contrast, her knowledge tends toward the spiritual, folkloric and physical. Discuss her piece as rhetoric, and comment on the differences in her ways of knowing versus her audience's.

2. Discuss the piece in terms of style. What language skills does she use to create emphasis in her speech?

NOBODY MEAN MORE TO ME THAN YOU[1] AND THE FUTURE LIFE OF WILLIE JORDAN

June Jordan

> *This article by professor, poet, essayist and playwright June Jordan originally appeared in* On Call, *a collection of her political essays. Jordan's subject here is the power of language, both "Standard English" and "Black English." Within the essay, she narrates events from a course she taught in Black English, placing those events in relation to (and contrast with) the killing by police of Reggie Jordan, her student Willie Jordan's brother.*

Black English is not exactly a linguistic buffalo; as children, most of the thirty-five million Afro-Americans living here depend on this language for our discovery of the world. But then we approach our maturity inside a larger social body that will not support our efforts to become anything other than the clones of those who are neither our mothers nor our fathers. We begin to grow up in a house where every true mirror shows us the face of somebody who does not belong there, whose walk and whose talk will never look or sound "right," because that house was meant to shelter a family that is alien and hostile to us. As we learn our way around this environment, either we hide our original word habits, or we completely surrender our own voice, hoping to please those who will never respect anyone different from themselves: Black English is not exactly a linguistic buffalo, but we should understand its status as an endangered species, as a perishing, irreplaceable system of community intelligence, or we should expect its extinction, and, along with that, the extinguishing of much that constitutes our own proud, and singular, identity.

What we casually call "English," less and less defers to England and its "gentlemen." "English" is no longer a specific matter of geography or an element of class privilege; more than thirty-three countries use this tool as a means of "intranational communication."[2] Countries as disparate as Zimbabwe and Malaysia, or Israel and Uganda, use it as their non-native currency of convenience. Obviously, this tool, this "English," cannot function inside thirty-three discrete societies on the basis of rules and values absolutely determined somewhere else, in a thirty-fourth other country, for example.

In addition to that staggering congeries of non-native users of English, there are five countries, or 333,746,000 people, for whom this thing called "English" serves as a native tongue.[2] Approximately 10 percent of these native speakers of "English" are Afro-American citizens of the U.S.A. I cite these numbers and varieties of human beings dependent on "English" in order, quickly, to suggest how strange and how tenuous is any concept of "Standard English." Obviously, numerous forms of English now operate inside a natural, an uncontrollable, continuum of development. I would suppose "the standard" for English in Malaysia is not the same as "the standard" in Zimbabwe. I know that standard forms of English for Black people in this country do not copy that of Whites. And, in fact, the structural differences between these two kinds of English have intensified, becoming more Black, or less White, despite the expected homogenizing effects of television[3] and other mass media.

Nonetheless, White standards of English persist, supreme and unquestioned, in these United States. Despite our multi-lingual population, and despite the deepening Black and White cleavage within that conglomerate, White standards control our official and popular judgements of verbal proficiency and correct, or incorrect, language skills, including speech. In contrast to India, where at least fourteen languages co-exist as legitimate Indian languages, in contrast to Nicaragua, where all citizens are legally entitled to formal school instruction in their regional or tribal languages, compulsory education in America compels accommodation to exclusively White forms of "English." White English, in America, is "Standard English."

This story begins two years ago. I was teaching a new course, "In Search of the Invisible Black Woman," and my rather large class seemed evenly divided among young Black women and men. Five or six White students also sat in attendance. With unexpected speed and enthusiasm we had moved through historical narration of the 19th century to literature by and about Black women, in the 20th. I then assigned the first forty pages of Alice Walker's *The Color Purple*, and I came, eagerly, to class that morning:

"So!" I exclaimed, aloud. "What did you think? How did you like it?"

The students studied their hands, or the floor. There was no response. The tense, resistant feeling in the room fairly astounded me.

At last, one student, a young woman still not meeting my eyes, muttered something in my direction:

"What did you say?" I prompted her.

"Why she have them talk so funny. It don't sound right."

"You mean the language?"

Another student lifted his head: "It don't look right, neither. I couldn't hardly read it."

At this, several students dumped on the book. Just about unanimously, their criticisms targeted the language. I listened to what they wanted to say and silently marvelled at the similarities between their casual speech patterns and Alice Walker's written version of Black English.

But I decided against pointing to these identical traits of syntax. I wanted not to make them self-conscious about their own spoken language—not while they clearly felt it was "wrong." Instead I decided to swallow my astonishment. Here was a negative Black reaction to a prize-winning accomplishment of Black literature that White readers across the country had selected as a best seller. Black rejection was aimed at the one irreducibly Black element of Walker's work: the language—Celie's Black English. I wrote the opening lines of *The Color Purple* on the blackboard and asked the students to help me translate these sentences into Standard English:

You better not never tell nobody but God. It'd kill your mommy.

Dear God,
   I am fourteen years old. I have always been a good girl. Maybe you can give me a sign letting me know what is happening to me.

> Last spring after Little Lucious come I heard them fussing. He was pulling on her
> arm. She say it too soon, Fonso. I ain't well. Finally he leave her alone. A week go by,
> he pulling on her arm again. She say, Naw, I ain't gonna. Can't you see I'm already
> half dead, an all of the children.[4]

Our process of translation exploded with hilarity and even hysterical, shocked laughter: The Black writer, Alice Walker, knew what she was doing! If rudimentary criteria for good fiction include the manipulation of language so that the syntax and diction of sentences will tell you the identity of speakers, the probable age and sex and class of speakers, and even the locale—urban/rural/southern/western—then Walker had written, perfectly. This is the translation in Standard English that our class produced:

Absolutely, one should never confide in anybody besides God. Your secrets could
prove devastating to your mother.

Dear God,
   I am fourteen years old. I have always been good. But now, could you help me to
understand what is happening to me?
   Last spring, after my little brother, Lucious, was born, I heard my parents fighting. My father kept pulling at my mother's arm. But she told him, "it's too soon for
sex, Alfonso. I am still not feeling well." Finally, my father left her alone. A week went
by, and then he began bothering my mother, again: Pulling her arm. She told him,
"No, I won't! Can't you see I'm already exhausted from all of these children?"

(Our favorite line was "It's too soon for sex, Alfonso.")
   Once we could stop laughing, once we could stop our exponentially wild improvisations on the theme of Translated Black English, the students pushed to explain their own negative first reactions to their spoken language on the printed page. I thought it was probably akin to the shock of seeing yourself in a photograph for the first time. Most of the students had never before seen a written facsimile of the way they talk. None of the students had ever learned how to read and write their own verbal system of communication: Black English. Alternatively, this fact began to baffle or else bemuse and then infuriate my students. Why not? Was it too late? Could they learn how to do it, now? And, ultimately, the final test question, the one testing my sincerity: Could I teach them? Because I had never taught anyone Black English and, as far as I knew, no one, anywhere in the United States, had ever offered such a course, the best I could say was "I'll try."

*   *   *

He looked like a wrestler.
   He sat dead center in the packed room and, every time our eyes met, he quickly nodded his head as though anxious to reassure, and encourage me.
   Short, with strikingly broad shoulders and long arms, he spoke with a surprisingly high, soft voice that matched the soft bright movement of his eyes. His name was Willie Jordan. He would have seemed even more unlikely in the context of Contemporary Women's Poetry, except that ten or twelve other Black men were taking the course, as well. Still, Willie was conspicuous. His extreme fitness, the muscular density of his pres-

ence underscored the riveted, gentle attention that he gave to anything anyone said. Generally, he did not join the loud and rowdy dialogue flying back and forth, but there could be no doubt about his interest in our discussions. And, when he stood to present an argument he'd prepared, overnight, that nervous smile of his vanished and an irregular stammering replaced it, as he spoke with visceral sincerity, word by word.

That was how I met Willie Jordan. It was in between "In Search of the Invisible Black Women" and "The Art of Black English." I was waiting for departmental approval and I supposed that Willie might be, so to speak, killing time until he, too, could study Black English. But Willie really did want to explore contemporary women's poetry and, to that end, volunteered for extra research and never missed a class.

Towards the end of that semester, Willie approached me for an independent study project on South Africa. It would commence the next semester. I thought Willie's writing needed the kind of improvement only intense practice will yield. I knew his intelligence was outstanding. But he'd wholeheartedly opted for "Standard English" at a rather late age, and the results were stilted and frequently polysyllabic, simply for the sake of having more syllables. Willie's unnatural formality of language seemed to me consistent with the formality of his research into South African apartheid. As he projected his studies, he would have little time, indeed, for newspapers. Instead, more than 90 percent of his research would mean saturation in strictly historical, if not archival, material. I was certainly interested. It would be tricky to guide him into a more confident and spontaneous relationship both with language and apartheid. It was going to be wonderful to see what happened when he could catch up with himself, entirely, and talk back to the world.

September, 1984: Breezy fall weather and much excitement! My class, "The Art of Black English," was full to the limit of the fire laws. And in Independent Study, Willie Jordan showed up weekly, fifteen minutes early for each of our sessions. I was pretty happy to be teaching, altogether!

I remember an early class when a young brother, replete with his ever-present porkpie hat, raised his hand and then told us that most of what he'd heard was "all right" except it was "too clean." "The brothers on the street," he continued, "they mix it up more. Like 'fuck' and 'motherfuck.' Or like 'shit.'" He waited. I waited. Then all of us laughed a good while, and we got into a brawl about "correct" and "realistic" Black English that led to Rule 1.

Rule 1: *Black English is about a whole lot more than mothafuckin.*
As a criterion, we decided, "realistic" could take you anywhere you want to go. Artful places. Angry places. Eloquent and sweetalkin places. Polemical places. Church. And the local Bar & Grill. We were checking out a language, not a mood or a scene or one guy's forgettable mouthing off.

It was hard. For most of the students, learning Black English required a fallback to patterns and rhythms of speech that many of their parents had beaten out of them. I mean *beaten*. And, in a majority of cases, correct Black English could be achieved only by striving for *incorrect* Standard English, something they were still pushing at, quite uncertainly. This state of affairs led to Rule 2.

Rule 2: *If it's wrong in Standard English it's probably right in Black English, or, at least, you're hot.*
It was hard. Roommates and family members ridiculed their studies, or remained incredulous, "You *studying* that shit? At school?" But we were beginning to feel the companionship of pioneers. And we decided that we needed another rule that would establish each one of us as equally important to our success. This was Rule 3.

Rule 3: *If it don't sound like something that come out somebody mouth then it don't sound right. If it don't sound right then it ain't hardly right. Period.*
This rule produced two weeks of compositions in which the students agonizingly tried to spell the sound of the Black English sentence they wanted to convey. But Black English is, preeminently, an oral/spoken means of communication. *And spelling don't talk.* So we needed Rule 4.

Rule 4: *Forget about the spelling. Let the syntax carry you.*
Once we arrived at Rule 4 we started to fly, because syntax, the structure of an idea, leads you to the worldview of the speaker and reveals her values. The syntax of a sentence equals the structure of your consciousness. If we insisted that the language of Black English adheres to a distinctive Black syntax, then we were postulating a profound difference between White and Black people, *per se*. Was it a difference to prize or to obliterate?

There are three qualities of Black English—the presence of life, voice, and clarity—that intensify to a distinctive Black value system that we became excited about and self-consciously tried to maintain.

1. Black English has been produced by a pre-technocratic, if not anti-technological, culture. More, our culture has been constantly threatened by annihilation or, at least, the swallowed blurring of assimilation. Therefore, our language is a system constructed by people constantly needing to insist that we exist, that we are present. Our language devolves from a culture that abhors all abstraction, or anything tending to obscure or delete the fact of the human being who is here and now/the truth of the person who is speaking or listening. Consequently, *there is no passive voice construction possible in Black English.* For example, you cannot say, "Black English is being eliminated." You must say, instead, "White people eliminating Black English." The assumption of the presence of life governs all of Black English. Therefore, overwhelmingly, *all action takes place in the language of the present indicative.* And every sentence assumes the living and active participation of at least two human beings, the speaker and the listener.

2. A primary consequence of the person-centered values of Black English is the delivery of voice. If you speak, or write Black English, your ideas will necessarily possess that otherwise elusive attribute, *voice.*

3. One main benefit following from the person-centered values of Black English is that of *clarity.* If your idea, your sentence, assumes the pres-

ence of at least two living and active people, you will make it under-
standable, because the motivation behind every sentence is the wish to
say something real to somebody real.

As the weeks piled up, translation from Standard English into Black English or
vice versa occupied a hefty part of our course work.

Standard English (hereafter S.E.): "In considering the idea of studying Black English those questioned suggested—"

(What's the subject? Where's the person? Is anybody alive in here, in that idea?)

Black English (hereafter B.E.): "I been asking people what you think about somebody studying Black English and they answer me like this."

But there were interesting limits. You cannot "translate" instances of Standard English
preoccupied with abstraction or with nothing/nobody evidently alive, into Black English.
That would warp the language into uses antithetical to the guiding perspective of its community of users. Rather you must first change those Standard English sentences, themselves, into ideas consistent with the person-centered assumptions of Black English.

Guidelines for Black English

1. Minimal number of words for every idea: This is the source for the apho-
    ristic and/or poetic force of the language; eliminate every possible word.

2. Clarity: If the sentence is not clear it's not Black English.

3. Eliminate use of the verb *to be* whenever possible. This leads to the
    deployment of more descriptive and, therefore, more precise verbs.

4. Use *be* or *been* only when you want to describe a chronic, ongoing state
    of things.

    He *be* at the office, by 9. (He is always at the office by 9.)

    He *been* with her since forever.

5. Zero copula: Always eliminate the verb *to be* whenever it would com-
    bine with another verb, in Standard English.

    S.E.: She is going out with him.

    B.E.: She going out with him.

6. Eliminate *do* as in:

    S.E.: What do you think? What do you want?

    B.E.: What you think? What you want?

Rules number 3, 4, 5, and 6 provide for the use of the minimal number of verbs
per idea and, therefore, greater accuracy in the choice of verb.

7. In general, if you wish to say something really positive, try to formulate
    the idea using emphatic negative structure.

    S.E.: He's fabulous.

    B.E.: He bad.

8. Use double or triple negatives for dramatic emphasis.

S.E.: Tina Turner sings out of this world.

B.E.: Ain nobody sing like Tina.

9. Never use the *ed* suffix to indicate the past tense of a verb.

   S.E.: She closed the door.

   B.E.: She close the door. Or, she have close the door.

10. Regardless of intentional verb time, only use the third person singular, present indicative, for use of the verb *to have*, as an auxiliary.

    S.E.: He had his wallet then he lost it.

    B.E.: He have him wallet then he lose it.

    S.E.: We had seen that movie.

    B.E.: We seen that movie. Or, we have see that movie.

11. Observe a minimal inflection of verbs. Particularly, never change from the first person singular forms to the third person singular.

    S.E.: Present Tense Forms: He goes to the store.

    B.E.: He go to the store.

    S.E.: Past Tense Forms: He went to the store.

    B.E.: He go to the store. Or, he gone to the store. Or, he been to the store.

12. The possessive case scarcely ever appears in Black English. Never use an apostrophe ('s) construction. If you wander into a possessive case component of an idea, then keep logically consistent: *ours, his, theirs, mines.* But, most likely, if you bump into such a component, you have wandered outside the underlying worldview of Black English.

    S.E.: He will take their car tomorrow.

    B.E.: He taking they car tomorrow.

13. Plurality: Logical consistency, continued: If the modifier indicates plurality then the noun remains in the singular case.

    S.E.: He ate twelve doughnuts.

    B.E.: He eat twelve doughnut.

    S.E.: She has many books.

    B.E.: She have many book.

14. Listen for, or invent, special Black English forms of the past tense, such as: "He losted it. That what she felted." If they are clear and readily understood, then use them.

15. Do not hesitate to play with words, sometimes inventing them: e.g. "astropotomous" means huge like a hippo plus astronomical and, therefore, signifies real big.

16. In Black English, unless you keenly want to underscore the past tense nature of an action, stay in the present tense and rely on the overall context of your ideas for the conveyance of time and sequence.

17. Never use the suffix -*ly* form of an adverb in Black English.

    S.E.: The rain came down rather quickly.

    B.E. The rain come down pretty quick.

18. Never use the indefinite article *an* in Black English.

    S.E.: He wanted to ride an elephant.

    B.E.: He wanted to ride him a elephant.

19. Invariant syntax: in correct Black English it is possible to formulate an imperative, an interrogative, and a simple declarative idea with the same syntax:

    B.E.: You going to the store?

    You going to the store.

    You going to the store!

Where was Willie Jordan? We'd reached the mid-term of the semester. Students had formulated Black English guidelines, by consensus, and they were now writing with remarkable beauty, purpose, and enjoyment:

> I ain hardly speakin for everybody but myself so understan that.
> —KIM PARKS

Samples from student writings:

Janie have a great big ole hole inside her. Tea Cake the only thing that fit that hole. . . .

That pear tree beautiful to Janie, especial when bees fiddlin with the blossomin pear there growin large and lovely. But personal speakin, the love she get from starin at that tree ain the love what starin back at her in them relationship. (Monica Morris)

Love a big theme in, *They Eye Was Watching God*. Love show people new corners inside theyself. It pull out good stuff and stuff back bad stuff . . . Joe worship the doing uh his own hand and need other people to worship him too. But he ain't think about Janie that she a person and ought to live like anybody common do. Queen life not for Janie. (Monica Morris)

In both life and writin, Black womens have varietous experience of love that be cold like a iceberg or fiery like a inferno. Passion got for the other partner involve, man or women, seem as shallow, ankle-deep water or the most profoundest abyss. (Constance Evans)

Family love another bond that ain't never break under no pressure. (Constance Evans)

You know it really cold/When the friend you/Always get out the fire/Act like they don't know you/When you in the beat. (Constance Evans)

Big classroom discussion bout love at this time. I never take no class where us have any long arguin for and against for two or three day. New to me and great. I find the class time talkin a million time more interestin than detail bout the book. (Kathy Esseks)

As these examples suggest, Black English no longer limited the students, in any way. In fact, one of them Philip Garfield, would shortly "translate" a pivotal scene from Ibsen's *A Doll House*, as his final term paper.

Nora: I didn't gived no shit. I thinked you a asshole back then, too, you make it so hard for me save mines husband life.

Krogstad: Girl, it clear you ain't any idea what you done. You done exact what I once done, and I losed my reputation over it.

Nora: You asks me believe you once act brave save you wife life?

Krogstad: Law care less why you done it.

Nora: Law must suck.

Krogstad: Suck or no, if I wants, judge screw you wid dis paper.

Nora: No way, man. (Philip Garfield)

But where was Willie? Compulsively punctual, and always thoroughly prepared with neat typed compositions, he had disappeared. He failed to show up for our regularly scheduled conference, and I received neither a note nor a phone call of explanation. A whole week went by. I wondered if Willie had finally been captured by the extremely current happenings in South Africa: passage of a new constitution that did not enfranchise the Black majority and militant Black South African reaction to that affront. I wondered if he'd been hurt somewhere. I wondered if the serious workload of weekly readings and writings had over whelmed him and changed his mind about independent study. Where was Willie Jordan?

One week after the first conference that Willie missed, he called: "Hello, Professor Jordan? This is Willie. I'm sorry I wasn't there last week. But something has come up and I'm pretty upset. I'm sorry but I really can't deal right now."

I asked Willie to drop by my office and just let me see that he was okay. He agreed to do that. When I saw him I knew something hideous had happened. Something had hurt him and scared him to the marrow. He was all agitated and stammering and terse and incoherent. At last, his sadly jumbled account let me surmise, as follows: Brooklyn police had murdered his unarmed, twenty-five-year-old brother, Reggie Jordan. Neither Willie nor his elderly parents knew what to do about it. Nobody from the press was interested. His folks had no money. Police ran his family around and around, to no point. And Reggie was really dead. And Willie wanted to fight, but he felt helpless.

*   *   *

With Willie's permission I began to try to secure legal counsel for the Jordan family. Unfortunately, Black victims of police violence are truly numerous, while the resources available to prosecute their killers are truly scarce. A friend of mine at the Center for Constitutional Rights estimated that just the preparatory costs for bringing the cops into court normally approaches $180,000. Unless the execution of Reggie Jordan became a major community cause for organizing and protest, his murder would simply become a statistical item.

Again, with Willie's permission, I contacted every newspaper and media person I could think of. But the Bastone feature article in *The Village Voice* was the only result from that canvassing.

Again, with Willie's permission, I presented the case to my class in Black English. We had talked about the politics of language. We had talked about love and sex and child abuse and men and women. But the murder of Reggie Jordan broke like a hurricane across the room.

There are few "issues" as endemic to Black life as police violence. Most of the students knew and respected and liked Jordan. Many of them came from the very neighborhood where the murder had occurred. All of the students had known somebody close to them who had been killed by police, or had known frightening moments of gratuitous confrontation with the cops. They wanted to do everything at once to avenge death. Number One: They decided to compose a personal statement of condolence to Willie Jordan and his family, written in Black English. Number Two: They decided to compose individual messages to the police, in Black English. These should be prefaced by an explanatory paragraph composed by the entire group. Number Three: These individual messages, with their lead paragraph, should be sent to *Newsday*.

The morning after we agreed on these objectives, one of the young women students appeared with an unidentified visitor, who sat through the class, smiling in a peculiar, comfortable way.

Now we had to make more tactical decisions. Because we wanted the messages published, and because we thought it imperative that our outrage be known by the police, the tactical question was this: Should the opening, group paragraph be written in Black English or Standard English?

I have seldom been privy to a discussion with so much heart at the dead beat of it. I will never forget the eloquence, the sudden haltings of speech, the fierce struggle against tears, the furious throwaway, and useless explosions that this question elicited.

That one question contained several others, each of them extraordinarily painful to even contemplate. How best to serve the memory of Reggie Jordan? Should we use the language of the killer—Standard English—in order to make our ideas acceptable to those controlling the killers? But wouldn't what we had to say be rejected, summarily, if we said it in our own language, the language of the victim, Reggie Jordan? But if we sought to express ourselves by abandoning our language wouldn't that mean our suicide on top of Reggie's murder? But if we expressed ourselves in our own language wouldn't that be suicidal to the wish to communicate with those who, evidently, did not give a damn about us/Reggie/police violence in the Black community?

At the end of one of the longest, most difficult hours of my own life, the students voted, unanimously, to preface their individual messages with a paragraph composed in the language of Reggie Jordan. "*At least we don't give up nothing else. At least we stick to the truth: Be who we been. And stay all the way with Reggie.*"

It was heartbreaking to proceed, from that point. Everyone in the room realized that our decision in favor of Black English had doomed our writings, even as the distinctive reality of our Black lives always has doomed our efforts to "be who we been" in this country.

I went to the black board and took down this paragraph dictated by the class:

YOU COPS!

WE THE BROTHER AND SISTER OF WILLIE JORDAN, A FELLOW STONY
BROOK STUDENT WHO THE BROTHER OF THE DEAD REGGIE JORDAN.
REGGIE, LIKE MANY BROTHER AND SISTER, HE A VICTIM OF BRUTAL
RACIST POLICE, OCTOBER 25, 1984. US APPALL, FED UP, BECAUSE THAT
ANOTHER SENSELESS DEATH WHAT OCCUR IN OUR COMMUNITY. THIS
WHAT WE FEEL, THIS, FROM OUR HEART, FOR WE AIN'T STAYIN' SILENT
NO MORE.

With the completion of this introduction, nobody said anything. I asked for comments. At this invitation, the unidentified visitor, a young Black man, ceaselessly smiling, raised his hand. He was, it so happens, a rookie cop. He had just joined the force
in September and he said, he thought he should clarify a few things. So he came forward and sprawled easily into a posture of barroom, or fire-side, nostalgia:

"See," Officer Charles enlightened us, "Most times when you out on the street and
something come down you do one of two things. Over-react or under-react. Now, if
you under-react then you can get yourself kilt. And if you over-react then maybe you
kill somebody. Fortunately it's about nine times out of ten and you will over-react. So
the brother got kilt. And I'm sorry about that, believe me. But what you have to
understand is what kilt him: Over-reaction. That's all. Now you talk about Black people and White police but see, now, I'm a cop myself. And (big smile) I'm Black. And
just a couple months ago I was on the other side. But it's the same for me. You a cop,
you the ultimate authority: the Ultimate Authority. And you on the street, most of the
time you can only do one of the two things: over-react or under-react. That's all it is
with the brother. Over-reaction. Didn't have nothing to do with race."

That morning Officer Charles had the good fortune to escape without being
boiled alive. But barely. And I remember the pride of his smile when I read about the
fate of Black policemen and other collaborators, in South Africa. I remember him,
and I remember the shock and palpable feeling of shame that filled the room. It was
as though that foolish, and deadly, young man had just relieved himself of his foolish, and deadly, explanation, face to face with the grief of Reggie Jordan's father and
Reggie Jordan's mother. Class ended quietly. I copied the paragraph from the blackboard, collected the individual messages and left to type them up.

Newsday rejected the piece.

The Village Voice could not find room in their "Letters" section to print the individual messages from the students to the police.

None of the TV news reporters picked up the story.

Nobody raised $180,000 to prosecute the murder of Reggie Jordan.

Reggie Jordan is really dead.

I asked Willie Jordan to write an essay pulling together everything important to
him from that semester. He was still deeply beside himself with frustration and
amazement and loss. This is what he wrote, unedited, and in its entirety:

Throughout the course of this semester I have been researching the effects of oppression and exploitation along racial lines in South Africa and its neighboring countries. I have become aware of South African police brutalization of native Africans beyond the extent of the law, even though the laws themselves are catalyst affliction upon Black men, women and children. Many Africans die each year as a result of the deliberate use of police force to protect the white power structure.

Social control agents in South Africa, such as policemen, are also used to force compliance among citizens through both overt and covert tactics. It is not uncommon to find bold-faced coercion and cold-blooded killings of Blacks by South African police for undetermined and/or inadequate reasons. Perhaps the truth is that the only reasons for this heinous treatment of Blacks rests in racial differences. We should also understand that what is conveyed through the media is not always accurate and may sometimes be construed as the tip of the iceberg at best.

I recently received a painful reminder that racism, poverty, and the abuse of power are global problems which are by no means unique to South Africa. On October 25, 1984 at approximately 3:00 p.m. my brother, Mr. Reginald Jordan, was shot and killed by two New York City policemen from the 75th precinct in the East New York section of Brooklyn. His life ended at the age of twenty-five. Even up to this current point in time the Police Department has failed to provide my family, which consists of five brothers, eight sisters, and two parents, with a plausible reason for Reggie's death. Out of the many stories that were given to my family by the Police Department, not one of them seems to hold water. In fact, I honestly believe that the Police Department's assessment of my brother's murder is nothing short of ABSOLUTE BULLSHIT, and thus far no evidence had been produced to alter perception of the situation.

Furthermore, I believe that one of three cases may have occurred in this incident. First, Reggie's death may have been the desired outcome of the police officer's action, in which case the killing was premeditated. Or, it was a case of mistaken identity, which clarifies the fact that the two officers who killed my brother and their commanding parties are all grossly incompetent. Or both of the above cases are correct, i.e., Reggie's murderers intended to kill him and the Police Department behaved insubordinately.

Part of the argument of the officers who shot Reggie was that he had attacked one of them and took his gun. This was their major claim. They also said that only one of them had actually shot Reggie. The facts, however, speak for themselves. According to the Death Certificate and autopsy report, Reggie was shot eight times from point-blank range. The Doctor who performed the autopsy told me himself that two bullets entered the side of my brother's head, four bullets were sprayed into his back, and two bullets struck him in the back of his legs. It is obvious that unnecessary force was used by the police and that it is extremely difficult to shoot someone in his back when he is attacking or approaching you.

After experiencing a situation like this and researching South Africa I believe that to a large degree, justice may only exist as rhetoric. I find it difficult to talk of true justice when the oppression of my people both at home and abroad attests to the fact that inequality and injustice are serious problems whereby Blacks and Third World people are perpetually short-changed by society. Something has to be done about the way in which this world is set up. Although it is a difficult task, we do have the power to make a change.

—*WILLIE J. JORDAN, JR.*
EGL 487, SECTION 58, NOVEMBER 14, 1984

Notes

1. Black English aphorisms crafted by Monica Morris, a junior at S.U.N.Y., Stony Brook, October, 1984.

2. *English Is Spreading, But What Is English?* A presentation by Professor S. N. Sridhar, Department of Linguistics, S.U.N.Y., Stony Brook, April 9, 1985: Dean's Convocation Among the Disciplines.

3. *New York Times*, March 15, 1985, Section One, p. 14: Report on Study by Linguists at the University of Pennsylvania.

4. Alice Walker. *The Color Purple* (New York: Harcourt Brace Jovanovich, 1982), p. 11.

Questions:

1. Jordan's students felt strongly about whether to preface their letters to the police officers in Standard English or Black English. Why did they ultimately choose Black English? What were the benefits? The drawbacks? In more general terms, what are the benefits to having and using Standard English? What are its drawbacks?

2. Many of us use different "voices" to speak to different people. For example, we often find ourselves speaking to teachers and employers in a more formal manner, while we speak to friends and parents in a less formal way. Certainly, too, there are other differences between the way we address friends and the way we address parents. Why might that be the case? How is it that we make decisions about how best to speak to others?

3. Jordan's students spent much time translating texts from Standard English to Black English and vice versa. Why did they do that, and what did they learn in the process?

4. Translation can take many forms. It can take the more traditional form, as when someone translates from English to Spanish, for example. There are also the more typical, less obvious forms, as when someone translates the lyrics to a song for parents who aren't familiar with today's "slang," or when a doctor translates a medical condition into language that the typical patient can understand. Think back to the last time you had to do some sort of "translating." Why was it necessary to translate? What did you think about as you were deciding how to present the material you were translating? What was the process like? Was anything lost or gained in the translation?

II

Audience and Schema

NYU APPLICATION ESSAY

Hugh Gallagher

The following is quoted from "an actual essay written by a college applicant. The author, Hugh Gallagher, is reputed to attend NYU."

3a.   ESSAY: in order for the admission staff of our college to get to know you, the applicant, better, we ask that you answer the following questions: are there any significant experiences you have had, or accomplishments you have realized, that have helped to define you as a person?

I am a dynamic figure, often seen scaling walls and crushing ice. I have been known to remodel train stations on my lunch break, making them more efficient in the area of heat retention. I translate ethnic slurs for Cuban refugees, I write award-winning operas, I manage time efficiently. Occasionally, I tread water for three days in a row. I woo women with my sensuous and godlike trombone playing, I pilot bicycles up severe inclines with unflagging speed, and I cook Thirty-Minute Brownies in twenty minutes. I am an expert in stucco, a veteran in love, and an outlaw in Peru. Using only a hoe and a large glass of water, I once single-handedly defended a small village in the Amazon Basin from a horde of ferocious army ants. I play bluegrass cello, I was once scouted by the Mets, I am the subject of numerous documentaries. When I'm bored, I build large suspension bridges in my yard. I enjoy urban hang gliding. On Wednesdays, after school, I repair electrical appliances free of charge. I am an abstract artist, a concrete analyst, and a ruthless bookie. Critics worldwide swoon over my original line of corduroy eveningware. I don't perspire. I am a private citizen, yet I receive fan mail. I have been caller number nine and have won the weekend passes. Last summer, I toured New Jersey with a traveling centrifugal-force demonstration.

I bat .400. My deft floral arrangements have earned me fame in the international botany circles. Children trust me. I can hurl tennis rackets at small moving objects with deadly accuracy. I once read Paradise Lost, Moby Dick, and David Copperfield in one day and still had time to refurbish an entire dining room that evening. I know the exact location of every food item in the supermarket. I have performed several covert operations for the CIA, I sleep once a week; when I do sleep, I sleep in a chair. While on vacation in Canada, I successfully negotiated with a group of terrorists who had seized a small bakery. The laws of physics do not apply to me. I balance, I weave, I dodge, I frolic, and my bills are paid. On weekend, to let off steam, I participate in full-contact Origami. Years ago, I discovered the meaning of life, but forgot to write it down. I have made extraordinary four course meals using only a mouli and a toaster oven. I breed prizewinning clams. I have won bullfights in San Juan, cliff-diving competitions in Sri Lanka, and spelling bees at the Kremlin. I have played Hamlet, I have performed open-heart surgery, and I have spoken with Elvis. But I have not yet gone to college. Not a bad essay, I would say, as one who has done almost none of these things.

Questions:

1. Consider Gallagher's audience. What reaction do you imagine a college admission board would have to such an essay? Is there evidence that Gallagher was aware of his audience? If so, what?

2. Imagine (or recall) writing a college admission essay of your own. What are your audience's schemas for such an essay? What steps would you take to present a credible ethos?

MEGA BUYS

Franklin Saige

> *The following is an excerpt from an essay Saige wrote for* Plain, *a publication that advocates an ethic of simple living. Use clues from the essay to construct a fuller picture of the audience to whom Saige is writing. When you've finished reading, consider how Saige might have written to an audience with an opposing point of view.*

A television ad for MCI reportedly features a child star chanting, "There will be a road. It will not connect two points. It will connect all points. It will not go from here to there. There will be no there. We will all only be here." Maybe this is actually a profound utterance, if we listen carefully, rather than the baloney it appears to be. Because even though the rumble of the bulldozers clearing the way for the information superhighway is fairly distant, perhaps it's time to listen, and then ask just where exactly is this "here" where we will all be?

One of the perils of modern technology is that it is invented to be sold, as opposed to most earlier inventions, which were made to be used by the inventor, the inventor's patron, or the community. Modern technology comes clothed in seductive imagery in order to make the sale, but it can take away our freedom once we buy into it. It takes away our freedom by reducing our ability to choose—our ability to choose not to think in terms of "organization" or having our schedules "managed," for example. It takes away our freedom by narrowing our options to a set of preprogrammed choices. It removes the sensory complexity that is the most obvious characteristic of the lived world.

Of course, there is another school of thought on this question: Most people believe that technology barely influences how we live our lives. "It's what we *do* with technology that counts," they say. In other words, it depends on our moral fitness, our will to master the machine.

I suppose that even the most seductive forms of technology can be resisted, at least for a while. People resisted using automobiles at first. Many people thought the automobile would be too noisy, too fast, too pretentious, and just too expensive to fit the existing social fabric. Initially, most people did not buy one. But even though their fears about the automobile were quickly realized, soon everyone who could afford to own one, did. Then these automobiles were used in ways that gradually led to the weakening of the family and the community, not to mention the destruction of the landscape.

If hundreds of millions of car owners supposedly could choose how they would use this technology, what happened to make them choose destructive rather than supportive uses? Did they simply change their values on a whim? Or could something inherent in the technology have pulled them in a particular direction?

What does the automobile do *best*: pull families apart, cause urban sprawl, distort our sense of distance, or make travel more convenient? Only the last—convenience— is proven false every morning at rush hour, yet the car was sold to us on metaphors of speed and convenience. If we want to know where the information superhighway is leading us, maybe we should ask ourselves what it will do best.

To follow this road, we need to know that the term "information superhighway" is strictly the creation of the advertising muse. It was coined to piggyback onto the prestige of the "information highway" of interactive (meaning two-way) networked computers sharing text and data known as the Internet. What makes the superhighway super is that it will be a commercially run interactive video network put together by the mega telecommunication and cable television industries. "Interactive pay TV" would be a more accurate name for it, though the Internet and similar data networks will undoubtedly be incorporated and offered as incidental services. A true definition of the information superhighway would focus on its somewhat less lofty pursuits: video shopping, pay-per-view movies on demand (presently a $10 billion annual market for video rental stores), and two-way videophones.

Once the billions of dollars to build the system have been spent, every marketer will be in your living room and inside your head; your entertainment viewing choices, and especially your video shopping buying preferences, will be monitored and analyzed so that advertisers can turn around and market to you in a very targeted manner. Imagine one day using your television to purchase cloth diapers from the Virtual Wal-Mart. Then you switch to an entertainment program and *voila!* the commercials are all for Pampers, piped to your household as a result of your latest purchasing profile. That is the commercial dream, very interactive, through not exactly in the poetic way it is being portrayed.

Whatever the specific route the superhighway takes, it is obviously going to be *best* at invading your private life. Ultimately, its best use will be driving up consumption, which appeals to marketers more than to me, concerned as I am about the condition of the planet and my soul. I don't know about you, but I need less temptation to buy things, not more. And I don't want to be constantly sold to.

In *In the Absence of the Sacred*, Jerry Mander lists "Ten Recommended Attitudes About Technology." Along with number one ("Since most of what we are told about new technology comes from its proponents, be deeply skeptical of all claims") and number two ("Assume all technology guilty until proven innocent"), my favorite is number five: "Never judge a technology by the way it benefits you personally. Seek a holistic view of its impacts. The operative question is not if it benefits you, but who benefits most? And to what end?"

Since people appear to be more enslaved in their work and home lives than ever before, we could ask whether the problems their computers and electronic media seem to alleviate can be traced to the advent of computers themselves. Have computers and television speeded up economic life and undermined the social fabric?

None of the electronic technologies would be here if not for their utility as pillars of the consuming society. An ambulance is a "good" use for an internal combustion engine, but it takes a whole society of energy-guzzling car buyers addicted to mobility and speed to provide commercial reasons to make an internal combustion engine industry happen.

We are presently being assured that stepping into the virtual reality of the information superhighway and opening our minds to it is a good thing. Doubtless there will be many examples of this good: Grandparents will be able to see the grandkids on the videophone. The disabled will have more opportunities to be included.

And we will hear more and more about "virtual communities"—an exciting concept because, after all, the real ones have nearly disappeared. Perhaps almost-real ones will suffice, but I am unwilling to be part of a technology that can only exist if it drives me to consume more, which drains my will to seek out real community.

A woman at an organic farming conference I attended told the program speaker, who was against most new technologies, that even though she, too, thought these technologies might be harmful to the social fabric, still she felt she had to keep up with them: "Since this is what's going on in the world, don't we have to participate, just to survive?" No one could answer her then, and I have only part of the answer myself. I can only say I'm unwilling to drive the superhighway, and I sense that many others are deciding whether to continue on this ride or find an exit. On the other hand, the people I glimpse in their cubicles, or sitting around their TV hearths at home, don't seem too dissatisfied. What will wake them up? How can I help them reverse direction and get back out of the machine?

I have no interest in being part of a "movement" to "ban" or "boycott." To do that, I would have to become like my friends in the ecology movement, *connected* to a computer network in order to *exchange information* and get *organized*. I see the technology encouraging in them precisely the way of relating to lived experience that has brought about the crises that they seek to alleviate.

My strategy for exiting the information superhighway is simply never to enter it. The only "direct action" I can take is to live a real life, in real time, without viewing or networking or overconsuming anything. No input, no output. And I am going to tell anyone who will listen that real life, in a real community, in real reality, is better than the virtual reality of the information superhighway any day of the week.

Questions:

1. What specific details within the essay reveal the audience to whom Saige is writing? What are the values and concerns of that audience?

2. How might Saige have approached this essay if he had been writing to a hostile audience? What do you imagine he could have done to persuade them?

3. Do you agree or disagree with Saige's predictions for the future regarding the information superhighway? To what extent has the Internet already proven him right? Wrong?

4. If you read June Jordan's essay earlier in the reader, can you make some comparisons between Saige's solution and the Jordan class's solution? In each case, the answer seems to be not to participate in the oppressive instrument (here the Internet, there Standard English). Does that seem to be a good solution? In Saige's case, what are the benefits? The risks? Again, if you read the Jordan piece, what are the differences between the two situations that make a comparison risky?

ALL IVANA ALL THE TIME

Peter Carlson

> *The following short piece originally appeared in the "Magazine Reader"*
> *section of* The Washington Post, *where it was printed as a review of*
> *Ivana Trump's new magazine,* Ivana's Living in Style. *As you read, con-*
> *sider who the audience for this piece is. Just as important, consider who*
> *the audience for Trump's new magazine might be.*

One aspect of New York that isn't adequately covered in *The New Yorker* is the plague
of obnoxious, tasteless, egomaniacal rich people who infest the more fashionable
neighborhoods of Manhattan. But this oversight is more than rectified in the debut
issue of Ivana Trump's new magazine, *Ivana's Living in Style*, which turns out to be a
devastatingly scathing portrait of one of those people—Ivana herself.

"Welcome to the first issue of my new magazine," Ivana writes. "It's packed full of
informative but fun guides to the latest fashion trends, the best beauty buys, stylish
home decorating and easy wining and dining—all accompanied by pages and pages
of beautiful photographs."

What she doesn't say is that most of her photographs are of herself. The crack
Magazine Reader research staff (my daughter Emily) actually counted the number of
photos of Ivana in this 84-page mag. Guess how many there were . . . Wrong. Guess
higher . . . No, higher . . . The answer is 58! And that doesn't include six pictures that
just show Ivana's legs.

Ivana is very proud of her legs. She quotes her "boyfriend," Count Roffredo Gae-
tani, talking about her "fabulous legs" and she quotes her daughter Ivanka talking
about those same "amazing legs."

But Ivana doesn't show off just her gams. She also shows off her clothes, her Manhattan apartment, her special leopard-motif bedroom and the red Ferrari sports car
that the count bought for her—the one with the vanity plate that reads IVANA.

Of course the mag is not composed *entirely* of photos of Ivana. There are also
articles, like the one that tells readers how to pose for photos. It is illustrated with
photos of Ivana posing for photos. Another article tells how to frame photos. It is
illustrated with photos of Ivana's photos of Ivana.

Ivana does not reveal how often her magazine will appear. But one thing is certain: As long as she has a mirror, she'll never run out of story ideas.

Questions:

1. Who is the audience for this article? What evidence can you find for
   your answer?

2. Who seems to be the audience for *Ivana's Living in Style?* Again, what
   evidence can you supply?

CLASS ACTION

Dave Barry

> *What follows appears to be a commencement address written to the*
> *class of 1995, and it follows many of the conventions of such a piece of*
> *writing. In actuality, this is an article written by popular columnist*
> *Dave Barry, which appeared in* The Washington Post Magazine. *As*
> *you read, note what Barry states as his thesis. Is this really his point, or*
> *is he actually saying something very different?*

Commencement Address to the High School Class of 1995

I am especially pleased to be addressing you, the Class of 1995, because it just so happens that I graduated from Pleasantville (N.Y.) High School in 1965, which is exactly 30 million years ago.

A lot has changed since 1965, young people. For example, in those days, most schools did not have modern technology such as the Xerox brand copier machine. When teachers wanted to give us a test, they'd run it off on a "mimeograph" machine, which was a device originally developed by spies for the purpose of smearing ink so thoroughly that enemy code-breakers would never figure out what the original words were. The teachers would hand us students a piece of paper with questions that consisted mostly of purple smears, with an occasional word sprinkled in, like this:

"1. Assuming that (smear) and (smear) (smear) Renaissance (smear), helium (smear) Treaty of (smear) (smear) (smear) cosine. Cite three examples."

We'd ponder the question, then generally write down: "The Tigris and Euphrates rivers." Surprisingly often this turned out to be the correct answer, even in algebra.

Also, back in those days some schools still had real desks, solid wooden structures roomy enough to house Third World families and covered with the initials of students dating back to the original 12 disciples. Students traditionally carved these initials with a device called a "compass," which every student was required, for some mysterious scholastic reason, to buy (along with a "protractor"), and which seemed to have no practical purpose other than to carve initials into desks.

The best feature of these desks was that they had hinged tops, so that in critical classroom situations you could hide your head inside. We'd be sitting in class, and the teacher would be writing on the blackboard, imparting some fascinating and vital piece of information such as how many acute angles there are in an isosceles triangle (correct answer: the Tigris and Euphrates rivers), and in the back of the room a student such as Walter Gorski would stick his hand under his shirt and make a noise by forming an acute angle with his armpit, and the rest of us, rendered helpless by the almost unbearable humor of the situation, would quickly raise our desktops and duck our heads inside, ostrichlike, and the teacher would whirl around to face a roomful of vibrating bodies with desks for heads, emitting the kind of wet snorting sounds normally associated with severely congested horses.

Yes, we members of the Class of 1965 sometimes "acted up," but in the end we "toed the line," because back in those days, American society was different. It had a quality that you simply do not see today—a quality that I would define, for lack of a better term, as "Anthony Sabella." Mr. Sabella was the assistant principal at Pleasantville High. He was a stocky, stern-faced individual, approximately the width of Kansas, who had more authority than the U.S. Supreme Court, in the sense that if you were a male student who came to school wearing really tight pants, the U.S. Supreme Court was not empowered to explain the Pleasantville High Dress Code to you while holding you completely off the ground by your neck, whereas Mr. Sabella was.

At this juncture I'm sure the question that is on the minds of you young people is: "You wore tight pants?"

Yes, we did. We were not like you young males today, walking around in giant pants that are structurally identical to a Sears brand four-person mountain tent with pockets. Back in 1965 we preferred extremely tight pants, the kind that you never put your hands in the pockets of, because you'd never get them back out. We did not wear those pants because of some trivial passing "fad": we wore them because the Beatles wore them.

We idolized the Beatles, except for those of us who idolized the Rolling Stones, who in those days still had many of their original teeth. We argued passionately about which band was better, Beatles vs. Stones, because WE CARED ABOUT ISSUES. It's not like you young people today, listening passively, in your giant pants, to bands such as "Big Head Todd." What kind of name is THAT, young people? Back in our day, bands had names that STOOD for something, such as "Sam the Sham and the Pharaohs." You heard that name, and you knew instantly that this was a band with more than one dimension: a Sam the Sham dimension, and a Pharaohs dimension. When this band sang, the Class of '65 sang right along, with genuine feeling: "Wooly BULLLLLY, Wooly Bully; Wooly Bully, Wooly Bully, Wooly Bully." Call us idealistic, but those words MEANT something to us back in 1965, and I can still hear them ringing in my head today, even when I double my sedative dosage. Young people, these are words that speak across the generations from my class to yours, the Class of 1995, and that is why, as you prepare to remove your rental gowns and go out into the world, I want to end my speech by asking you to remember one very, very, very important thing, but I forgot what. Thank you: good luck: and somebody should wipe up this drool.

Questions:

1. Barry's stated thesis seems to be that "A lot has changed since 1965." What "evidence" does he provide to prove his point? Is this evidence compelling? Why or why not?

2. At the article's beginning, it seems as though the graduating class of 1995 is Barry's audience. Does that seem true? Might he actually be addressing another audience? If so, who? (In answering this question, you might consider, especially, the place of publication.)

3. What, by the end of the article, do we discover is Barry's *actual* thesis? Do you agree with his conclusion? Why or why not?

CHIPS, DIP AND DEEP THOUGHTS:
DOCTORS OF THINKOLOGY

Cathy Alter

> *Alter's piece, a generally playful description of her encounter with a convention held for members of the American Philosophical Association, originally appeared in* The Washington Post. *What becomes clear is that Alter's ideas about what conventions are for and how to have fun are in no way similar to the convention participants'.*

If, according to Plato, wonder is the feeling of a philosopher, and philosophy begins in wonder, then I wonder what I'm doing here.

The here in question, if there really is a here at all, is a reception for the American Philosophical Association, whose members descended upon Washington one winter week for their annual meeting. (I'll pause for a moment while you draw your own ironies.) During the APA's four-day conference and interview marathon, more than 2,300 philosophy graduate students, professors and academic glitterati attended talks with provocative titles like "Can Factualists Solve the Self-Location Problem?"; "The Boredom of His Days, or: Transformations in/of Heidegger's Moods"; and, proving tautologically that philosophers can too coin a phrase, "Zombanimals: Why Robots Are Just Zombie Animals."

Though I am not a philosopher, or even particularly thoughtful, I, too, have come here in question. Not the "Is God Dead?" "Do I exist?" "What is Time?" sort of fare. What business is that of mine? No, my question is: "What do philosophers do for dumb fun?"

"No, no, no. We don't have fun," disclaims my friend, the proud owner of multiple letters after his name. "But that doesn't mean you can't have some. Ask them what the difference is between analytic and continental philosophy. It'll drive them all nuts."

The Hatfields and the McCoys; the Sharks and the Jets; the Analytics and the Continentals. A rivalry as old as, well, I didn't know, but I had my $64,000 question and I was running with it.

For the evening reception, the International Ballroom at the Washington Hilton is dressed for an existential bar mitzvah. Soda straight or cut with the harder stuff, is drunk from plastic cups. Numbered tables are armed with bowls of chips and pretzels. At these tables, young philosophers-for-hire mingle with university faculty, who in turn, bombard each other with ideas, *ideas*, IDEAS!

Since the analytics are housed in the majority of U.S. philosophy departments, the continentals are definitely outnumbered here. I have no idea what a continental is—are we talking Maurice Chevalier types in ascots waving cigarette holders?—but I've got it on good authority that Northwestern's table is filled with them.

"Don't expect a one-word answer from them," warns a professor from Georgetown, who in her own circular discourse has managed to evade my analytic/continental question.

Northwestern's table, No. 37—a prime number, *coincidence?*—is occupied by two women and two men, who, even sitting down, exude such imposing intellectual rigor that I'm afraid to approach them. Averting my eyes, I hurry past, and aim for the potted plant, where I can collect myself. There I meet Neal, a graduate student from Oxford.

When I tell him I was too chicken to ask the Northwestern continentals how they "do philosophy," he rolls his eyes in disgust. "I bet they thought they were so cool. Probably had on nice clothes, good hair. Acting like they were English professors. The jerks."

"Does that mean you're an analytic?"

He fixed me with a stare and arched his eyebrows, well, archly. "Does it?"

At the University of Maryland table, a group is gathered around a cocktail napkin. "I really want to show you my graph of degrees of abstraction," says a woman in giant eyeglasses, pointing to the napkin. Her graph consists of two axes and a small black dot.

A man who looks like Harold Ramis adds, "It's a sketch of a novel mechanism schema."

"Well," counters Harold, "there can be how-actually dispossibilities."

When there's a standoff at the napkin, I drop my bombshell. "Are you guys analytics or continentals?"

Dead silence is followed by some shoe gazing.

"Well, I'm not a continental," says a new addition to the table, a man with an exceedingly bad comb-over.

"So you're an analytic?" I ask.

"What makes you say that?" he volleys back.

I should have known better than to assume a post hoc fallacy.

I'm hoping that Table 10, the North American Nietzsche Society, will have something to say on the matter. I wander my way across the room picking up snippets of conversation. At Table 51, a pretty blonde from the Society for Women in Philosophy comments over her wine, "There are a lot of dummies out there—both sexes."

Over by the bar, an ancient man with crazy Einstein hair says, "It's like the one-eyed fly landing on the window."

"Visual illusions seem not to have much impart on our motor," answers his friend.

I don't overhear a single person talking about slasher movies, the Web, or Monica.

I bump into Drew, who has just taped a segment of "No Dogs or Philosophers Allowed," a television talk show that discusses burning philosophical issues like consciousness, blasphemy and computer ethics.

"Do you know the difference between analytic and continental philosophy?" I ask.

"It's basically your alives versus your deads. Your Russells versus your Heideggers."

"I don't know," I start, "that seems sort of funny to me."

"What is fun?"

I walk away feeling a spreading void. When I finally find Nietzsche's table, it is totally deserted. I hear the sound of one hand clapping.

Questions:

1. What are Alter's expectations—her schema—regarding conferences and conventions? How do her preconceived notions of what happens at a conference affect how she functions at the APA reception?

2. Think of an instance where you found yourself in a situation that was different from what you expected. (Your first time in college classes might be one example. Other examples might include attending a meeting, cultural celebration, or religious service of a type with which you were not previously familiar.) How did you make sense of the situation? Were you able, for example, to draw comparisons between that situation and another you were more familiar with? What else helped?

3. Imagine explaining something unfamiliar—perhaps your English 101 class, or your answer to question number 2—to a friend. What steps would you take in your writing to be sure that s/he is able to understand?

HAPPY CAMPERS

Christopher Buckley

> *Christopher Buckley's "Happy Campers," which originally appeared in*
> The New Yorker, *is an obvious parody of a more traditional informa-*
> *tional letter to the parents of young campers. As you read, consider who*
> *the audience might actually be and why Buckley might be writing this*
> *"letter."*

Dear Camper Parents,

Thank you for the $5,000 down payment for your child's upcoming three-week
stay at Camp Earwig. We are looking forward to meeting him/her! In the meantime,
please fill out the following questionnaire:

Extras *(Rates are for three-week rental)*

Bed	$500
Drinking water:	
Lake	$5
Tap	$25
Bottled	$200
Soap *(large bar)*	$20
Food *(recommended)*	
raw	$750
cooked	$2,000
Mosquito-netting rental:	
wide-mesh type	$15
fine-mesh type	$150
Tennis racquet *(rec'd for killing bats)*	$50
Personal tear-gas supply *(rec'd for bears, moose, porcupines, etc.)*	$70
.357 Magnum pistol *(see above)*	$400
Marshmallows	$120
Roasting stick *(see above)*:	
knobbly pine	$10
splinter-free Burmese mahogany	$75
Staff tips	$1,500

Character Assessment

1. How would you describe your child's personality? (a) superb; (b) average; (c) better than cousins'; (d) sociopathic.

2. On a scale of 1 to 10, how willing and eager is your child when it comes
   to chores like cleaning up toxic waste or re-roofing the house?

3. Is your child pierced? If so, indicate where: (a) ears; (b) nose; (c) mouth; (d) would rather not say.

4. Is your child a finicky eater when it comes to such foods as squirrel, badger, and king snake?

5. Can your child "hack" into a bank's computer system and transfer money from one account to another? (*May qualify for special discount*).

Homesickness and Phone Calls

It may take some time for your child to adjust to the camp experience. To assist in this important transition, we ask that you not make contact with your child in any way during the three-week duration. Further, should your child manage to get a message to the outside, we ask that you ignore it. Remember that Earwig campers are prone to exaggeration, especially with concern to alleged instances of hazing, food poisoning, binge-drinking by counsellors, etc.

Optional Activities and Excursions

1. Three-Day Highway-Maintenance Field Trip. Children will work alongside seasoned state-correctional-facility inmates, learning how to pick up litter and clear away underbrush along scenic interstate highways. Teamwork, endurance, and "getting the heck out of the way" of oncoming vehicles are just some of the skills learned, along with getting to know people from different walks of life. $450.

2. Two-Day Junior-Smoke-Jumper Trip. Children will be dropped out of planes at a low altitude into the path of an exciting "out of control" forest fire as it advances on Camp Earwig. They quickly acquire lifesaving skills such as wind-shift detection, fire-wall digging, and running "like the dickens." $900. (*Includes parachute, flame-retardant suit, oxygen, and shovel*).

3. Five-Day, Six-Night Field Trip to Local Native American Casino. Children will work closely with counsellors as they try to "break the bank" at nearby Magua's Revenge Casino, run by the proud—and still fierce—Mashmaquoddy Nation. Includes workshops on card-counting, roulette-wheel fixing, and bartering your wristwatch for credit. $5,000. (*Cash only.*)

4. Seven-Day Blackfly-Eradication Program. As part of our continuing effort to bring about our own Silent Spring, campers will "take the war to the enemy," spending a rigorous but exhilarating week wading through nearby Swamp Eecheeatchoo (Mashmaquoddy for "Can't We Look for Food Somewhere Else?"), spraying insect breeding grounds with the latest in no-nonsense insecticides cooked up by Counsellor Andy (Anthrax) Widgely. Workshops include poisonous-snake identification, heat prostration, and coping with Giardia. $600. (*Emergency helicopter evacuation available for extra charge.*)

5. Three-Week House-Renovation Field Trip. Campers will learn how to renovate a decrepit house in a marginal neighborhood of a major American urban center. Working under the close supervision of a general contractor, campers will live on-site and experience the joys—and frustrations!—of putting in eighteen-hour days transforming "this old house" into a beautiful house with a "Sold!" sign out front. Conducted exclusively at the winter lodgings of Camp Director Big Mike Bargle. $200. (*Materials extra.*)

See you soon!

Questions:

1. At first sight, Buckley's article appears to be a letter to parents of children who are enrolled in a summer camp. What are that audience's interests and concerns?

2. It quickly becomes clear that Buckley's audience is really not what it appears. Who is his actual audience? What evidence can you find to support your claim?

3. "Happy Campers," we discover shortly after we begin reading, is a parody of the type of letter parents of campers might actually expect to receive. While Buckley is careful to reproduce many of the conventions of such a letter, he violates those conventions in other ways. In what ways does Buckley write according to our schema? In what ways does he disrupt our schema for such letters?

4. If you read Dave Barry's "Class Action," you likely noticed some similarities in his and Buckley's use of irony and humor to make a deeper, more serious point. What do you think of this tactic? Is it helpful, or does it ultimately weaken a writer's ability to be taken seriously in any way? (How) does this tactic depend on the author's intended audience?

THE DRUDGE-ON-THE-HIDE

Diane Gifford-Gonzalez

> *"The Drudge-on-the-Hide" originally appeared in* Archaeology. *In it, Diane Gifford-Gonzalez argues calls for a different visual representation of prehistoric women, one more in line with our growing knowledge of Stone Age gender roles. As you read, consider your own schemas regarding prehistoric life. What do you know of Stone Age women? Are your schemas similar to the ones the author is arguing against?*

Most of us would question a museum display with a heading that read: "In the Stone Age, men hunted, made tools and houses, created art, and performed rituals. Women stayed home, held babies, and scraped hides. Old people and children just hung out because they weren't useful, like men." Yet depictions of prehistoric life that accompany many displays and that appear in books convey that impression. This raises an intriguing question: our knowledge of Stone Age prehistory and the diversity of gender roles among modern foragers has grown during this century— why have visual artists failed to keep pace?

I recently studied 135 drawings of Cro-Magnon people in books intended for the general public. Stereotypical portrayals of men and women prevail. Man-the-Hunter and Man-the-Toolmaker, fit and in their prime, predominate. Women, unless young, decorative, and unclothed, work on hides and appear in the background along with the useless children and old folks. Woman as hide-worker is an extraordinarily potent symbol of primordial womanhood and female labor. I call her the Drudge-on-the-Hide. On her hands and knees, scraping a bloody hide, she is part of the scenery, doing dull and nasty work. To make matters worse, the Drudge is seldom shown using scraping tools, which makes her look not only irrelevant but incompetent. Hides are never stretched on frames, and women never work sitting or standing. They crouch or kneel, confronting the hide with, at best, a flake of stone. The image of a woman crouched on all fours conveys subservience and animality, with sexual overtones. Remember the rape scenes in *Quest for Fire* and *Clan of the Cave Bear?* Both feature unwilling female victims crouched on all fours, a blatant evocation of the Drudge's animality.

And what about the men? Consumed with hunting, toolmaking, and performing rituals, they never hold a baby, make ornaments, or, heaven forfend, relax. Do artists creating dioramic representations of early humans deliberately select subjects and viewpoints that marginalize women, children, and the elderly? Or do some of them, by following long-entrenched iconographic conventions, simply re-create prehistoric social conventions they themselves might, upon further reflection, call into question? I suspect that the latter is the case.

Those most responsible for these distorted images are scientific experts—people like me. We rush to correct an anachronistic tool or wrong-shaped skull in such renderings, but remain blind to the cultural messages these images send. We have not challenged artists on scientific grounds, nor have we offered alternative visions. Highly creative and more probable images have been created by French illustrator Véronique creative and more probable images have been created by French illustrator Véronique Ageorges and former Smithsonian artist John Gurche, both of whom are well-versed in archaeology and physical anthropology. Their "ancestors" include capable elders, active children, and strong women who create rock art, dance, make tools, and forage away from camp. Their men sometimes wear ornaments, smile, even sit idle.

The challenge for illustrators and experts is not to produce politically correct, quota-system illustration, e.g., Guys-on-Hides. Instead, we need to re-envision our ancestors, to think of prehistory as more than a repetitious set of "guy things." This requires knowledge of archaeological and fossil evidence, and an understanding of anthropology, ecology, and other relevant fields. Illustrations that reveal learned speculation about the past will stimulate rather than stultify. One such illustration by Ageorges had a profound effect on me. A handsome, slightly weathered Cro-Magnon couple sit at a fire. He gnaws on a roast rib. She squats at the fire cutting rib meat with a flint knife. Her muscular arms are bare and flexed, her brow a little furrowed as she speaks. Her face and arms suggest a world of strong women. I like that. Women had to be strong to survive in those times. If they had been as abject as the Drudge, we never would have made it out of the Stone Age. A creative illustrator can make this point with a few strokes of the brush.

Questions:

1. What are your schemas regarding prehistoric gender roles? Where did you develop those schemas?

2. Did the information Gifford-Gonzalez presents here change your mind regarding women of the Stone Age? Why or why not?

3. For most of us, representations of prehistoric women are not controversial, and as we learn more about them, our schemas are likely to shift with little resistance. Try imagining a more volatile subject, however. Think about how you might approach an argument which attempts to persuade an audience to change a schema in which they are heavily invested. For example, imagine trying to persuade a literature teacher who teaches Shakespeare and believes that he is the greatest writer of all time that, in fact, Toni Morrison is the greatest writer. Alternatively, imagine trying to persuade a friend who has a deep commitment to environmental preservation to invest in a company that has a record of killing large numbers of wildlife and destroying forest-rich areas, all in order to build low-cost housing for people in need. In each of those cases, what might you say to argue for a shift in schema (the first being a schema regarding "greatness" of an author, the second being a schema regarding what constitutes a preserving of the environment) ? How might you be able to demonstrate sensitivity to your audience's schema while still persuading them that a shift is necessary?

III

Encomia

THE AMAZING MRS. CLINTON

"The Amazing Mrs. Clinton" first appeared in The Economist *(a British publication) in October of 1998. It serves as a fine example of an encomium in the sense that it presents First Lady Hillary Rodham Clinton not just as a good woman, or even an excellent first lady, but rather as among the very best of public figures. As you read, pay special attention to the original topics of praise contained within, as well as the anecdote that begins the article.*

One summer weekend two years ago, America's newspapers and talk shows shared a jolly laugh at the expense of Hillary Clinton. A new book claimed that the first lady had communicated, through a spirit medium, with the dead Eleanor Roosevelt; and the image of this super-rational lawyer resorting to psychic comfort was cruelly entertaining. The following Monday, Mrs Clinton was due to appear in public for the first time since her humiliation, to address a conference in Nashville. The audience waited, cringing on her behalf. Then a beaming figure appeared upon the stage. "This conference is a terrific way of bringing together people," she purred; "I had one of my conversations with Mrs Roosevelt, and she thinks this is a terrific idea as well." Journalists and conference-goers dissolved into laughter, and any lingering psychic embarrassment was instantly forgotten.

Nobody, save perhaps her husband, shrugs off public humiliation as elegantly as Mrs Clinton. Time and again since she drove down to Arkansas to manage her future husband's 1974 congressional campaign, she has had to confront allegations of his infidelity; with Gennifer Flowers and Paula Jones; with a host of long-forgotten names; and now with Monica Lewinsky. Time and again she has done more than merely stick with him; she has defended him. Had she done otherwise, Bill Clinton might never have reached the White House; had she denounced him over the Lewinsky affair, his career might now be over. Future historians will remember the current scandal in many ways: for the president's childish squandering of huge political talents, for the obsessive inquisition conducted by Ken Starr, for the disturbing influence of Internet-borne leaks, for the gap between the chattering classes and the public. But future biographers will focus on America's remarkable first lady.

When Ms Flowers sold her story of a 12-year affair with candidate Clinton to a supermarket tabloid, Mrs Clinton dismissed the whole business as "trash for cash", and compared rumours about her husband's sex life to UFO sightings. When Mrs Jones sued President Clinton for sexual harassment, Mrs Clinton advised him to settle out of court, despite the humiliation that would follow from her husband's implied admission of infidelity. When the Lewinsky story surfaced in January, some thought this would be the last straw: they worried that Mrs Clinton would march out, destroying her husband both emotionally and politically. But Mrs Clinton stuck by him again, blaming the allegations on a "vast right-wing conspiracy". Now, even though the worst Lewinsky rumours have proved true, Mrs Clinton is still there, loudly defending her husband's record.

This would be remarkable enough. But Mrs Clinton does all this without asking anyone for sympathy. She refuses to discuss her feeling; indeed, she reveals nothing of herself whatever. On a recent money-raising campaign swing, she assured anybody impertinent enough to ask that she was "Just fine!" Even officials who have worked with her for years seem mystified by her. One White House aide, no great Hillary fan, recalls a tete-a-tete with the First Lady at a particularly bad moment in the Lewinsky saga. Throughout lunch she was "completely calm, chatting about life". Her self-control, her knack of sweeping problems into some corner-cabinet of her mind, is even more amazing than her husband's.

Through all this, moreover, she manages to be popular. She exudes as much empathy as a management consultant with flu; she is the most ruthless of her husband's spin doctors; she has, in short, the qualities that would doom most public figures. But she has recently become the most popular speaker at Democratic fund-raising events. According to one recent poll, 54% of men see her as a good role model, and 66% of women feel that way about her. It used to be that Mrs Clinton was especially popular among career women who identified with this lawyer-mum, but less so among housewives. Now the polls suggest that non-career women are Mrs Clinton's keenest supporters.

There is a message in this popularity, and it is not the one that seems most obvious. It would be tempting to conclude that Mrs Clinton's image-makers have successfully disguised her ambitious side, conning Middle America into identifying with her. Over the years, Mrs Clinton has forsaken frizzy brown hair in favour of soft blond locks; she has traded nerdish spectacles for contact lenses; she has even boasted about her low-fat cookie recipe. After a bad spell as a front-line wonk, leading her husband's failed effort to reform health care, she has retreated to safely feminine issues like children. And yet, despite this careful repositioning of her brand, it would be wrong to think that Americans have been taken in. They do not see her as a traditional wife, standing meekly by an abusive man. On the contrary, 48% of Americans view the Clintons' marriage as a practical career relationship; and, because of this 56% expect her to divorce Bill Clinton when he leaves office.

In short, Americans see Mrs Clinton for what she is: a laser-brained careerist, who met her future husband in the Yale law library and has propelled him, not always scrupulously, to the White House. They are prepared to believe that she skirted the law in a property deal known as Whitewater; they may not entirely dismiss the extreme view, put about in recent days, that she defends her husband because she needs a presidential pardon to save her from indictment. And yet, seeing her this way, a majority of Americans remain fond of her. The conventional wisdom holds that politicians must be packaged as feeling family types, rather than thick-skinned, sharp-elbowed machines dedicated to self-advancement. But America thrives on a healthy respect for ambition, even in its raw extremes. It would be a lesser place if it did not admire the amazing Mrs Clinton.

CLASSICAL ROMANCE FROM AWADAGIN PRATT

T. Brooks Shepard

As T. Brooks Shepard reveals, Awadagin Pratt is by no means an ordinary musician. As a classical pianist, Pratt's style and demeanor are unconventional—courageous and brilliant, Shepard suggests. Add to that the fact that Pratt is an African American in a circle of musicians that typically does not include African Americans, and he seems nothing short of extraordinary.

This review originally appeared in American Visions, *a publication marketed to an African American readership. As you read, notice the ways in which Shepard writes to that particular audience. T. Brooks Shepard is a freelance writer in Boston.*

Although he is the first African American since the great Andre Watts to achieve international acclaim in the heady, elite world of classical piano, Awadagin Pratt lacks pretension, as indicated by his casual, unaffected attire. Without the customary, boring tuxedo and black bow tie, Pratt takes the stage at Boston's Jordan Hall in a subtle but colorful green-and-lavender striped and checked shirt. His black pants reveal a dash of whimsicality below the cuffs: socks adorned with a portrait of Van Gogh. But once the brother begins to play, once he cuts loose after his brief moment of meditation, he could be wearing baggy pants with untied Timberlands and sitting on a whoopee cushion with his hat on backward! It wouldn't matter.

His break with the norm—Pratt even eschews the typical piano bench, instead performing on his own cushionless, hand-carved wooden seat, which is at least a foot shorter than the usual bench—is a testament to his individuality, courage and confidence.

The astonishing brilliance and beauty, the romance and lyricism, the incredible technique and prodigious talent, and his superb and imaginative repertoire transport listeners, levitating them into a spiritual dimension, where materials are immaterial. Hyperbole, you say? Uh-uh, Pratt is just that good.

Born in Pittsburgh, Pa., in 1966 and raised in Normal, Ill., he began playing the piano at age 6, switched to violin at 9, and played both instruments upon entering the University of Illinois at 16. He decided that piano was his forte and enrolled in Baltimore's renowned Peabody Conservatory of Music. He was the first student in the history of that institution to earn certificates in piano and violin and a graduate diploma in conducting.

Pratt recalls that his father, a physics professor born in Sierra Leone and educated in the United States, and his mother, a professor of sociology from Texas, had always impressed upon him and his sister the importance of being "as prepared as possible to face life" and that "to be considered as good as others, you have to be better."

Otherwise influenced primarily by Leonard Bernstein, Glenn Gould and Beethoven, Pratt has had amazingly limited exposure to (and virtually no interest in) the top ten, for a person who grew up in the United States. "I started listening to a little bit of popular music when I was 16 or 17," he says, "and I've listened to it a little bit more. But all I listened to growing up was classical music."

Didn't the nexus of disposable pop culture and peer pressure affect his socialization? "There was no socialization, so it was irrelevant," Pratt states succinctly. "The nature of our household was very organized. With a schedule of practicing music and playing a lot of tennis, there really wasn't a lot of time for it." He was totally busy and has no regrets about not running with the crowd: "I was comfortable with what I was doing."

Pratt's career made a "great leap forward" in 1992, when he became the first African-American classical musician to win the prestigious international Naumberg Competition, which included six other finalists. The recognition that accompanies the prize made him such a hot commodity and created so much demand that he gave more than 40 performances that year. The following year, Pratt gave more than 70 solo piano performances.

In 1994 he not only enjoyed the release of his first EMI Classics CD, *A Long Way From Normal*, featuring compositions by Liszt, but he was also awarded the $10,000 Avery Fisher Career Grant, and he had his premiere with the New York Philharmonic at Lincoln Center.

Since then, Pratt has performed with the Cleveland Orchestra and the Tokyo and Chicago symphonies. He plays 80 concerts a year now, both in the States and abroad. Somehow, despite his hectic schedule, he found time to record two more CDs: *Beethoven Piano Sonatas* (EMI, 1995) and *Live From South Africa* (EMI, 1996), which was recorded in Cape Town.

Relishing international travel, this piano virtuoso is always delighted at the prospect of meeting new people and exploring new cultures. Traveling to South Africa in 1996 placed a positive imprint on his consciousness. "It's a place of tremendous potential," he says. "In Cape Town you can walk down a single block and hear every conceivable point of view. Nothing is swept under the rug." He describes his trip there as "healthy."

The creative impulse—that cosmic voice within each artist that says, "Don't do that; do this"—defies definition and is beyond analysis. On the other hand, the creative process can be observed. Pratt's approach is unusual for a musician because his choices are based on neither the sound of a given work nor its audience appeal. Rather his decisions are defined by passion. He's not necessarily looking for marriage, but he's definitely looking for love.

"I select music based on a complicated process," he explains. "For example, I have a list of certain pieces that I enjoy but haven't played in a long time. I examine those pieces to find out if they are pieces that I want to live with for nine months, a year, or a year and a half. I have to find out if I can live with whatever expression is contained in those pieces. Then I try to put those pieces together in a manner that is coherent. One would have to take my programs cumulatively, probably as long as I've been playing, to find out where the center is."

He's disciplined and he's romantic. The beauty, intelligence or popularity of the piece won't move him; he's got to be in love to serve it up.

Uncorrupted by fame, Pratt today maintains the same yeoman's dedication to his craft that carried him to this present plateau: "I practice pretty much every day, although travel days are tough. The hours I practice are variable, I'll practice anywhere from 2 or 3 hours. After a certain number, I have no awareness of how many hours I've been practicing. It's not important for me to count."

He's serious about music, but he's not all about work. A hard-core Knicks fan, he plays basketball three days a week on his New Mexico home front, digs dinner with friends, and is always on the lookout for fine restaurants. "I love good food," he says.

*   *   *

The delicious sense of anticipation that greeted Pratt onstage in Boston is still there as the concert draws to a close. He opened the program with a stunning interpretation of Passacaglia and Fugue, BWV 582, an 18th-century J.S. Bach piece that he had arranged. Then he demonstrated his prowess with the alternately complex, then simple 19th-century Brahms composition Variations and Fugue in B-flat on a Major Theme. (By this time, he had seduced the sparkling, nine-foot black Steinway grand and made it his own.)

Completing the 16th and final movement of a particularly engaging and incandescent 19th-century Moussorgsky masterpiece that he'd flirted with for eight years before adding to his program last spring, Pratt amazed his audience with his astonishing memory. He had just played 16 movements of various keys, tempos, melodies and emotions.

As the piano rings silent, Pratt bows to a standing ovation. During the third ovation, does the audience detect a wee smile on that handsome black face?

The crowd is hungry, almost manic. They want more music, and they are not to be denied. After the fourth "standing O," Pratt, ever the smart showman, plays some soothing, somewhat sentimental audience cool-out music. Then he stands for his last bow and departs.

Yes! (The few black folks in the audience have a special secret joy. Pratt has proved that he's a class act, and they are proud of him.) As the smiling faces exit, one gentleman says, his voice resonating with wonder. "Well, I guess he's the real thing." Yes, Pratt has convinced everyone tonight that he is, indeed, "the real thing," and that real thing is called genius.

SPIELBERG'S WAR IS HELL

Stephen Hunter

This review of Steven Spielberg's "Saving Private Ryan" was written by Washington Post *Staff Writer Stephen Hunter. Upon its release, the gory opening scenes of the movie sparked a slight controversy. However, Hunter finds those scenes, along with many other elements of the film, to be precisely what puts this movie in a class of its own. Notice, as you read, how Hunter's use of descriptive, well-paced language adds a liveliness to the review and helps to make his admiration of Spielberg's movie clear.*

There are movies and then there are movies. And then there is Steven Spielberg's "Saving Private Ryan." Searing, heartbreaking, so intense it turns your body into a single tube of clenched muscle, this is simply the greatest war movie ever made, and one of the great American movies. In one stroke, it makes everything that came before—with the exception of two or three obscure European variants on the same theme—seem dated and unwatchable. And it redefines the way we look at war.

Generically, it could be called the last example of that vanished category, the unit tribute film. But this unit is not the 2nd Ranger Battalion or the 101st Airborne. Rather, it is a generation: those men born in the late 1910s and early '20s, who, when asked, simply put aside their tools and settled the great issue of the century, determining who would administer the industrial revolution, dictatorship or democracy. They did this without complaint, bitterness, anger or remorse. Then they came home and picked up their tools again. To this day, few will talk about what they saw and did, and Spielberg shows us why.

In the first seconds you understand you are in a different place than you've ever been before, unless you survived the Normandy Invasion. You're in a Higgins boat in the gray dawn of June 5, 1944, wet and cold and already exhausted, scudding through the sloppy surf, and all around you men are puking. The noise is astonishing. Your hands tremble; your breath comes in dry, hurtful spurts.

Then the landing gate falls and in the very first instant, zeroed German machine gun fire spits through the boat. At this moment you'll wish you were elsewhere, as did surely every man in the real thing. In Spielberg's terrifying version, the bullets seem somehow angry—they pierce the air, trailing a whine or a streak of neon illumination, and when they strike sand or steel, they kick up big, vicious geysers; and there are so many of them, and they come so fastfastfast. But when they strike flesh, they strike it with a thudding finality that reduces a man to maimed meat in a sixth of a second, and takes it all away from him, so that he falls forward obedient only to gravity. He dies like a sack of potatoes falling off a shelf.

Spielberg's ability to capture the palpable madness of all this borders on the incredible. The first 25 minutes of the film—a re-creation of Omaha Beach from the point of view of an all-too-human Ranger captain, who's been here and done this, but not at this level of violence—is surely one of the great tours de force of world cinema. From the spillage of viscera, the shearing of limbs, the gushing of blood and the psychotic whimsy of the bullets, to a final kind of fog of panic and soul-deep fear, he makes you glad it was your daddy's job, and not yours.

But Spielberg also understands war's deepest reality, which is that being there is not enough, and being willing to die for your country is also not enough; you have to be willing to kill for your country. So much of the battle carnage pictured in "Saving Private Ryan" is based on the craft of close-quarter, small-unit combat: It's watching men maneuver across terrain for geometrical superiority, hunting for a position to vector fire in on the enemy. He who shoots from the best position and brings the most fire to bear, he's the winner. The thermodynamics of infantry combat: Shoot well, shoot fast, shoot often.

Where does this unprecedented version of war come from? It may come out of a few other movies, ironically all of them German. I think of "Das Brucke" ("The Bridge"). "The Winter War" (actually Finnish, about the short, brutal Russo-Finn war of 1940), or "Stalingrad" or even "Das Boot"—all movies that portrayed unflinchingly the iron randomness of war. But more vividly, it has clearly been informed by a close study of as much archival footage of The Real Thing as can be had. In this sense, it's ersatz documentary, with desaturated '40s color, jittery, terrified camera movement (you feel the cameraman's fear of getting hit) and the sensation of overwhelming chaos.

It's mean, terrifying, exhausting and quipless. There's no spunk and very little humor. Morale is nonexistent. It's a grinding, debasing job carried out in physical misery in an environment—mud, rain, cold—that is itself an enemy. It's Bill Mauldin's Willie and Joe without the punch lines, but with a lot of dead GIs and a crushing melancholy hanging over everything like smoke.

But this will become evident only in time. Initially, we are in such a fog from the intensity of the invasion sequence that fatigue is the only response: A few survivors eat K-rations and try to decompress from the pressurized brutality they've both suffered and dealt. Word comes: a mission.

Here the movie broadens somewhat, for just a moment: Two Ryan brothers have died in the invasion and a third has just perished in New Guinea. Mrs. Ryan, of Every Farm, U.S.A., will get three letters on the same day. But it seems there's a fourth Ryan, James (Matt Damon), the youngest, somewhere with the advance units of the 101st Airborne in the small French towns that cover the approach to the beaches. No less a personage than George C. Marshall himself, the chief of staff (played by Harve Presnell with a less kitschy quality than might be expected), orders that a unit be sent out to pluck this boy from battle and return him to the farm. It's typical of Spielberg that this position is not treated glibly, as another bit of idiocy by "the brass." In a spirit of decency and in accordance with what seems to be his career-long recognition of benevolent authority, he makes us see on what basis Marshall makes his decision, and how, no matter how it plays out, it represents the best of the American spirit, not the worst.

Eight men—that heroic captain, John Miller (Tom Hanks in another of his quietly brilliant everyman roles), a sergeant (Tom Sizemore), a Browning Automatic Rifleman (Edward Burns), a sniper (Barry Pepper), a medic (Giovanni Ribisi), two riflemen (Vin Diesel and Adam Goldberg) and an interpreter (Jeremy Davies)—are charged to cross the dangerous ground between the beachhead and the town, locate Private Ryan and bring him back alive. Or bring back his dog tags.

As pure story, the movie has a swiftness to it that goes far beyond the sheer fidelity of the battle sequences. The narrative has been expertly configured; it moves us through a variety of experiences—squad assault, town battle, sniper duel, a final stand against armored units—while at the same time keeping precise track of the overall story situation. Simultaneously, the personalities of the men are expressing themselves, in small ways. Even Damon's Ryan, who could be the font of sentimentality, turns out to be just another kid, low-key and quietly furiously decent. (Damon, like all the actors, is excellent in this lesser role.) But its no flashback-o-rama, in the fashion of "The Naked and the Dead," where each man's life is summed up in a banal recollection. Rather—this is a point Spielberg makes over and over—these men have essentially given up on their civilian personalities—with the exception of the unit intellectual, the interpreter played by Davies—for the duration. They know the drill. They know what to do. They can hold it together. They've become, in Stephen Ambrose's wonderful term, complete Citizen Soldiers.

In this way, the film approaches its true subject, which isn't heroism, but duty, which is to say, repression. Its about men who make a conscious decision that the self does not matter: the "personality" is irrelevant; feelings are dangerous. Thus they become what they must, to survive, to kill and to win: sealed-off beings locked away, hoarding their emotions, giving vent only to rage. They let nothing hang out because hanging out can get you killed. And Spielberg dramatizes this point twice, explicitly, in episodes where two soldiers yield to compassion. In this cruelest of worlds, the result is catastrophe. This movie is about a generation that put its heart on the shelf, dialed its minds down into a small, cold tunnel, and fought with its brains.

All the way through you can feel Spielberg flirting with cliche, almost daring us to recognize it and then at the last moment pulling it away from us and leaving us open-mouthed. But the biggest cliche that the movie assaults is the very conceit upon which war movies have been eternally built: It is the idea that somehow, combat is cool. There's always been an athletic grace to battle as the movies have portrayed it, a kind of photogenic sportiness. Even in the most violent of battle sequences, a little boy in you thought, "Hey, that's kinda neat." You know, dropping grenades on the German high command trapped underground in "The Dirty Dozen" or spray-painting Nazis red with your Thompson in "The Longest Day." And there was that Hollywood thing where the hero ran through blizzards of fire and somehow was never touched, because, after all, he was the hero.

That's all gone here. Not merely because of its gore but far more because of its cruelty, the war here will inspire no enlistees and no one will relive it in private later. It's flat-out terrifying, and the emotion it finally produces in you is more than another film has gotten, but about one-thousandth of what the infantrymen of 1944 must have felt after one day on the line: utter exhaustion. You feel bled out, and at least emotionally, you have been.

So in the end, this one is for the boys of Pointe-du-Hoc, and also the boys of Utah and Omaha, Salemo, Monte Cassino, Iwo, the boys who took the long walk ashore at Tarawa through the Japanese fire, the boys whose last moments were spent in a flaming fortress over Schweinfurt, or whatever, wherever, between the years 1941 and 1945. Take a bow, little guy, it says to them.

And to us, their inheritors, it says: Hey, look what your daddies did, what they went through, what they survived or didn't survive—and be proud. And it also asks us the hardest of all questions: Are we worthy of them?

THE SKY LINE: NOW ARRIVING

The restoration of Grand Central Terminal is a triumphant validation of an ambitious urban idea.

Paul Goldberger

> *"Now Arriving" is written in praise of New York City's Grand Central Terminal. While students of architecture and urban planning may be familiar with some of the warrants for admiration that Goldberger includes, others may be surprised to learn what it is that he finds praiseworthy in the newly-restored building. Perhaps his audience— readers of* The New Yorker—*were surprised as well. As you read, pay particular attention to those topics of praise, all of which lead Goldberger to conclude that the Terminal is "the poster building for every landmark in the United States."*

Grand Central Terminal was never as overpowering or as grandiose as the late Pennsylvania Station, which was torn down in 1965, and that may be why it has survived. It wove its way into the fabric of New York City so subtly and so tightly that it couldn't be ripped out. The real brilliance of the place—for all its architectural glory—is the way in which it confirms the virtues of the urban ensemble. Grand Central was conceived as the monumental center of a single composition, with hotels and streets and towers and subways arrayed around it. When it opened, in 1913, it was New York's clearest embodiment of the essential urban idea—that different kinds of buildings work together to make a whole that is far greater than any of its parts.

If Penn Station was built mainly to send a message about the splendor of arrival, then Grand Central was conceived to make clear the choreography of connection. Railway trains, automobiles, subways, office buildings, hotels—everything that made the early-twentieth-century city a collage of movement—were brought together here, seamlessly. Not that the terminal is a cold-blooded testament to functionalism. The sumptuous Beaux-Arts façade and the great space of the main concourse possess beauty as rich as any to be found in the public realm. But the building was designed with clarity and simplicity. Originally, for instance, long-distance passengers could carry their baggage from Forty-second Street to the train platforms without a single change of level. City traffic wraps around the building on viaducts that eliminate the congestion a huge building in the center of town could cause, and underground pedestrian passageways tether surrounding buildings to the terminal at their center.

John Belle, of Beyer Blinder Belle, the architect who has been supervising the spectacular restoration of Grand Central under the aegis of the Metropolitan Transportation Authority, understands completely how the terminal is at once an exalted symbol and a kind of urban operating system, and he has managed to enhance the place on both counts. Thanks to his work and to the M.T.A.'s belated understanding of what Grand Central is, the restoration of the terminal is a triumphant moment in the modern history of New York.

It is also sweet revenge, given that Grand Central was almost lost in the nineteen-seventies, when the struggling Penn Central railroad commissioned Marcel Breuer to turn its financially draining terminal into a paying real-estate proposition by putting a huge skyscraper on the roof. The Landmarks Preservation Commission's decisive rejection of that plan led to a lawsuit that ended up in the United States Supreme Court, the first landmarks case ever to do so. In 1978, the Court ruled that the commission had acted appropriately, thus upholding the right of a city to save its most valued buildings, even if they are privately owned and their land could be put to more profitable uses. Grand Central is the poster building for every landmark in the United States.

*   *   *

Whitney Warren, the gifted and socially well-connected architect who is credited as the terminal's main designer, gave the magnificent concourse its shape and the dignified façade its form, but the real begetter of Grand Central as a figure nearly lost to history—William J. Wilgus, the chief engineer of the New York Central railway company, the predecessor of the Penn Central. Wilgus enthusiastically promoted the conversion of the New York Central system from the noisy, sooty, and dangerous steam locomotives that were the legacy of the nineteenth century to the electrically powered trains that would prevail in the twentieth. He designed the New York Central's electrification system, and conceived of the duplex arrangement of tracks in Grand Central. He also foresaw the profound implications of the new system. The old-fashioned coal-fired trains let off great blasts of steam and had to be parked outside or in enormous sheds, where the products of combustion would dissipate. Since the new trains could run underground, the conversion to electricity would free block upon block of land for development. Wilgus proposed that the railroad start a realty company to exploit the value of the land above the tracks. He all but invented the concept of air rights. His plan created the modern Park Avenue; a boulevard set on the roof of railroad tracks. Since the blocks south of Fifty-sixth Street were developed by the New York Central—originally that whole area was to be called Terminal City—the buildings there evolved as a coherent group.

Wilgus's ambitious urban plan needed a great building at its heart, and in 1903 the railroad invited several architects to submit designs, including McKim, Mead & White and Daniel H. Burnham. The winner was the firm of Reed & Stem, whose senior partner, Charles Reed, happened to be William Wilgus's brother-in-law. That familial connection was overshadowed, however, by the fact that William K. Vanderbilt, the New York Central's chairman, was Whitney Warren's cousin. The firms of both Warren and Reed were hired. They formed an awkward association, with Reed & Stem's scheme providing the basis for the urban design and Warren designing most of the building itself.

Although Grand Central was created by a private corporation, it turned out to be one of the most ambitious public works in the history of New York. The terminal alone required two and a half times the amount of steel used to build the Eiffel Tower, and cost eighty million dollars, or roughly two billion in today's dollars. Because monumental space was no longer needed to house the trains, the impulse toward architectural grandeur played itself out not in a huge glass train shed but in more usable public spaces like Grand Central's main concourse, which is two hundred and seventy feet long, a hundred and twenty feet wide, and a hundred and twenty-five feet high—longer, wider, and higher than the nave of the Cathedral of Notre-Dame. The project gave twentieth-century form to midtown Manhattan.

*   *   *

Much of the strength of Wilgus's urban plan remains visible today, though it has been badly compromised by gargantuanism in the form of the Metropolitan Life Building—the fifty-nine-story slab that was known until recently as the Pan Am Building—and by vulgarity in the form of the Grand Hyatt Hotel, the Trump-sponsored metamorphosis of the Commodore Hotel from dignified order into cheap garishness. In almost every other way, however, Grand Central and its neighborhood have never been in better shape than they are right now. John Belle, who describes his job as "peeling off the excrescences," has spiffed up the terminal to look more elegant than it has at any time since the nineteen-twenties, when the first in a long series of destructive alterations began. But the restoration has brought additions, too, ranging from the imposing staircase placed at the east end of the main concourse to new (and still unfinished) entrances at Park and Madison Avenues that will give commuters direct access to the north end of the underground train platforms. The staircase is the most controversial part of the project, since it is not a restoration. Whitney Warren built a grand staircase at the west end of the main concourse to give access to Vanderbilt Avenue, and proposed a similar staircase at the east end to lead to the lobby of a medium-sized office tower that was contemplated for atop the terminal. When the office tower did not get built, neither did the stairs, leaving an empty and inaccessible balcony at the east end of the main concourse for eighty-five years.

The balcony is now to be used for cafes and restaurants, and Belle reasoned that the most logical thing to do was resurrect the idea for a staircase there, giving the concourse a degree of symmetry it never had. He has designed the new staircase to be almost, but not precisely, the same as the one on the west side. The detailing on the balustrades is very slightly simpler. New stores and restaurants and a lower-level food court have also been added, but discreetly; Belle and the M.T.A. have stripped away most of the advertising signs that for years turned the main concourse into a kind of covered version of Times Square. They have managed the trick of making Grand Central look virginal while making it more commercial.

No more Kodak sign, no more huge clock, lots of architecture. You can wallow in the main concourse now; it is pure space. It's even tempting to say that Belle has treated the interior too much like a cathedral, especially since its original purpose, to serve travelers crossing the continent on great trains, has long been archaic. Grand Central is now just a big commuter station. And who needs all this architecture if you are merely heading for Stamford?

Well, nobody needs it. But without Grand Central, or with Grand Central reduced to being the base of a monstrous office block, New York City would be a vastly diminished place. Grand Central teaches us that monumental architecture can transcend issues of refinement and enrich the minutiae of daily life. The building, with its swarming crowds, is an oasis of calm, a serene eye in the midst of the swirling city. If you doubt this, look at how many people are not rushing through the main concourse but stopping to contemplate it. And it is somehow inherent in the nature of the space that, however large the crowds, people direct themselves around each other, intuitively; the concourse is not a hectic passageway of jostling throngs but an immense dance floor.

Now that Grand Central no longer functions as a place for long-distance arrivals and departures, it is more like a town square. Its clarity and its serenity, as well as its majesty, belong to everyone, and not, as they once did, primarily to those coming to board the Twentieth Century Limited. A transcendent experience is there for the taking, even if you're only walking through.

The Following Questions for Discussion Pertain to Each of the Encomia You Have Read:

1. What are the topics of praise for the given subject?
2. Do those topics of praise seem relevant to the given audience? Why?
3. Are there other ways in which the author attempts to reach the audience?
4. If the article was written strictly as an encomium for your English 101 class, what information would you exclude from the text? Is there other information that you might add?
5. Comment on the way the author crafted his language. Does it seem appropriate to the audience and occasion for writing? Why or why not?
6. If the author uses anecdotes to support any of the included warrants for admiration, do those anecdotes seem appropriate? (How) will they help maintain audience interest?

UNIT TWO

Rhetorical Analysis

INTRODUCTION

We are constantly bombarded with persuasive discourse —any time you drive by a billboard or flip through advertisements in a magazine, any time you hear a campaign speech or a State of the Union Address, any time you read through the editorials of a newspaper or listen to talk radio, any time someone tries to convince you to do something, say something, buy something, or think something. We know when we hear an argument or see an advertisement or listen to a speech that is persuasive, that "works." We know it is persuasive because it makes us think, because it moves us. But do we know *why* it moves us? What is it that makes an argument effective?

Conducting insightful rhetorical analysis helps us to answer those very questions, helps us to discover why certain arguments move us and why others, well, we'd rather move aside. Analyzing persuasive texts challenges us to understand the strategies behind argumentation. An artful and empowering skill, rhetorical analysis provides us with the necessary language to make sense of the discourses that comprise contemporary society. More importantly, however, when we are able to discern what makes a persuasive argument persuasive we can apply that knowledge to our own writing and, in turn, write our own effective arguments. Thus, we can make our voices heard. We can move others.

Analyzing a persuasive text rhetorically means, quite literally, taking it apart. An argument is a lot like a complicated machine: it does something, but it can only accomplish its goal if all its inside gears and parts are working — and working together. When you analyze an argument, you are looking "inside" to see that all its components — its evidence, its appeals to emotion, its proof of the author's credibility — are working. Of course, all those components are interrelated, working together like a complicated gear system which gets the argument to do its job: to persuade. Your job, when analyzing a persuasive text, is to determine which gears could use a bit of tinkering and which are doing most of the work. And, your job will also be to always ask *how* and *why*.

Because we must take as a constant that engaging in the rhetoric of others will assist us in becoming stronger, more efficient, and more intelligent communicators in this — and any other — academic and professional venue, this unit provides you with a host of readings to analyze. The first part provides you with readings in which you can explore the complex effects of an author's credibility on persuasive discourse. The second part of this unit contains essays for straightforward rhetorical analysis. The third and fourth subsections contain essay pairs (and, in some cases, essay clusters) which invite you to compare your rhetorical analyses from one essay to another so that you may make evaluative judgments on which argument is more persuasive and why. Ultimately, when you complete this unit, you'll be able to make more informed choices as you strategize your own written arguments.

Dina L. Longhitano

I

Ethos

"GIVE CHILDREN THE VOTE."

Vita Wallace

Vita Wallace lives in Philadelphia, where she is a writer. This article originally appeared in The Nation *(14 October 1991), a liberal publication, when Wallace was sixteen years old. As you read, consider how her age has shaped this argument.*

I first became interested in children's rights two years ago, when I learned that several states had passed laws prohibiting high school dropouts from getting driver's licenses. I was outraged, because I believe that children should not be forced to go to school or be penalized if they choose not to, a choice that is certainly the most sensible course for some people.

I am what is called a home schooler. I have never been to school, having always learned at home and in the world around me. Home schooling is absolutely legal, yet as a home schooler, I have had to defend what I consider to be my right to be educated in the ways that make the most sense to me, and so all along I have felt sympathy with people who insist on making choices about how they want to be educated, even if that means choosing not to finish high school. Now this choice is in jeopardy.

Since first learning about the discriminatory laws preventing high school dropouts from getting driver's licenses that have been passed by some state legislatures, I have done a lot of constitutional and historical research that has convinced me that children of all ages must be given the same power to elect their representatives that adults have, or they will continue to be unfairly treated and punished for exercising the few legal options they now have, such as dropping out of high school.

Most people, including children themselves, probably don't realize that children are the most regulated people in the United States, In addition to all the laws affecting adults, including tax laws, children must comply with school attendance laws, child labor laws, and alcohol and cigarette laws. They are denied driver's licenses because of their age, regardless of the dropout issue; they are victims of widespread child abuse; and they are blatantly discriminated against everywhere they go, in libraries, restaurants, and movie theaters. They have no way to protect themselves: Usually they cannot hire lawyers or bring cases to court without a guardian, and they are not allowed to vote.

The child labor and compulsory schooling laws were passed by well-meaning people to protect children from exploitation. Child labor laws keep children from being forced to work, and compulsory schooling allows all children to get an education. But the abolition of slavery in 1865 didn't end the exploitation of black people. They needed the right to vote and the ability to bring lawsuits against their employers. Children need those rights too. Without them, laws that force children to go to school and generally do not allow them to work may be necessary to prevent exploitation, but they also take away children's rights as citizens to life, liberty, and the pursuit of happiness. In my case, the compulsory education laws severely limited my right to pursue the work that is important to me (which is surely what "the pursuit of happiness" referred to in the Declaration of Independence).

I am sixteen now, still not old enough to vote. Like all children, then, the only way I can fight for children's rights is by using my freedom of speech to try to convince adults to fight with me. While I am grateful that I have the right to speak my mind, I believe that it is a grave injustice to deny young people the most effective tool they could have to bring about change in a democracy. For this reason, I suggest that the right of citizens under 18 to vote not be denied or abridged on account of age.

Many people argue that it would be dangerous to let loose on society a large group of new voters who might not vote sensibly. They mean that children might not vote for the right candidates. The essence of democracy, however, is letting people vote for the wrong candidates. Democratic society has its risks, but we must gamble on the reasonableness of all our citizens, because it is less dangerous than gambling on the reasonableness of a few. That is why we chose to be a democracy instead of a dictatorship in the first place.

As it is, only 36 to 40 percent of adults who are eligible to vote actually vote in nonpresidential years, and about 25 percent of the population is under 18. As you can see, our representatives are elected by a very small percentage of our citizens. That means that although they are responsible for all of us, they are responsible to only a few of us. Politicians usually do all they can to keep that few happy, because both voters and politicians are selfish, and a politician's reelection depends on the well-being of the voters. Large segments of society that are not likely or not allowed to vote are either ignored or treated badly because of this system. It would be too much to expect the few always to vote in the interests of the many. Under these circumstances, surely the more people who vote the better, especially if they are of both sexes and of all races, classes, and ages.

People also claim that children are irresponsible. Most of the teenagers who act irresponsibly do so simply because they are not allowed to solve their problems in any way that would be considered responsible—through the courts or legislature. They fall back on sabotage of the system because they are not allowed to work within it.

Some people believe that children would vote the way their parents tell them to, which would, in effect, give parents more votes. Similarly, when the Nineteenth Amendment was passed in 1920, giving women the vote, many people thought women would vote the way their husbands did. Now women are so independent that the idea of women voting on command seems absurd. The Nineteenth Amendment was a large part of the process that produced their independence. I think a similar and equally desirable result would follow if children were allowed to vote. They are naturally curious, and most are interested in the electoral process and the results of the elections even though they are not allowed to vote. Lacking world-weary cynicism, they see, perhaps even more clearly than their elders, what is going on in their neighborhoods and what is in the news.

Suffragist Belle Case La Follette's comment that if women were allowed to vote there would be a lot more dinner-table discussion of politics is as true of children today. More debate would take place not only in the home but among children and adults everywhere. Adults would also benefit if politics were talked about in libraries, churches, stores, laundromats, and other places where children gather.

People may argue that politicians would pander to children if they could vote, promising for instance that free ice cream would be distributed every day. But if kids were duped, they would not be duped for long. Children don't like to be treated condescendingly.

Even now, adults try to manipulate children all the time in glitzy TV ads or, for example, in the supposedly educational pamphlets that nuclear power advocates pass out in school science classes. Political candidates speak at schools, addressing auditoriums full of captive students. In fact, schools should be no more or less political than workplaces. Children are already exposed to many different opinions, and they would likely be exposed to even more if they could vote. The point is that with the vote, they would be better able to fight such manipulation, not only because they would have the power to do so but because they would have added reason to educate themselves on the issues.

What I suggest is that children be allowed to grow into their own right to vote at whatever rate suits them individually. They should not be forced to vote, as adults are not, but neither should they be hindered from voting if they believe themselves capable, as old people are not hindered.

As for the ability to read and write, that should never be used as a criterion for eligibility, since we have already learned from painful past experience that literacy tests can be manipulated to ensure discrimination. In any case, very few illiterate adults vote, and probably very few children would want to vote as long as they couldn't read or write. But I firmly believe that, whether they are literate or not, the vast majority of children would not attempt to vote before they are ready. Interest follows hand in hand with readiness, something that is easy to see as a home schooler but that is perhaps not so clear to many people in this society where, ironically, children are continually taught things when they are not ready, and so are not interested. Yet when they are interested, as in the case of voting, they're told they are not yet ready. I think

I would not have voted until I was eight or nine, but perhaps if I had known I could vote I would have taken an interest sooner.

Legally, it would be possible to drop the voting-age requirements. In the Constitution, the states are given all powers to set qualifications for voters except as they defy the equal protection clause of the Fourteenth Amendment, in which case Congress has the power to enforce it. If it were proved that age requirements "abridge the privileges or immunities of citizens of the United States" (which in my opinion they do, since people born in the United States or to U.S. citizens are citizens from the moment they are born), and if the states could not come up with a "compelling interest" argument to justify a limit at a particular age, which Justices Potter Stewart, Warren Burger, and Harry Blackmun agreed they could not in *Oregon v. Mitchell* (the Supreme Court case challenging the 1970 amendment to the Voting Rights Act that gave 18-year-olds the vote), then age requirements would be unconstitutional. But it is not necessary that they be unconstitutional for the states to drop them. It is within the power of the states to do that, and I believe that we must start this movement at the state level. According to *Oregon v. Mitchell*, Congress cannot change the qualifications for voting in state elections except by constitutional amendment, which is why the Twenty-sixth Amendment setting the voting age at eighteen was necessary. It is very unlikely that an amendment would pass unless several states had tried eliminating the age requirement and had good results. The experience of Georgia and Kentucky, which lowered their age limits to eighteen, helped to pass the Twenty-sixth Amendment in 1971.

Already in our country's history several oppressed groups have been able to convince the unoppressed to free them. Children, who do not have the power to change their situation, must now convince the adults who do to allow them that power.

Questions:

1. After you read this essay, were you surprised by Wallace's age?
2. How does Wallace assert herself as credible?
3. How does Wallace's continuous use of the term *children* affect her argument?
4. Consider Wallace's audience. In paragraph 6, she writes: "I am sixteen now, still not old enough to vote. Like all children, then, the only way I can fight for children's rights is by using my freedom of speech to try to convince adults to fight with me." Do you think she has convinced the adult readers of *The Nation* to fight with her?

WHO SHOT JOHNNY?

Debra Dickerson

> *Debra Dickerson is a lawyer living in Washington, D.C. This essay orig-*
> *inally appeared in* The New Republic *on 1 January 1996.*

Given my level of political awareness, it was inevitable that I would come to view the everyday events of my life through the prism of politics and the national discourse. I read *The Washington Post, The New Republic, The New Yorker, Harper's, The Atlantic Monthly, The Nation, National Review, Black Enterprise* and *Essence* and wrote a weekly column for the Harvard Law School Record during my three years just ended there. I do this because I know that those of us who are not well-fed white guys in suits must not yield the debate to them, however well-intentioned or well-informed they may be. Accordingly, I am unrepentant and vocal about having gained admittance to Harvard through affirmative action; I am a feminist, stoic about my marriage chances as a well-educated, 36-year-old black woman who won't pretend to need help taking care of herself. My strength flags, though, in the face of the latest role assigned to my family in the national drama. On July 27, 1995, my 16-year-old nephew was shot and paralyzed.

Talking with friends in front of his home, Johnny saw a car he thought he recognized. He waved boisterously—his trademark—throwing both arms in the air in a full-bodied, hip-hop Y. When he got no response, he and his friends sauntered down the walk to join a group loitering in front of an apartment building. The car followed. The driver got out, brandished a revolver and fired into the air. Everyone scattered. Then he took aim and shot my running nephew in the back.

Johnny never lost consciousness. He lay in the road, trying to understand what had happened to him, why he couldn't get up. Emotionlessly, he told the story again and again on demand, remaining apologetically firm against all demands to divulge the missing details that would make sense of the shooting but obviously cast him in a bad light. Being black, male and shot, he must, apparently, be gang- or drug-involved. Probably both. Witnesses corroborate his version of events.

Nearly six months have passed since that phone call in the night and my night-marish, headlong drive from Boston to Charlotte. After twenty hours behind the wheel, I arrived haggard enough to reduce my mother to fresh tears and to find my nephew reassuring well-wishers with an eerie sangfroid.

I take the day shift in his hospital room; his mother and grandmother, a clerk and cafeteria worker, respectively, alternate nights there on a cot. They don their uniforms the next day, gaunt after hours spent listening to Johnny moan in his sleep. How often must his subconscious replay those events and curse its hosts for saying hello without permission, for being carefree and young while a would-be murderer hefted the weight of his uselessness and failure like Jacob Marley's chains? How often must he watch himself lying stubbornly immobile on the pavement of his nightmares while the sound of running feet syncopate his attacker's taunts?

I spend these days beating him at gin rummy and Scrabble, holding a basin while he coughs up phlegm and crying in the corridor while he catheterizes himself. There are children here much worse off than he. I should be grateful. The doctors can't, or won't, say whether he'll walk again.

I am at once repulsed and fascinated by the bullet, which remains lodged in his spine (having done all the damage it can do, the doctors say). The wound is undramatic—small, neat and perfectly centered—an impossibly pink pit surrounded by an otherwise undisturbed expanse of mahogany. Johnny has asked me several times to describe it but politely declines to look in the mirror I hold for him.

Here on the pediatric rehab ward, Johnny speaks little, never cries, never complains, works diligently to become independent. He does whatever he is told; if two hours remain until the next pain pill, he waits quietly. Eyes bloodshot, hands gripping the bed rails. During the week of his intravenous feeding when he was tormented by the primal need to masticate, he never asked for food. He just listened while we counted down the days for him and planned his favorite meals. Now required to dress himself unassisted, he does so without demur, rolling himself back and forth valiantly on the bed and shivering afterwards, exhausted. He "ma'am"s and "sir"s everyone politely. Before his "accident," a simple request to take out the trash could provoke a firestorm of teenage attitude. We, the women who have raised him, have changed as well; we've finally come to appreciate those boxer-baring, oversized pants we used to hate—it would be much more difficult to fit properly sized pants over his diaper.

He spends a lot of time tethered to rap music still loud enough to break my concentration as I read my many magazines. I hear him try to soundlessly mouth the obligatory "mothafuckers" overlaying the funereal dirge of the music tracks. I do not normally tolerate disrespectful music in my or my mother's presence, but if it distracts him now . . .

"Johnny," I ask later, "do you still like gangster rap?" During the long pause I hear him think loudly, *I'm paralyzed Auntie, not stupid.* "I mostly just listen to hip hop," he says evasively into his *Sports Illustrated.*

Miserable though it is, time passes quickly here. We always seem to be jerking awake in our chairs just in time for the next pill, his every-other-night bowel program, the doctor's rounds. Harvard feels a galaxy away—the world revolves around Family Members Living With Spinal Cord Injury class, Johnny's urine output and strategizing with my sister to find affordable, accessible housing. There is always another long-distance uncle in need of an update, another church member wanting to pray with us or Johnny's little brother in need of some attention.

We Dickerson women are so constant a presence the ward nurses and cleaning staff call us by name and join us for cafeteria meals and cigarette breaks. At Johnny's birthday pizza party, they crack jokes and make fun of each other's husbands (there are no men here). I pass slices around and try not to think, "17 with a bullet."

Oddly, we feel little curiosity or specific anger toward the man who shot him. We have to remind ourselves to check in with the police. Even so, it feels pro forma, like sending in those $2 rebate forms that come with new pantyhose: you know your request will fall into a deep, dark hole somewhere but, still, it's your duty to try. We push for an arrest because we owe it to Johnny and to ourselves as citizens. We don't think about it otherwise—our low expectations are too ingrained. A Harvard aunt notwithstanding, for people like Johnny, Marvin Gaye was right that only three things are sure: taxes, death and trouble. At least it wasn't the second.

We rarely wonder about or discuss the brother who shot him because we already know everything about him. When the call came, my first thought was the same one I'd had when I'd heard about Rosa Parks's beating: a brother did it. A non-job-having, middle-of-the-day malt-liquor-drinking, crotch-clutching, loud-talking brother with many neglected children born of many forgotten women. He lives in his mother's basement with furniture rented at an astronomical interest rate, the exact amount of which he does not know. He has a car phone, an $80 monthly cable bill and every possible phone feature but no savings. He steals Social Security numbers from unsuspecting relatives and assumes their identities to acquire large TV sets for which he will never pay. On the slim chance that he is brought to justice, he will have a colorful criminal history and no coherent explanation to offer for this act. His family will raucously defend him and cry cover-up. Some liberal lawyer just like me will help him plea bargain his way to yet another short stay in a prison pesthouse that will serve only to add another layer to the brother's sociopathology and formless, mindless nihilism. We know him. We've known and feared him all our lives.

As a teenager, he called, "Hey, baby, gimme somma that boodie!" at us from car windows. Indignant at our lack of response, he followed up with, "Fuck you, then, 'ho!" He called me a "white-boy lovin' nigger bitch oreo" for being in the gifted program and loving it. At 27, he got my 17-year-old sister pregnant with Johnny and lost interest without ever informing her that he was married. He snatched my widowed mother's purse as she waited in pre-dawn darkness for the bus to work and then broke into our house while she soldered on an assembly line. He chased all the small entrepreneurs from our neighborhood with his violent thievery, and put bars on our windows. He kept us from sitting on our own front porch after dark and laid the foundation for our periodic bouts of self-hating anger and racial embarrassment. He made our neighborhood a ghetto. He is the poster fool behind the maddening community knowledge that there are still some black mothers who raise their daughters but merely love their sons. He and his cancerous carbon copies eclipse the vast majority of us who are not sociopaths and render us invisible. He is the Siamese twin who has died but cannot be separated from his living, vibrant sibling; which of us must attract more notice? We despise and disown this anomalous loser but, for many, he *is* black America. We know him, we know that he is outside the fold, and we know that he will only get worse. What we didn't know is that, because of him, my little sister would one day be the latest hysterical black mother wailing over a fallen child on TV.

Alone, lying in the road bleeding and paralyzed but hideously conscious, Johnny had lain helpless as he watched his would-be murderer come to stand over him and offer this prophecy: "Betch'ou won't be doin' nomo' wavin', motha' fucker."

Fuck you, asshole. He's fine from the waist up. You just can't do anything right, can you?

Questions:

1. What is Dickerson's argument in this essay?
2. Is Dickerson's description of "the brother who shot him" a stereotype? Would her claims read differently were she not a black woman?
3. How does Dickerson establish her ethos? Is it effective? Why?

II

Single Selections for Rhetorical Analysis

PLAY-DOCTORS ON THE HILL

They diagnose the vote potential in demographically correct diseases.

Charles Krauthammer

> *This article originally appeared in* The Washington Post. *As you read, underline or highlight the points in Krauthammer's argument which you find most persuasive. Why are those parts effective?*

In the age of Clinton, the relentless pursuit of yet new areas for the play of governmental compassion continues. The latest fad is the medical mandate: the promise of superior care if you have a politically correct condition. Last year's fashion was childbirth, which Washington, in its kindness, decreed should merit—uniquely, among human conditions—a guaranteed 48-hour hospital stay. Today it is breast cancer.

In case you missed it, the president somewhere deep in his State of the Union address, deplored the dangerous and demeaning practice of premature hospital discharges after mastectomy and asked Americans to "guarantee that a woman can stay in the hospital for 48 hours after a mastectomy."

On this issue, though, Clinton was running to catch up, compassion-wise, with the Republicans. Sen. Alfonse D'Amato and Rep. Susan Molinari had already proposed legislation to do just that. Indeed, their legislation guarantees not just a measly 48 hours, but an *indefinite* post-mastectomy hospital stay.

Before you howl at my insensitivity and hard-heartedness, answer me this: By what measure of compassion, by what rule of logic, by what principle of justice should this right and privilege extend only to women with post-breast cancer mastectomy?

Molinari offers no guidance. Under her "Women's Health and Cancer Rights Act" the breast cancer patient "in consultation with her physician, determines when it is medically appropriate to be discharged following a mastectomy. Rather than leaving the decision to insurance companies or even to Congress [!] this crucial decision is [to be] made by these personally involved."

Lovely sentiment. Now I repeat: Why just mastectomy?

Molinari: "Patients should never be denied the opportunity to be covered by insurance in this frightening situation." And "there are few procedures which are of such a sensitive nature as mastectomies."

I can name a few. Facial surgery following disfiguring trauma. Skin grafts for third-degree burns. Castration for testicular cancer. Colostomy (the diversion of the digestive tract so it empties not at the anus but out through the skin of the abdomen). Amputation.

Forgive my rudeness in producing this brief excerpt from the catalogue of horrors that life can visit upon the human body. But I am sorely provoked by the arrogance of a chamberful of lawyers stretching out its magic wand to anoint with special protection one, and only one, tragic affliction.

Maybe lawmakers should be sentenced to spend a week or two at a children's burn unit or a ward for diabetic amputees. They might then be a little more humble in deciding who earns the designation of sufferer from a "sensitive" or "frightening" condition.

I know because I served my time: three years as a resident doctor at the Massachusetts General Hospital and another, even more instructive, as a patient there. I spent that year in a four-bed hospital room. One of my many roommates was a double amputee. One of my ward mates, a fellow medical student, had suffered a terrible brain injury. He screamed at night.

Can we measure the anguish of this young man or my amputee buddy against that of a woman suffering from breast cancer? Of course not. So why is Congress doing so? Why is it playing favorites?

The answer is obvious. It is the crudest of group politics. What cheaper way for the gender-gapped Republicans to get credit for sensitivity to women? What better way for Clinton to reward his most crucial constituency?

Why breast cancer? After all, more women die of lung cancer, far more of heart disease. But alas, preferential treatment for these conditions would extend to millions of men as well. We can't have that. Hence the fashion for women-only breast cancer.

Consider: Preference-by-diagnosis began last year with the 48-hour stay for childbirth—a nice election-year gift to women between, say, 18 and 40.

Then last week, the Senate instructed the NIH to essentially reverse the finding of its own scientific panel and recommend mammograms for women between 40 and 50.

And now the mastectomy bill would grant an extraordinary hospital privilege for an illness that particularly targets women over 50.

Let's see now: 18–40, 40–50 and 50 and over. Taken together, these three congressional mandates on medical practice offer perfect demographic coverage for the entire constituency of voting-age women. It's a wonder Dick Morris hasn't taken credit for this yet.

Why is this bad? Because it is thoroughly and fundamentally unfair. Because these intrusive, often ignorant mandates (the 98–0 mammogram vote is a monument of know-nothing willfulness) are cynical pandering dressed up as compassion.

Is there a politician who will stand up to the women's groups and breast cancer lobby and declare that either all Americans live under the constraints of our wondrous but now cost-conscious medical system—or no one does? That you don't get a special pass merely because your diagnosis is now in political fashion.

I doubt it.

HENRY THE FIFTH (EXCERPT)

William Shakespeare

> *Delivered by King Henry V in order to inspire his troops to fight in the battle of Agincourt (1415) against the French, this excerpt is considered by many to be one of the most powerful motivational speeches in literature. Before you read, put yourself in the general position of the speaker and think about what kinds of arguments you would make to get a reluctant army to fight.*

—*The Complete Pelican Shakespeare, Ed: Alfred Harbage, New York, Viking, 1969.*

IV, ii

GRANDPRE

46 With torch-staves in their hand; and their poor jades
47 Lob down their heads, dropping the hides and hips,
48 The gum down roping from their pale-dead eyes,
49 And in their pale dull mouths the gimmaled bit
    Lies foul with chawed grass, still and motionless;
51 And their executors, the knavish crows,
    Fly o'er them all, impatient for their hour.
    Description cannot suit itself in words
    To demonstrate the life of such a battle
55 In life so lifeless as it shows itself.

CONSTABLE

56 They have said their prayers, and they stay for death.

DAUPHIN

    Shall we go send them dinners and fresh suits
    And give their fasting horses provender,
    And after fight with them?

CONSTABLE

60 I stay but for my guard. On to the field!
61 I will the banner from a trumpet take
    And use it for my haste. Come, come away!
63 The sun is high, and we outwear the day.
            Exeunt.

IV, iii

        Enter Gloucester, Bedford, Exeter, Erpingham with all his Host, Salisbury, and Westmoreland.

GLOUCESTER

    Where is the king?

BEDFORD

2   The king himself is rode to view their battle.

WESTMORELAND

    Of fighting men they have full three-score thousand.

EXETER

    There's five to one; besides, they all are fresh.

SALISBURY

    God's arm strike with us! 'Tis a fearful odds.

    God bye you, princes all; I'll to my charge.

    If we no more meet till we meet in heaven,

    Then joyfully, my noble Lord of Bedford,

    My dear Lord Gloucester, and my good Lord Exeter,

    And my kind kinsman, warriors all, adieu!

BEDFORD

    Farewell, good Salisbury, and good luck go with thee!

EXETER

    Farewell, kind lord: fight valiantly to-day;

    And yet I do thee wrong to mind thee of it,

14   For thou art framed of the firm truth of valor.

           [Exit Salisbury.]

BEDFORD

    He is as full of valor as of kindness,

    Princely in both.

           [Enter the King.]

WESTMORELAND

    O that we now had here

    But one ten thousand of those men in England

    That do no work to-day!

KING

    What's he that wishes so?

    My cousin Westmoreland? No, my fair cousin.

20   If we are marked to die, we are enow

    To do our country loss; and if to live,

    The fewer men, the greater share of honor.

    God's will! I pray thee wish not one man more.

    By Jove, I am not covetous for gold,

    Nor care I who doth feed upon my cost;

    It yearns me not if men my garments wear;

    Such outward things dwell not in my desires:

    But if it be a sin to covet *honor,*

    I am the most offending soul alive.

30   No, faith, my coz, wish not a man from England.

    God's peace! I would not lose so great an *honor*

    As one man more methinks would share from me

    For the best hope I have. O, do not wish one more!

    Rather proclaim it, Westmoreland, through my host,

    That he which hath no stomach to this fight,

Let him depart; his passport shall be made,
37 And crowns for convoy put into his purse.
We would not die in that man's company
39 That fears his fellowship to die with us.
40 This day is called the Feast of Crispian.
He that outlives this day, and comes safe home,
Will stand a-tiptoe when this day is named
And rouse him at the name of Crispian.
He that shall see this day, and live old age,
Will yearly on the vigil feast his neighbors
And say, 'To-morrow is Saint Crispian.'
Then will he strip his sleeve and show his scars,
[And say, 'These wounds I had on Crispin's day.']
Old men forget; yet all shall be forgot,
50 But he'll remember, with advantages,
What feats he did that day. Then shall our names,
Familiar in his mouth as household words—
Harry the King, Bedford and Exeter,
Warwick and Talbot, Salisbury and Gloucester—
Be in their flowing cups freshly rememb'red.
This story shall the good man teach his son;
And Crispin Crispian shall ne'er go by,
From this day to the ending of the world,
But we in it shall be remembered—
We few, we happy few, we band of brothers;
For he to-day that sheds his blood with me
62 Shall be my brother. Be he ne'er so vile,
63 This day shall gentle his condition;
And gentlemen in England now abed
Shall think themselves accursed they were not here,
And hold their manhoods cheap whiles any speaks
That fought with us upon Saint Crispin's day.
        Enter Salisbury.
SALISBURY
My sovereign lord, bestow yourself with speed.
The French are bravely in their battles set
70 And will with all expedience charge on us.
KING
All things are ready, if our minds be so.
WESTMORELAND
Perish the man whose mind is backward now!
KING
Thou dost not wish more help from England, coz?
WESTMORELAND
God's will, my liege! would you and I alone,

Without more help, could fight this royal battle!

Notes

46   *torch-staves,* tapers

47   *Lob,* droop

48   *roping* (cf. III, v, 23)

49   *gimmaled,* jointed

51   *executors,* disposers of the remains

55   *In life,* in actuality

56   *stay,* wait

60   *guard* (including color-bearer)

61   *trumpet,* trumpeter

63   *outwear,* waste

IV, iii The English Camp

2   *battle,* army

14   *framed . . . truth,* i.e. made of the authentic stuff

20-21   *enow,* To do enough to cause

26   *yearns,* moves, grieves

30   *coz,* cousin, kinsman

37   *convoy,* transport

39   *fellowship* i.e. fraternal right

40   *Feast of Crispian,* October 25 (the brothers Crispianus and Crispinus were martyred A.D. 487; they became the patron saints of shoemakers)

50   *advantages* i.e. embellishments

62   *vile,* low-born

63   *gentle his condition* i.e. achieve gentility

70   *expedience,* expedition

Question:

To what value, concern, or interest does King Henry primarily appeal? Is this appropriate given his audience?

EXCERPT FROM *PATTON*

The following speech has been excerpted from the film Patton *(1970) starring George C. Scott in the title role. The film, noted for its historical accuracy, details the life and times of World War II General George Patton, who often met with controversy for his intense speaking style. Scott won an Oscar in 1971 for his portrayal of the General.*

Now, I want you to remember that no bastard ever won a war by dying for his country. He won it by making the other poor, dumb bastard die for his country.

Men, all this talk about America not wanting to fight, wanting to stay out of the war is a lot of horse dung. Americans traditionally love to fight. All real Americans love the sting of battle. When you were kids, you all admired the champion marble shooter, the fastest runner, the big league ball players, the toughest boxers. Americans love a winner and will not tolerate a loser. Americans play to win all the time. I wouldn't give a hoot in hell for a man who lost and laughed. That's why Americans have never lost and will never lose a war: because the thought of losing is hateful to Americans.

Now, an army is a team. It lives, eats, sleeps, fights as a team. This individuality stuff is a bunch of crap. The bilious bastards who wrote that stuff about individuality for *The Saturday Evening Post* don't know anything more about real battle than they do about fornicating.

Now, we have the finest food and equipment, the best spirit and the best men in the world. You know, by God, I actually pity those poor bastards we are going up against. By God, I do. We're not just going to shoot the bastard. We're going to cut out their living guts and use them to grease the treads of our tanks. We are going to murder those lousy Hun bastards by the bushel.

Now, some of you boys, I know, are wondering whether or not you will chicken out under fire. Don't worry about it. I can assure you that you will do your duty. The Nazis are the enemy. Wade into them. Spill their blood. Shoot them in the belly. When you put your hand into a bunch of goo that a moment before was your best friend's face, you will know what to do.

Now, there's another thing I want you to remember. I don't want to get any messages saying that we are holding our position. We're not holding anything. Let the Hun do that. We are advancing constantly and we are not interested in holding on to anything except the enemy. We're going to hold on to him by the nose and we're going to kick him in the ass. We're going to kick the hell out of him all the time and we're going to go through him like crap through a goose.

Now there's one thing that you men will be able to say when you get back home and you may thank God for it. Thirty years from now when you are sitting around your fireside with your grandson on your knee and he asks you "What did you do in the great World War II?" you won't have to say, "Well, I shoveled shit in Louisiana."

All right you sons of bitches, you know how I feel. Oh, I will be proud to lead you wonderful guys into battle anytime, anywhere. That's all.

Questions:

1. What is the speaker trying to accomplish with this speech? What is the thesis?
2. Is the speaker persuasive?
3. Does Patton present himself as credible? How?
4. To which rhetorical appeal (ethos, logos, or pathos) does Patton primarily appeal?

LETTER FROM BIRMINGHAM JAIL

Martin Luther King, Jr.

> *Martin Luther King, Jr. (1929–1968) was an ordained minister with a doctorate in theology who led a boycott of the Montgomery bus system in 1955, resulting in the Supreme Court's ruling that Alabama's bus segregation laws were unconstitutional. In 1957, King organized the Southern Christian Leadership Conference (SCLC) as a way to promote a nonviolent platform for equality and justice for black Americans. Over the next thirteen years, he led numerous protests and met with much criticism: he was stabbed, had his house bombed three times, and was frequently arrested and jailed. This famous letter was written from a jail cell in 1963 after King had been arrested at a sit-in demonstration in a segregated diner in Birmingham, Alabama. It is directly addressed to King's fellow clergy who were critical of his activism. As you read, think about whether this specific audience is the only one King addresses in this letter.*
>
> *Deemed one of the most prominent and charismatic leaders for black civil rights in America, King is distinguished for his zealous commitment to nonviolence. He is also known for his strong moral vision and powerful eloquence. In 1964 he was awarded the Nobel Peace Prize for his efforts to transform America, the youngest (at age 35) to receive it. Just four years later, while demonstrating in Memphis for striking sanitation workers, he was assassinated by a white man, James Earl Ray. Ray died in late April 1998, while serving a ninety-nine-year prison sentence.*

My Dear Fellow Clergymen:[1]

While confined here in the Birmingham city jail, I came across your recent statement calling my present activities "unwise and untimely." Seldom do I pause to answer criticism of my work and ideas. If I sought to answer all the criticisms that cross my desk, my secretaries would have little time for anything other than such correspondence in the course of the day, and I would have no time for constructive work. But since I feel that you are men of genuine good will and that your criticisms are sincerely set forth, I want to try to answer your statements in what I hope will be patient and reasonable terms.

I think I should indicate why I am here in Birmingham, since you have been influenced by the view which argues against "outsiders coming in." I have the honor of serving as president of the Southern Christian Leadership Conference, an organization operating in every southern state, with headquarters in Atlanta, Georgia. We have some eighty-five affiliated organizations across the South, and one of them is the Alabama Christian Movement for Human Rights. Frequently we share staff, educational, and financial resources with our affiliates. Several months ago the affiliate here in Birmingham asked us to be on call to engage in a nonviolent direct-action program if such were deemed necessary. We readily consented, and when the hour came we lived up to our promise. So I, along with several members of my staff, am here because I was invited here. I am here because I have organizational ties here.

But more basically, I am in Birmingham because injustice is here. Just as the prophets of the eighth century B.C. left their villages and carried their "thus saith the Lord" far beyond the boundaries of their home towns, and just as the Apostle Paul left his village of Tarsus and carried the gospel of Jesus Christ to the far corners of the Greco-Roman world, so am I compelled to carry the gospel of freedom beyond my own home town. Like Paul, I must constantly respond to the Macedonian call for aid. Moreover, I am cognizant of the interrelatedness of all communities and states. I cannot sit idly by in Atlanta and not be concerned about what happens in Birmingham. Injustice anywhere is a threat to justice everywhere. We are caught in an inescapable network of mutuality, tied in a single garment of destiny. Whatever affects one directly, affects all indirectly. Never again can we afford to live with the narrow, provincial "outside agitator" idea. Anyone who lives inside the United States can never be considered an outsider anywhere within its bounds.

You deplore the demonstrations taking place in Birmingham. But your statement, I am sorry to say, fails to express a similar concern for the conditions that brought about the demonstrations. I am sure that none of you would want to rest content with the superficial kind of social analysis that deals merely with effects and does not grapple with underlying causes. It is unfortunate that demonstrations are taking place in Birmingham, but it is even more unfortunate that the city's white power structure left the Negro community with no alternative.

In any nonviolent campaign there are four basic steps: collection of the facts to determine whether injustices exist; negotiation; self-purification; and direct action. We have gone through all these steps in Birmingham. There can be no gainsaying the fact that racial injustice engulfs this community. Birmingham is probably the most thoroughly segregated city in the United States. Its ugly record of brutality is widely known. Negroes have experienced grossly unjust treatment in the courts. There have been more unsolved bombings of Negro homes and churches in Birmingham than in any other city in the nation. These are the hard, brutal facts of the case. On the basis of these conditions, Negro leaders sought to negotiate with the city fathers. But the latter consistently refused to engage in good-faith negotiation.

Then, last September, came the opportunity to talk with leaders of Birmingham's economic community. In the course of the negotiations, certain promises were made by the merchants—for example, to remove the stores' humiliating racial signs. On the basis of these promises, the Reverend Fred Shuttlesworth and the leaders of the Alabama Christian Movement for Human Rights agreed to a moratorium on all demonstrations. As the weeks and months went by, we realized that we were the victims of a broken promise. A few signs, briefly removed, returned; the others remained.

As in so many past experiences, our hopes had been blasted, and the shadow of deep disappointment settled upon us. We had no alternative except to prepare for direct action, whereby we would present our very bodies as a means of laying our case before the conscience of the local and the national community. Mindful of the difficulties involved, we decided to undertake a process of self-purification. We began a series of workshops on nonviolence, and we repeatedly asked ourselves: "Are you able to accept blows without retaliating?" "Are you able to endure the ordeal of jail?" We decided to schedule our direct-action program for the Easter season, realizing that except for Christmas, this is the main shopping period of the year. Knowing that a strong economic-withdrawal program would be the by-product of direct action, we felt that this would be the best time to bring pressure to bear on the merchants for the needed change.

Then it occurred to us that Birmingham's mayoralty election was coming up in March, and we speedily decided to postpone action until after election day. When we discovered that the Commissioner of Public Safety, Eugene "Bull" Connor, had piled up enough votes to be in the run-off we decided again to postpone action until the day after the run-off so that the demonstrations could not be used to cloud the issues. Like many others, we waited to see Mr. Connor defeated, and to this end we endured postponement after postponement. Having aided in this community need, we felt that our direct-action program could be delayed no longer.

You may well ask: "Why direct action? Why sit-ins, marches, and so forth? Isn't negotiation a better path?" You are quite right in calling for negotiation. Indeed, this is the very purpose of direct action. Nonviolent direct action seeks to create such a crisis and foster such a tension that a community which has constantly refused to negotiate is forced to confront the issue. It seeks to dramatize the issue that it can no longer be ignored. My citing the creation of tension as part of the work of the nonviolent-resister may sound rather shocking. But I must confess that I am not afraid of the word "tension." I have earnestly opposed violent tension, but there is a type of constructive, nonviolent tension which is necessary for growth. Just as Socrates felt that it was necessary to create a tension in the mind so that individuals could rise from the bondage of myths and half-truths to the unfettered realm of creative analysis and objective appraisal, so must we see the need for nonviolent gadflies to create the kind of tension in society that will help men rise from the dark depths of prejudice and racism to the majestic heights of understanding and brotherhood.

The purpose of our direct-action program is to create a situation so crisis-packed that it will inevitably open the door to negotiation. I therefore concur with you in your call for negotiation. Too long has our beloved Southland been bogged down in a tragic effort to live in monologue rather than dialogue.

One of the basic points in your statement is that the action that I and my associates have taken in Birmingham is untimely. Some have asked: "Why didn't you give the new city administration time to act?" The only answer that I can give to this query is that the new Birmingham administration must be prodded about as much as the outgoing one, before it will act. We are sadly mistaken if we feel that the election of Albert Boutwell as mayor will bring the millennium to Birmingham. While Mr. Boutwell is a much more gentle person than Mr. Connor, they are both segregationists, dedicated to maintenance of the status quo. I have hope that Mr. Boutwell will be reasonable enough to see the futility of massive resistance to desegregation. But he will not see this without pressure from devotees of civil rights. My friends, I must say to you that we have not made a single gain in civil rights without determined legal and nonviolent pressure. Lamentably, it is an historical fact that privileged groups seldom give up their privileges voluntarily. Individuals may see the moral light and voluntarily give up their unjust posture; but, as Reinhold Niebuhr has reminded us, groups tend to be more immoral than individuals.

We know through painful experience that freedom is never voluntarily given by the oppressor; it must be demanded by the oppressed. Frankly, I have yet to engage in a direct-action campaign that was "well timed" in the view of those who have not suffered unduly from the disease of segregation. For years now I have heard the word "Wait!" It rings in the ear of every Negro with piercing familiarity. This "Wait" has almost always meant 'Never." We must come to see, with one of our distinguished jurists, that "justice too long delayed is justice denied."

We have waited for more than 340 years for our constitutional and God-given rights. The nations of Asia and Africa are moving with jet-like speed toward gaining political independence, but we still creep at horse-and-buggy pace toward gaining a cup of coffee at a lunch counter. Perhaps it is easy for those who have never felt the stinging darts of segregation to say, "Wait." But when you have seen vicious mobs lynch your mothers and fathers at will and drown your sisters and brothers at whim; when you have seen hate-filled policemen curse, kick, and even kill your black brothers and sisters; when you see the vast majority of your twenty million Negro brothers smothering in an airtight cage of poverty in the midst of an affluent society; when you suddenly find your tongue twisted and your speech stammering as you seek to explain to your six-year-old daughter why she can't go to the public amusement park that has just been advertised on television, and see tears welling up in her eyes when she is told that Funtown is closed to colored children, and see ominous clouds of inferiority beginning to form in her little mental sky, and see her beginning to distort her personality by developing an unconscious bitterness toward white people; when you have to concoct an answer for a five-year-old son who is asking: "Daddy, why do white people treat colored people so mean?"; when you take a cross-country drive and find it necessary to sleep night after night in the uncomfortable corners of your automobile because no motel will accept you; when you are humiliated day in and day out by nagging signs reading "white" and "colored"; when your first name becomes "nigger," your middle name becomes "boy" (however old you are) and your last name becomes "John," and your wife and mother are never given the respected title "Mrs."; when you are harried by day and haunted by night by the fact that you are a Negro, living constantly at tiptoe stance, never quite knowing what to expect next, and are plagued with inner fears and outer resentments; when you are forever fighting a degenerating sense of "nobodiness"—then you will understand why we find it difficult to wait. There comes a time when the cup of endurance runs over, and men are no longer willing to be plunged into the abyss of despair. I hope, sirs, you can understand our legitimate and unavoidable impatience.

You express a great deal of anxiety over our willingness to break laws. This is certainly a legitimate concern. Since we so diligently urge people to obey the Supreme Court's decision of 1954 outlawing segregation in the public schools, at first glance it may seem rather paradoxical for us consciously to break laws. One may well ask: "How can you advocate breaking some laws and obeying others?" The answer lies in the fact that there are two types of laws: just and unjust. I would be the first to advocate obeying just laws. One has not only a legal but a moral responsibility to obey just laws. Conversely, one has a moral responsibility to disobey unjust laws. I would agree with St. Augustine that "an unjust law is no law at all"

Now, what is the difference between the two? How does one determine whether a law is just or unjust? A just law is a man-made code that squares with the moral law or the law of God. An unjust law is a code that is out of harmony with the moral law. To put it in the terms of St. Thomas Aquinas: An unjust law is a human law that is not rooted in eternal law and natural law. Any law that uplifts human personality is just. Any law that degrades human personality is unjust. All segregation statutes are unjust because segregation distorts the soul and damages the personality. It gives the segregator a false sense of superiority and the segregated a false sense of inferiority. Segregation, to use the terminology of the Jewish philosopher Martin Buber, substitutes an "I-it" relationship for an "I-thou" relationship and ends up relegating persons to the status of things. Hence segregation is not only politically, economically, and sociologically unsound, it is morally wrong and awful. Paul Tillich said that sin is separation. Is not segregation an existential expression of man's tragic separation, his awful estrangement, his terrible sinfulness? Thus it is that I can urge men to obey the 1954 decision of the Supreme Court, for it is morally right; and I can urge them to disobey segregation ordinances, for they are morally wrong.

Let us consider a more concrete example of just and unjust laws. An unjust law is a code that a numerical or power majority group compels a minority group to obey but does not make binding on itself. This is *difference* made legal. By the same token, a just law is a code that a majority compels a minority to follow and that it is willing to follow itself. This is *sameness* made legal.

Let me give another explanation. A law is unjust if it is inflicted on a minority that, as a result of being denied the right to vote, had no part in enacting or devising the law. Who can say that the legislature of Alabama which set up that state's segregation laws was democratically elected? Throughout Alabama all sorts of devious methods are used to prevent Negroes from becoming registered voters, and there are some counties in which, even though Negroes constitute a majority of the population, not a single Negro is registered. Can any law enacted under such circumstances be considered democratically structured?

Sometimes a law is just on its face and unjust in its application. For instance, I have been arrested on a charge of parading without a permit. Now, there is nothing wrong in having an ordinance which requires a permit for a parade. But such an ordinance becomes unjust when it is used to maintain segregation and to deny citizens the First Amendment privilege of peaceful assembly and protest.

I hope you are able to see the distinction I am trying to point out. In no sense do I advocate evading or defying the law, as would the rabid segregationist. That would lead to anarchy. One who breaks an unjust law must do so openly, lovingly, and with a willingness to accept the penalty. I submit that an individual who breaks a law that conscience tells him is unjust and who willingly accepts the penalty of imprisonment in order to arouse the conscience of the community over its injustice, is in reality expressing the highest respect for law.

Of course, there is nothing new about this kind of civil disobedience. It was evidenced sublimely in the refusal of Shadrach, Meshach, and Abednego to obey the laws

of Nebuchadnezzar, on the ground that a higher moral law was at stake. It was practiced superbly by the early Christians, who were willing to face hungry lions and the
excruciating pain of chopping blocks rather than submit to certain unjust laws of the
Roman Empire. To a degree, academic freedom is a reality today because Socrates
practiced civil disobedience. In our own nation, the Boston Tea Party represented a
massive act of civil disobedience.

We should never forget that everything Adolf Hitler did in Germany was "legal"
and everything the Hungarian freedom fighters did in Hungary was "illegal." It was
"illegal" to aid and comfort a Jew in Hitler's Germany. Even so, I am sure that, had I
lived in Germany at the time, I would have aided and comforted my Jewish brothers.
If today I lived in a Communist country where certain principles dear to the Christian faith are suppressed, I would openly advocate disobeying that country's antireli-
gious laws.

I must make two honest confessions to you, my Christian and Jewish brothers.
First, I must confess that over the past few years I have been gravely disappointed with
the white moderate. I have almost reached the regrettable conclusion that the Negro's
great stumbling block in his stride toward freedom is not the White Citizen's Coun-
ciler or the Ku Klux Klanner, but the white moderate, who is more devoted to "order"
than to justice; who prefers a negative peace which is the absence of tension to a positive peace which is the presence of justice; who constantly says: "I agree with you in
the goal you seek, but I cannot agree with your methods of direct action"; who pater-
nalistically believes he can set the timetable for another man's freedom; who lives by
a mythical concept of time and who constantly advises the Negro to wait for a "more
convenient season." Shallow understanding from people of good will is more frustrating than absolute misunderstanding from people of ill will. Lukewarm acceptance
is much more bewildering than outright rejection.

I had hoped that the white moderate would understand that law and order exist
for the purpose of establishing justice and that when they fail in this purpose they
become the dangerously structured dams that block the flow of social progress. I had
hoped that the white moderate would understand that the present tension in the South
is a necessary phase of the transition from an obnoxious negative peace, in which the
Negro passively accepted his unjust plight, to a substantive and positive peace, in which
all men will respect the dignity and worth of human personality. Actually, we who
engage in nonviolent direct action are not the creators of tension. We merely bring to
the surface the hidden tension that is already alive. We bring it out in the open, where
it can be seen and dealt with. Like a boil that can never be cured so long as it is covered up but must be opened with all its ugliness to the natural medicines of air and
light, injustice must be exposed, with all the tension its exposure creates, to the light of
human conscience and the air of national opinion before it can be cured.

In your statement you assert that our actions, even though peaceful, must be condemned because they precipitate violence. But is this a logical assertion? Isn't this like
condemning a robbed man because his possession of money precipitated the evil act
of robbery? Isn't this like condemning Socrates because his unswerving commitment
to truth and his philosophical inquiries precipitated the act by the misguided populace in which they made him drink hemlock? Isn't this like condemning Jesus because

his unique God-consciousness and never-ceasing devotion to God's will precipitated the evil act of crucifixion? We must come to see that, as the federal courts have consistently affirmed, it is wrong to urge an individual to cease his efforts to gain his basic constitutional rights because the quest may precipitate violence. Society must protect the robbed and punish the robber.

I had also hoped that the white moderate would reject the myth concerning time in relation to the struggle for freedom. I have just received a letter from a white brother in Texas. He writes: "All Christians know that the colored people will receive equal rights eventually, but it is possible that you are in too great a religious hurry. It has taken Christianity almost two thousand years to accomplish what it has. The teachings of Christ take time to come to earth." Such an attitude stems from a tragic misconception of time, from the strangely rational notion that there is something in the very flow of time that will inevitably cure all ills. Actually, time itself is neutral; it can be used either destructively or constructively. More and more I feel that the people of ill will have used time much more effectively than have the people of good will. We will have to repent in this generation not merely for the hateful words and actions of the bad people but for the appalling silence of the good people. Human progress never rolls in on wheels of inevitability; it comes through the tireless efforts of men willing to be co-workers with God, and without this hard work, time itself becomes an ally of the forces of social stagnation. We must use time creatively, in the knowledge that the time is always ripe to do right. Now is the time to make real the promise of democracy and transform our pending national elegy into a creative psalm of brotherhood. Now is the time to lift our national policy from the quicksand of racial injustice to be solid rock of human dignity.

You speak of our activity in Birmingham as extreme. At first I was rather disappointed that fellow clergymen would see my nonviolent efforts as those of an extremist. I began thinking about the fact that I stand in the middle of two opposing forces in the Negro community. One is a force of complacency, made up in part of Negroes who, as a result of long years of oppression, are so drained of self-respect and a sense of "somebodiness" that they have adjusted to segregation; and in part of a few middle class Negroes who, because of a degree of academic and economic security and because in some ways they profit by segregation, have become insensitive to the problems of the masses. The other force is one of bitterness and hatred, and it comes perilously close to advocating violence. It is expressed in the various black nationalist groups that are springing up across the nation, the largest and best-known being Elijah Muhammad's Muslim movement. Nourished by the Negro's frustration over the continued existence of racial discrimination, this movement is made up of people who have lost faith in America, who have absolutely repudiated Christianity, and who have concluded that the white man is an incorrigible "evil."

I have tried to stand between these two forces, saying that we need emulate neither the "do-nothingism" of the complacent nor the hatred and despair of the black nationalist. For there is the more excellent way of love and nonviolent protest. I am grateful to God that, through the influence of the Negro church, the way of nonviolence became an integral part of our struggle.

If this philosophy had not emerged, by now many streets of the South would, I am convinced, be flowing with blood. And I am further convinced that if our white brothers dismiss as "rabble-rousers" and "outside agitators" those of us who employ nonviolent direct action, and if they refuse to support our nonviolent efforts, millions of Negroes will, out of frustration and despair, seek solace and security in black-nationalist ideologies—a development that would inevitably lead to a frightening racial nightmare.

Oppressed people cannot remain oppressed forever. The yearning for freedom eventually manifests itself, and that is what has happened to the American Negro. Something within has reminded him of his birthright of freedom, and something without has reminded him that it can be gained. Consciously or unconsciously, he has been caught up by the *Zeitgeist*, and with his black brothers of Africa and his brown and yellow brothers of Asia, South America, and the Caribbean, the United States Negro is moving with a sense of great urgency toward the promised land of racial justice. If one recognizes this vital urge that has engulfed the Negro community, one should readily understand why public demonstrations are taking place. The Negro has many pent-up resentments and latent frustrations, and he must release them. So let him march; let him make prayer pilgrimages to the city hall; let him go on freedom rides—and try to understand why he must do so. If his repressed emotions are not released in nonviolent ways, they will seek expression through violence; this is not a threat but a fact of history. So I have not said to my people: "Get rid of your discontent." Rather, I have tried to say that this normal and healthy discontent can be channeled into the creative outlet of nonviolent direct action. And now this approach is being termed extremist.

But though I was initially disappointed at being categorized as an extremist, as I continued to think about the matter I gradually gained a measure of satisfaction from the label. Was not Jesus an extremist for love: "Love your enemies, bless them that curse you, do good to them that hate you, and pray for them which despitefully use you, and persecute you." Was not Amos an extremist for justice: "Let justice roll down like waters and righteousness like an ever-flowing stream." Was not Paul an extremist for the Christian gospel: "I bear in my body the marks of the Lord Jesus." Was not Martin Luther an extremist: "Here I stand; I cannot do otherwise, so help me God." And John Bunyan: "I will stay in jail to the end of my days before I make a butchery of my conscience." And Abraham Lincoln: "This nation cannot survive half slave and half free." And Thomas Jefferson: "We hold these truths to be self-evident, that all men are created equal. . . ." So the question is not whether we will be extremists, but what kind of extremists we will be. Will we be extremists for hate or for love? Will we be extremists for the preservation of injustice or for the extension of justice? In that dramatic scene on Calvary's hill three men were crucified. We must never forget that all three were crucified for the same crime—the crime of extremism. Two were extremists for immorality, and thus fell below their environment. The other, Jesus Christ, was an extremist for love, truth, and goodness, and thereby rose above his environment. Perhaps the South, the nation, and the world are in dire need of creative extremists.

I had hoped that the white moderate would see this need. Perhaps I was too optimistic; perhaps I expected too much. I suppose I should have realized that few members of the oppressor race can understand the deep groans and passionate yearnings of the oppressed race, and still fewer have the vision to see that injustice must be rooted out by strong, persistent, and determined action. I am thankful, however, that some of our white brothers in the South have grasped the meaning of this social revolution and committed themselves to it. They are still too few in quantity, but they are big in quality. Some—such as Ralph McGill, Lillian Smith, Harry Golden, James McBride Dabbs, Ann Braden, and Sarah Patton Boyle—have written about our struggle in eloquent and prophetic terms. Others have marched with us down nameless streets of the South. They have languished in filthy, roach-infested jails, suffering the abuse and brutality of policemen who view them as "dirty nigger lovers." Unlike so many of their moderate brothers and sisters, they have recognized the urgency of the moment and sensed the need for powerful "action" antidotes to combat the disease of segregation.

Let me take note of my other major disappointment. I have been so greatly disappointed with the white church and its leadership. Of course, there are some notable exceptions. I am not unmindful of the fact that each of you has taken some significant stands on this issue. I commend you, Reverend Stallings, for your Christian stand on this past Sunday, in welcoming Negroes to your worship service on a nonsegregated basis. I commend the Catholic leaders of this state for integrating Spring Hill College several years ago.

But despite these notable exceptions, I must honestly reiterate that I have been disappointed with the church. I do not say this as one of those negative critics who can always find something wrong with the church. I say this as a minister of the gospel, who loves the church; who was nurtured in its bosom; who has been sustained by its spiritual blessings and who will remain true to it as long as the cord of life shall lengthen.

When I was suddenly catapulted into the leadership of the bus protest in Montgomery, Alabama, a few years ago, I felt we would be supported by the white church. I felt that the white ministers, priests, and rabbis of the South would be among our strongest allies. Instead, some have been outright opponents, refusing to understand the freedom movement and misrepresenting its leaders; all too many others have been more cautious than courageous and have remained silent behind the anesthetizing security of stained-glass windows.

In spite of my shattered dreams, I came to Birmingham with the hope that the white religious leadership of this community would see the justice of our cause and, with deep moral concern, would serve as the channel through which our just grievances could reach the power structure. I had hoped that each of you would understand. But again I have been disappointed.

I have heard numerous Southern religious leaders admonish their worshipers to comply with a desegregation decision because it is the law, but I have longed to hear white ministers declare: "Follow this decree because integration is morally right and because the Negro is your brother." In the midst of blatant injustices inflicted upon the Negro, I have watched white churchmen stand on the sideline and mouth pious irrelevancies and sanctimonious trivialities. In the midst of a mighty struggle to rid our nation of racial and economic injustice, I have heard many ministers say: "Those are social issues, with which the gospel has no real concern." And I have watched many churches commit themselves to a completely otherworldly religion which makes a strange, and Biblical distinction between body and soul, between the sacred and the secular.

I have traveled the length and breadth of Alabama, Mississippi, and all the other Southern states. On sweltering summer days and crisp autumn mornings I have looked at the South's beautiful churches with their lofty spires pointing heavenward. I have beheld the impressive outlines of her massive religious-education buildings. Over and over I have found myself asking: "What kind of people worship here? Who is their God? Where were their voices when the lips of Governor Barnett dripped with words of interposition and nullification? Where were they when Governor Wallace gave a clarion call for defiance and hatred? Where were their voices of support when bruised and weary Negro men and women decided to rise from the dark dungeons of complacency to the bright hills of creative protest?"

Yes, these questions are still in my mind. In deep disappointment I have wept over the laxity of the church. But be assured that my tears have been tears of love. There can be no deep disappointment where there is not deep love. Yes, I love the church. How could I do otherwise? 1 am in the rather unique position of being the son, the grandson and the great-grandson of preachers. Yes, I see the church as the body of Christ. But, oh! How we have blemished and scarred that body through social neglect and through fear of being nonconformists.

There was a time when the church was very powerful—in the time when the early Christians rejoiced at being deemed worthy to suffer for what they believed. In those days the church was not merely a thermometer that recorded the ideas and principles of popular opinion; it was a thermostat that transformed the mores of society. Whenever the early Christians entered a town, the people in power became disturbed and immediately sought to convict the Christians for being "disturbers of the peace" and "outside agitators." But the Christians pressed on, in the conviction that they were "a colony of heaven," called to obey God rather than man. Small in number, they were big in commitment. They were too God intoxicated to be "astronomically intimidated." By their effort and example they brought an end to such ancient evils as infanticide and gladiatorial contests.

Things are different now. So often the contemporary church is a weak, ineffectual voice with an uncertain sound. So often it is an arch-defender of the status quo. Far from being disturbed by the presence of the church, the power structure of the average community is consoled by the church's silent and often even vocal sanction of things as they are.

But the judgment of God is upon the church as never before. If today's church does not recapture the sacrificial spirit of the early church, it will lose its authenticity, forfeit the loyalty of millions, and be dismissed as an irrelevant social club with no meaning for the twentieth century. Every day I meet young people whose disappointment with the church has turned into outright disgust.

Perhaps I have once again been too optimistic. Is organized religion too inextricably bound to the status quo to save our nation and the world? Perhaps I must turn my faith to the inner spiritual church, the church within the church, as the true *ekklesia* and the hope of the world. But again I am thankful to God that some noble souls from the ranks of organized religion have broken loose from the paralyzing chains of conformity and joined us as active partners in the struggle for freedom, They have left their secure congregations and walked the streets of Albany, Georgia, with us. They have gone down the highways of the South on torturous rides for freedom. Yes, they have gone to jail with us. Some have been dismissed from their churches, have lost the support of their bishops and fellow ministers. But they have acted in the faith that right defeated is stronger than evil triumphant. Their witness has been the spiritual salt that has preserved the true meaning of the gospel in these troubled times. They have carved a tunnel of hope through the dark mountain of disappointment.

I hope the church as a whole will meet the challenge of this decisive hour. But even if the church does not come to the aid of justice, I have no despair about the future. I have no fear about the outcome of our struggle in Birmingham, even if our motives are at present misunderstood. We will reach the goal of freedom in Birmingham and all over the nation, because the goal of America is freedom. Abused and scorned though we may be, our destiny is tied up with America's destiny. Before the pilgrims landed at Plymouth, we were here. Before the pen of Jefferson etched the majestic words of the Declaration of Independence across the pages of history, we were here. For more than two centuries our forebears labored in this country without wages; they made cotton king; they built the homes of their masters while suffering gross injustice and shameful humiliation—and yet out of a bottomless vitality they continued to thrive and develop. If the inexpressible cruelties of slavery could not stop us, the opposition we now face will surely fail. We will win our freedom because the sacred heritage of our nation and the eternal will of God are embodied in our echoing demands.

Before closing I feel impelled to mention one other point in your statement that has troubled me profoundly. You warmly commended the Birmingham police force for keeping "order" and "preventing violence." I doubt that you would have so warmly commended the police force if you had seen its dogs sinking their teeth into unarmed, nonviolent Negroes. I doubt that you would so quickly commend the policemen if you were to observe their ugly and inhumane treatment of Negroes here in the city jail; if you were to watch them push and curse old Negro women and young Negro girls; if you were to see them slap and kick old Negro men and young boys; if you were to observe them, as they did on two occasions, refuse to give us food because we wanted to sing our grace together. I cannot join you in your praise of the Birmingham police department.

It is true that the police have exercised a degree of discipline in handling the demonstrators. In this sense they have conducted themselves rather "nonviolently" in public. But for what purpose? To preserve the evil system of segregation. Over the past few years I have consistently preached that nonviolence demands that the means we use must be as pure as the ends we seek. I have tried to make clear that it is wrong to use immoral means to attain moral ends. But now I must affirm that it is just as wrong, or perhaps even more so, to use moral means to preserve immoral ends. Perhaps Mr. Connor and his policemen have been rather nonviolent in public, as was Chief Pritchett in Albany, Georgia, but they have used the moral means of nonviolence to maintain the immoral end of racial injustice. As T. S. Eliot has said: "The last temptation is the greatest treason: To do the right deed for the wrong reason."

I wish you had commended the Negro sit-inners and demonstrators of Birmingham for their sublime courage, their willingness to suffer, and their amazing discipline in the midst of great provocation. One day the South will recognize its real heroes. They will be the James Merediths, with the noble sense of purpose that enables them to face jeering and hostile mobs, and with the agonizing loneliness that characterizes the life of the pioneer. They will be old, oppressed, battered Negro women, symbolized in a seventy-two-year-old woman in Montgomery, Alabama, who rose up with a sense of dignity and with her people decided not to ride segregated buses, and who responded with ungrammatical profundity to one who inquired about her weariness: "My feets is tired, but my soul is at rest." They will be the young high school and college students, the young ministers of the gospel and a host of their elders, courageously and nonviolently sitting in at lunch counters and willingly going to jail for conscience' sake. One day the South will know that when these disinherited children of God sat down at lunch counters, they were in reality standing up for what is best in the American dream and for the most sacred values in our Judaeo-Christian heritage, thereby bringing our nation back to those great wells of democracy which were dug deep by the founding fathers in their formulation of the Constitution and the Declaration of Independence.

Never before have I written so long a letter. I'm afraid it is much too long to take your precious time. I can assure you that it would have been much shorter if I had been writing from a comfortable desk, but what else can one do when he is alone in a narrow jail cell, other than write long letters, think long thoughts and pray long prayers?

If I have said anything in this letter that overstates the truth and indicates an unreasonable impatience, I beg you to forgive me. If I have said anything that understates the truth and indicates my having a patience that allows me to settle for anything less than brotherhood, I beg God to forgive me.

I hope this letter finds you strong in the faith. I also hope that circumstances will soon make it possible for me to meet each of you, not as an integrationist or a civil rights leader but as a fellow clergyman and a Christian brother. Let us all hope that the dark clouds of racial prejudice will soon pass away and the deep fog of misunderstanding will be lifted from our fear-drenched communities, and in some not too distant tomorrow the radiant stars of love and brotherhood will shine over our great nation with all their scintillating beauty.

> Yours for the cause of Peace and Brotherhood,
> Martin Luther King, Jr.

Note

1. This response to a published statement by eight fellow clergymen from Alabama (Bishop C. C. J. Carpenter, Bishop Joseph A. Durick, Rabbi Hilton L. Grafman, Bishop Paul Hardin, Bishop Holan B. Harmon, the Reverend George M. Murray, the Reverend Edward V. Ramage, and the Reverend Earl Stallings) was composed under somewhat constricting circumstances. Begun on the margins of the newspaper in which the

statement appeared while I was in jail, the letter was continued on scraps of writing paper supplied by a friendly Negro trusty, and concluded on a pad my attorneys were eventually permitted to leave me. Although the text remains in substance unaltered, I have indulged in the author's prerogative of polishing it for publication.

Questions:

1. King is essentially writing to two audiences—both a hostile and a friendly one. How, then, does he address their multi-faceted concerns? Why do you think he chose to address the audiences he did?

2. Does King present himself as an authority on this subject? How? Does he vindicate himself to his hostile audience?

3. How does King define "nonviolent" action? Similarly, how does King distinguish between just and unjust laws? Is this logic effective?

4. Pay attention to King's strategy in addressing his opposition, especially as he presents it in paragraph 10. What is that strategy? Why does he use it? What is the effect on his audiences?

5. What does King suggest is the relationship between his nonviolent anti-racism campaign and Christianity? In terms of the argument he makes in this letter, why might he imply they complement one another?

6. Do you think this letter would have been effective if it were a speech? Explain.

III

Paired Selections for Rhetorical Analysis

THEY CAN BE A COUPLE, BUT NOT MARRIED

Jeff Jacoby

> *Jeff Jacoby is a regular columnist for the* Boston Globe. *This article originally appeared in the* Baltimore Sun *on 17 July 1996. In it, Jacoby addresses the then-recent Defense of Marriage Act, centering his argument around a traditional definition of marriage.*

Got to give Rep. Barney Frank credit. In his attack last week on the Defense of Marriage Act, which asserts as a matter of federal law that members of the same sex cannot "marry" each other, the homosexual Massachusetts congressman found himself arguing without benefit of facts, law, morality, history or common sense.

That might have intimidated lesser debaters, but not Mr. Frank. The most skillful polemicist in Congress simply changed the subject.

"How does the fact that I love another man and live in a committed relationship with him threaten your marriage?" he demanded in the House of Representatives. "Are your relations with your spouses of such fragility that the fact that I have a committed, loving relationship with another man jeopardizes them?"

A Phony Argument

As if that were the issue. No one ever suggested that Mr. Frank's unconventional love life is a danger to congressional marriages. But clever rhetoricians know that when you can't win the *real* argument, you try to maneuver your opponents into debating a phony one. In the end, the gambit didn't work—the Defense of Marriage Act passed the House, 342–67; now it moves to the Senate. Nice try, though.

The question that Mr. Frank and most gay activists would rather not answer is this: Why should the settled definition of marriage, which has been understood in virtually all places and times to mean the union of a man and woman, be overthrown?

The meaning of marriage is one of the few constants in human history, a point of agreement among cultures, religions and eras that share little else. If, after all these centuries, something as basic and universal as the definition of marriage is to be dramatically altered, there must be an irresistibly compelling reason to do so. What is it?

After all, it's not as if gay men and lesbians are barred from marrying. Many— perhaps most—men with homosexual tendencies *have* married women; many lesbians, despite their attraction to other women, have married men.

No doubt some of these marriages were mere shells; many more were genuine and lasting relationships, within which homes were built, children raised and life's joys and travails experienced together. The fact that these unions may not have been fully satisfying sexually is hardly a reason to rewrite the law of matrimony.

Plenty of men and women find the traditional boundaries of marriage constricting. Some men would prefer two or three wives. Others are attracted to their daughters, or their aunts, or the wife next door. Bisexuals might like a husband *and* a wife. There are women who crave an intimate relationship with their brothers. If marriage is to be redefined so that it includes same-sex unions, why shouldn't it be redefined to include *all* unions?

The hard reality—however much gay advocates evade it—is that there are only two options: Either marriage is restricted to one man plus one (unrelated) woman or it is not restricted at all. Change the law so that two men can be deemed "married," and what grounds can there possibly be not to deem three men married? Or three men and a woman? Or a brother and sister?

Another "alternative" marriage

This is not the first time in American history that practitioners of "alternative" marriage have been denied legal approval.

In 1849, the Mormon settlers of Utah—it was then called Deseret—applied to Congress for admission to the United States. Their petition was denied for 44 years largely because the federal government refused to sanction the Mormons' polygamous marriages. Not until the Mormons banned polygamy and wrote that ban into their constitution were they allowed to join the Union.

Is there any argument made today for redefining marriage to encompass same-sex unions that would not have applied with equal force to the multiple-wife marriages of Deseret? Those were loving, stable, supportive relationships, entered into by sober people who wanted to spend their lives together. "How does the fact that I love four women and live with them in a committed relationship," a 19th-century Mormon Barney Frank might have asked, "threaten your marriage?"

But threats have nothing to do with it. Society is under no obligation to radically revise its most fundamental institution just because a small number of activists demands it. The burden of proof is on the revisionists, be they Mormons in the 1850s or homosexuals in the 1990s.

Let Mr. Frank and his partner call themselves "spouses," if they like; this is a free and tolerant country. (A lot freer and more tolerant than it was for the polygamous Mormons, many of whom went to prison for violating anti-bigamy laws.) But freedom and tolerance don't entitle them to a marriage license.

They may love each other and live for each other; their hearts may beat as one. But in the eyes of American law, of Western civilization and of an emphatic moral code dating back 3,500 years, they are not married.

For at its irreducible minimum, marriage is the exclusive union of one man and one woman. If it doesn't mean that, it doesn't mean anything. How dismaying that it should require an act of Congress to say so.

GAY 'MARRIAGE' OBFUSCATION

Thomas Sowell

> *An economist and senior fellow at the Hoover Institution, Thomas Sowell is a nationally syndicated columnist. This article originally appeared in* The Washington Times *in July 1996.*
>
> *Sowell also addresses the Defense of Marriage Act, arguing that it is not exclusionary since "any state that wants to apply any or all of this legislation to homosexual unions remains free to do so."*

On an issue where misleading and dishonest statements have been the norm, it should hardly be surprising that the headline on the San Francisco Chronicle read: "House Votes Against Gay Marriages." The story claimed that the bill passed by the House was "a bill to restrict gay marriage."

In reality, after this vote you can still have all the gay marriages you want and any state that wants to recognize these marriages remains free to do so. What Congress refused to do was to force all 50 states to accord same-sex relationships the whole sweeping range of legislation that has been passed over the centuries, based on the assumption that this legislation would apply to a union between a man and a woman, who have the prospect of producing children that would have to be taken care of by them or by the society.

Any state that wants to apply any or all of this legislation to homosexual unions remains free to do so after the House vote. What the gay activists and their allies in the liberal media wanted was for all states to be forced to do so, if any single state decided to recognize homosexual unions as marriages, superseding the previously defined sense of the term.

In other words, what they wanted was an end-run around the democratic process, so they could piggyback onto legislation passed with entirely different situations in mind.

This is what the House of Representatives rejected—and rightly so. If homosexuals want to participate in the democratic process and convince state legislatures to apply some or all of the laws that were passed for husband-wife unions and their offspring to same-sex relationships as well, they have every right to do so.

They do not have a right to sneak in through the back door, pretending to be somebody else, just by using a word.

The issue of gay marriages exposes the hypocrisy of what was once the homosexuals' strongest argument—that what consenting adults do in private is nobody else's business. Now it is suddenly everybody else's business to recognize these liaisons and to confer on them all the legal prerogatives created for others.

Serious changes in the law and public policy should be discussed seriously, not evaded by the verbal sleight-of-hand of using the word "marriage." Marriage is more than a contract between two individuals. It is an assertion of an interest in those people's relationship, and its possible offspring, by the society at large.

Gay activists are trying to have it both ways. If it is none of my business what they do, then it is none of their business what I think about it. Nor should I be forced to recognize it in word or deed.

Emotional assertions of how much homosexual relationships mean to those involved are relevant only to those people themselves, who are free to make whatever contractual relationships they wish with one another, and to solemnize their relationship in whatever ceremony they prefer. But that is very different from trying to drag the rest of us into this, willy-nilly, through laws which our elected representatives never agreed to apply to them.

In a sense, the gay marriage issue is only a further extension of the notion that a "family" means whatever anybody wants it to mean. But there would never have been such a word in the language in the first place if any group of people, with any kind of relationship to one another, was considered the same as any other.

Families are not baseball teams, corporations, marching bands or computer clubs. What the law has evolved over centuries of experience with families need not apply to any other kind of association. Calling other kinds of relationships "families" is playing games with words, submerging the very concept in a sea of verbal mush.

What our laws, our values, and our analyses have said about families was not meant to apply to any old set of people that might later be fashionably analogized to families. Such word games may be very clever, but all they boil down to is that all things are the same, except for the differences, and different except for the similarities.

Gay activists have also thrived on the confusion between homosexuals and members of racial or ethnic minorities. But you are black or white or Chinese or Cuban, regardless of how you behave. Homosexuality is defined by behavior.

It is one thing to say all people have the same rights, as the 14th Amendment does, and something very different to say that all behavior has the same rights. There is no reason why the law should make all behavior equally acceptable to all people or surround all behavior with legal obligations on others. Once more the call for "equal rights" has masked an attempt to get special privileges, without having to play by the rules.

SHOULD SAME-SEX COUPLES BE PERMITTED TO MARRY?

Anna Quindlen

Evan's Two Moms

> *Anna Quindlen made her name as a writer for* The New York Times, *writing a widely praised, regularly syndicated column for it for a number of years. In 1992, she won a Pulitzer prize for her commentary. She has written several books, including* Thinking Out Loud: On the Personal, the Political, the Public, and the Private *(1993), from which this essay has been extracted. The last line of Quindlen's essay states her premise most obviously: "Love and commitment are rare enough; it seems absurd to thwart them in any guise."*

Evan has two moms. This is no big thing. Evan has always had two moms—in his school file, on his emergency forms, with his friends. "Oooooh, Evan, you're lucky," they sometimes say. "You have two moms." It sounds like a sitcom, but until last week it was emotional truth without legal bulwark. That was when a judge in New York approved the adoption of a six-year-old boy by his biological mother's lesbian partner. Evan. Evan's mom. Evan's other mom. A kid, a psychologist, a pediatrician. A family.

The matter of Evan's two moms is one in a series of events over the last year that lead to certain conclusions. A Minnesota appeals court granted guardianship of a woman left a quadriplegic in a car accident to her lesbian lover, the culmination of a seven-year battle in which the injured woman's parents did everything possible to negate the partnership between the two. A lawyer in Georgia had her job offer withdrawn after the state attorney general found out that she and her lesbian lover were planning a marriage ceremony; she's brought suit. The computer company Lotus announced that the gay partners of employees would be eligible for the same benefits as spouses.

Add to these public events the private struggles, the couples who go from lawyer to lawyer to approximate legal protections their straight counterparts take for granted, the AIDS survivors who find themselves shut out of their partner's dying days by biological family members and shut out of their apartments by leases with a single name on the dotted line, and one solution is obvious.

Gay marriage is a radical notion for straight people and a conservative notion for gay ones. After years of being sledge-hammered by society, some gay men and lesbian women are deeply suspicious of participating in an institution that seems to have "straight world" written all over it.

But the rads of twenty years ago, straight and gay alike, have other things on their minds today. Family is one, and the linchpin of family has commonly been a loving commitment between two adults. When same-sex couples set out to make that commitment, they discover that they are at a disadvantage: No joint tax returns. No health insurance coverage for an uninsured partner. No survivor's benefits from Social Security. None of the automatic rights, privileges, and responsibilities society attaches to a marriage contract. In Madison, Wisconsin, a couple who applied at the Y with their kids for a family membership were turned down because both were women. It's one of those small things that can make you feel small.

Some took marriage statutes that refer to "two persons" at their word and applied for a license. The results were court decisions that quoted the Bible and embraced circular argument: marriage is by definition the union of a man and a woman because that is how we've defined it.

No religion should be forced to marry anyone in violation of its tenets, although ironically it is now only in religious ceremonies that gay people can marry, performed by clergy who find the blessing of two who love each other no sin. But there is no secular reason that we should take a patchwork approach of corporate, governmental, and legal steps to guarantee what can be done simply, economically, conclusively, and inclusively with the words "I do."

"Fran and I chose to get married for the same reasons that any two people do," said the lawyer who was fired in Georgia. "We fell in love; we wanted to spend our lives together." Pretty simple.

Consider the case of *Loving vs. Virginia*, aptly named. At the time, sixteen states had laws that barred interracial marriage, relying on natural law, that amorphous grab bag for justifying prejudice. Sounding a little like God throwing Adam and Eve out of paradise, the trial judge suspended the one-year sentence of Richard Loving, who was white, and his wife, Mildred, who was black, provided they got out of the State of Virginia.

In 1967 the Supreme Court found such laws to be unconstitutional. Only twenty-five years ago and it was a crime for a black woman to marry a white man. Perhaps twenty-five years from now we will find it just as incredible that two people of the same sex were not entitled to legally commit themselves to each other. Love and commitment are rare enough; it seems absurd to thwart them in any guise.

WHY I CHANGED MY MIND

Sidney Callahan

> *Sidney Callahan is a regular columnist for* Commonweal, *a biweekly journal of public affairs, literature, the arts, and religion that is generally associated with Catholicism and liberal politics. This essay, in which Callahan argues that homosexuals should be allowed to marry, was originally published in* Commonweal *in April 1994.*

Last month I came out of the closet and confessed at an evening lecture that I believed that homosexuals should be allowed to marry. The morning after I had second thoughts, but I'm afraid my reconsiderations were mostly the result of cowardice and churlishness.

First the cowardice. Yes, I undoubtedly dread getting into arguments, especially with people I admire. I'm also distinctly uneager to be harassed by true believers playing punitive hardball—whether on the right or the left. Already I've been denounced and disinvited for being a feminist, and been greeted by banners unfurled to protest my acceptance of birth control, this while delivering a prolife speech at a Catholic conference. Yet in other venues I've been picketed, booed, hissed, and raged at by abortion advocates. (At least the latter episodes have the excitement of being thrown to the lions in the arena.) Still, do I need to get into one more religious and cultural donnybrook?

As for churlishness, I must say that as much as I hate being disliked, I loathe even more being approved of by certain groups. Who wants to end up on the same side with aggressively secular ideologues? And how unappetizing to aid and abet militant gay groups who engage in gross anti-Catholic tactics? Most of all I hate agreeing with those mindless religious types (I have my little list) who regularly seem to sell out their Christian birthright, along with the lives of the unborn, for a mess of PC pottage.

Unfortunately, flailing about and grinding one's teeth availeth naught, it gets you nowhere. The only way out of moral paralysis is to forget extrinsic political considerations and enter into the necessary struggle. If we want to bring forth a Christworthy, coherent sexual ethic for the twenty-first century then we must all think hard, pray hard, and seek God's Spirit of Love and Truth. Where? In all the familiar places: in Scripture, in tradition, in natural law reasoning, and in the signs and sciences of the times. So what is the gospel truth regarding homosexuality?

At this point I've read thousands of pages written by assorted experts and theologians giving their views on what constitutes an adequate moral, legal, scientific, and/or scriptural-theological approach to homosexuality (including recent *Commonweal* exchanges). But since I'm in the confessional mode let me own up to the fact that I also try to decide difficult moral dilemmas by praying, meditating, and naively imagining what Christ would have done and wants now. If the mind of Christ is in us, we must be transformed rather than being conformed to the world.

As I try to draw all these various strands of thought, imagination, and prayer into some order, I find myself diverging from official Vatican teaching. Yes, we are all told to look upon homosexuals as equal children of God who must be protected from assault, bigotry, and infringement of their civil rights. Indeed, Christ loves and includes the gay in his kingdom. And almost everyone on all sides agrees that homosexuality is not freely chosen but a given condition. So, too, all acknowledge that personal qualities and the call to holiness are not determined by sexual orientation. So far, so good.

But why is it intrinsically disordered for homosexuals and lesbians to act on their sexual orientation, even if they would fulfill all the same moral conditions required of heterosexual marital activity, such as commitment, love, and lifelong fidelity? After all, some heterosexual marriages need not, nor can be biologically procreative. I just cannot imagine Christ asking such an unequal sacrifice from homosexual persons with beloved partners who have not been called to vowed celibacy.

Those who do assign this burden in Christ's name describe the deprivation as morally and religiously necessary. They speak of maintaining the family for the common good, of how gender complementarity is necessary for marital bonding across genders. Of the importance of embodiment and being a part of the ongoing procreative narrative. The pope denounces "the false families" of homosexuals and lesbians. Well, of course, I agree that a viable society must support and privilege procreative families, but I don't see why this positive support necessitates barring the marriage of gay couples.

Good Catholic parents of adult children I know welcome their gay children's life long partners as "in-laws," who are part of their family. Doesn't it seem a confirmation of the Christian teaching on the goodness of monogamous marriage that gay couples eschew promiscuity and desire to regularize and ritualize their loving commitment to one another?

Assertions about the complementarity of the two genders appear to be false to new psychological insights on the range of gender variability and overlapping similarities, as well as to the Christian call to transcend gender in Christian unity where "there is neither male nor female." If the symbol of Christ as male bridegroom in union with the church is used too literally as the form for marriage, then could only females (as brides) be church members? (Rigid overestimation of gender is also the fallacy that bans women from ordination.)

Any two persons must struggle to obtain loving unity, but when you take into account the multitude of inevitable differences in temperament, intelligence, taste, talents, and moral maturity, gender can be a minor consideration.

Affirming embodiment and respect for the symbolic language of the body is important, but I'd say the grammar book includes a wider range of syntax and idiom than is officially published. In fact I've come (finally) to see the rejection of loving gay erotic expression as a rejection of embodiment and another form of resistance to the goodness of sexual desire and pleasure. For most persons, gay or straight, chaste friendships and general charity cannot produce the same intense intimacy, bodily confirmation, mutual sanctification, and fulfilling happiness that come from making love with a faithful partner. (The inability of some celibates to accept the importance of freely expressing sexual and erotic marital love has produced the birth control impasse.)

Other rejections of the body also may be surfacing when whatever homosexuals do together is considered especially revolting and repugnant. Our stringent toilet, cleanliness, and touch taboos enforced in infancy can linger on in the feeling that certain parts or functions of the body are intrinsically disgusting. Some of the anti-gay articles I've been dutifully perusing are revealing. They begin with warnings against the "gay conspiracy" and "homosexual cult" that aim "to seduce our children" into its diseased and perverted "clutches." Then follow references to "debased," "mutual self-gratifications," "through what very definitely and clearly is nothing but a deathhole . . . it yields only dead matter." Lesbians are absent from these phallocentric fulminations, presumably because they possess no "life giving or sharing organ" to end up in the wrong orifice.

Well, it has taken centuries to get over the ancient convictions that menstruating females are unclean and ritually pollute the altar. If, that is, we have gotten over it. When you see some of the heated resistance to women's ordination, one wonders. Oh Christ, if we could only take your words to heart and learn what defiles a person and what doesn't.

This pair of articles was originally published next to each other in the 20 July 1992 issue of Time *magazine. Written in response to the heated controversy surrounding Ice-T's "Cop Killer," these brief arguments take the familiar pro/con format, where each takes a stand on the issues surrounding this song's controversial status. At the time, one side, led by such key players as Oliver North and actor Charlton Heston called for Warner Bros. Records to pull the song from Ice-T's album,* Body Count. *The alternative position, argued by actor Wesley Snipes, rappers Ice Cube, Public Enemy, and Cypress Hill, along with the Recording Industry of America, defended Ice-T and Warner Bros. in the name of freedom of expression. Ultimately, Ice-T agreed to remove the song from the album and was released from his recording contract with Warner Bros. following bomb threats and the potential boycott of Time Warner products. Ice-T noted that, "you can't be part of the system and make music against the system. . . . Time Warner cannot be in the business of black rage."*

ICE-T: IS THE ISSUE SOCIAL RESPONSIBILITY . . .

Michael Kinsley

How did the company that publishes this magazine come to produce a record glorifying the murder of police?

> I got my 12-gauge sawed off
> I got my headlights turned off
> I'm 'bout to bust some shots off
> I'm 'bout to dust some cops off . . .
> Die, Die, Die Pig, Die!

So go the lyrics to *Cop Killer* by the rapper Ice-T on the album *Body Count*. The album is released by Warner Bros. Records, part of the Time Warner media and entertainment conglomerate.

In a *Wall Street Journal* op-ed piece laying out the company's position, Time Warner CO-CEO Gerald Levin makes two defenses. First, Ice-T's *Cop Killer* is misunderstood. "It doesn't incite or glorify violence . . . . It's his fictionalized attempt to get inside a character's head. . . . *Cop Killer* is no more a call for gunning down the police than *Frankie and Johnny* is a summons for jilted lovers to shoot one another." Instead of "finding ways to silence the messenger," we should be "heeding the anguished cry contained in his message."

This defense is self-contradictory. Frankie and Johnny does not pretend to have a political "message" that must be "heeded." If *Cop Killer* has a message, it is that the murder of policemen is a justified response to police brutality. And not in self-defense, but in premeditated acts of revenge against random cops. ("I know your family's grievin'—f____ 'em.")

5 Killing policemen is a good thing—that is the plain meaning of the words, and no "larger understanding" of black culture, the rage of the streets or anything else can explain it away. This is not Ella Fitzgerald telling a story in song. As in much of today's popular music, the line between performer and performance is purposely blurred. These are political sermonettes clearly intended to endorse the sentiments being expressed. Tracy Marrow (Ice-T) himself has said, "I scared the police, and they need to be scared." That seems clear.

6 The company's second defense of *Cop Killer* is the classic one of free expression: "We stand for creative freedom. We believe that the worth of what an artist or journalist has to say does not depend on preapproval from a government official or a corporate censor."

7 Of course Ice-T has the right to say whatever he wants. But that doesn't require any company to provide him an outlet. And it doesn't relieve a company of responsibility for the messages it chooses to promote. Judgment is not "censorship." Many an "anguished cry" goes unrecorded. This one was recorded, and promoted, because a successful artist under contract wanted to record it. Nothing wrong with making money, but a company cannot take the money and run from the responsibility.

8 The founder of *Time*, Henry Luce, would snort at the notion that his company should provide a value-free forum for the exchange of ideas. In Luce's system, editors were supposed to make value judgments and promote the truth as they saw it. *Time* has moved far from its old Lucean rigidity—far enough to allow for dissenting essays like this one. That evolution is a good thing, as long as it's not a handy excuse for abandoning all standards.

9 No commercial enterprise need agree with every word that appears under its corporate imprimatur. If Time Warner now intends to be "a global force for encouraging the confrontation of ideas," that's swell. But a policy of allowing diverse viewpoints is not a moral free pass. Pro and con on national health care is one thing; pro and con on killing policemen is another.

10 A bit of sympathy is in order for Time Warner. It is indeed a "global force" with media tentacles around the world. If it imposes rigorous standards and values from the top, it gets accused of corporate censorship. If it doesn't, it gets accused of moral irresponsibility. A dilemma. But someone should have thought of that before deciding to become a global force.

11 And another genuine dilemma. Whatever the actual merits of *Cop Killer*, if Time Warner withdraws the album now the company will be perceived as giving in to outside pressure. That is a disastrous precedent for a global conglomerate.

12 The Time-Warner merger of 1989 was supposed to produce corporate "synergy": the whole was supposed to be more than the sum of the parts. The *Cop Killer* controversy is an example of negative synergy. People get mad at *Cop Killer* and start boycotting the movie *Batman Returns*. A reviewer praises *Cop Killer* ("Tracy Marrow's poetry takes a switchblade and deftly slices life's jugular," etc.), and *Time* is accused of corruption instead of mere foolishness. Senior Time Warner executives find themselves under attack for—and defending—products of their company they neither honestly care for nor really understand, and doubtless weren't even aware of before controversy hit.

Pathos

13 Anyway, it's absurd to discuss *Cop Killer* as part of the "confrontation of ideas"— or even as an authentic anguished cry of rage from the ghetto. *Cop Killer* is a cynical commercial concoction, designed to titillate its audience with imagery of violence. It merely exploits the authentic anguish of the inner city for further titillation. Tracy Marrow is in business for a buck, just like Time Warner. *Cop Killer* is an excellent joke on the white establishment, of which the company's anguished apologia ("Why can't we hear what rap is trying to tell us?") is the punch line.

. . . OR IS IT CREATIVE FREEDOM?

Barbara Ehrenreich

Ice-T's song *Cop Killer* is as bad as they come. This is black anger—raw, rude and cruel—and one reason the song's so shocking is that in postliberal America, black anger is virtually taboo. You won't find it on TV, not on the *McLaughlin Group* or *Crossfire*, and certainly not in the placid features of Arsenio Hall or Bernard Shaw. It's been beaten back into the outlaw subcultures of rap and rock, where, precisely because it is taboo, it sells. And the nastier it is, the faster it moves off the shelves. As Ice-T asks in another song on the same album, "Goddamn what a brotha gotta do/To get a message through/To the red, white and blue?"

But there's a gross overreaction going on, building to a veritable paroxysm of white denial. A national boycott has been called, not just of the song or Ice-T, but of all Time Warner products. The President himself has denounced Time Warner as "wrong" and Ice-T as "sick." Ollie North's Freedom Alliance has started a petition drive aimed at bringing Time Warner executives to trial for "sedition and anarchy."

Much of this is posturing and requires no more courage than it takes to stand up in a VFW hall and condemn communism or crack. Yes, *Cop Killer* is irresponsible and vile. But Ice-T is as right about some things as he is righteous about the rest. And ultimately, he's not even dangerous—least of all to the white power structure his songs condemn.

The "danger" implicit in all the uproar is of empty-headed, suggestible black kids, crouching by their boom boxes, waiting for the word. But what Ice-T's fans know and his detractors obviously don't is that *Cop Killer* is just one more entry in pop music's long history of macho hyperbole and violent boast. Flip to the classic-rock station, and you might catch the Rolling Stones announcing "the time is right for violent revolooshun!" from their 1968 hit *Street Man Fighting*. And where were the defenders of our law-enforcement officers when a white British group, the Clash, taunted its fans with the lyrics: "When they kick open your front door/How you gonna come/With your hands on your head/Or on the trigger of your gun?"

"Die, Die, Die Pig" is strong speech, but the Constitution protects strong speech, and it's doing so this year more aggressively than ever. The Supreme Court has just downgraded cross burnings to the level of bonfires and ruled that it's no crime to throw around verbal grenades like "nigger" and "kike." Where are the defenders of decorum and social stability when prime-time demagogues like Howard Stern deride African Americans as "spear chuckers"?

More to the point, young African Americans are not so naïve and suggestible that they have to depend on a compact disc for their sociology lessons. To paraphrase another song from another era, you don't need a rap song to tell which way the wind is blowing. Black youths know that the police are likely to see them through a filter of stereotypes as miscreants and potential "cop killers." They are aware that a black youth is seven times as likely to be charged with a felony as a white youth who has committed the same offense, and is much more likely to be imprisoned.

They know, too, that in a shameful number of cases, it is the police themselves who indulge in "anarchy" and violence. The U.S. Justice Department has received

47,000 complaints of police brutality in Los Angeles, documenting 40 cases of "torture or cruel, inhuman or degrading treatment."

Menacing as it sounds, the fantasy in *Cop Killer* is the fantasy of the powerless and beaten down—the black man who's been hassled once too often ("a pig stopped me for nothin'!"), spread-eagled against a police car, pushed around. It's not even a "responsible" fantasy (fantasies seldom are). It's not even a very creative one. In fact, the sad thing about *Cop Killer* is that it falls for the cheapest, most conventional image of rebellion that our culture offers: the lone gunman spraying fire from his AK-47. This is not "sedition"; it's the familiar, All-American, Hollywood-style pornography of violence.

Which is why Ice-T is right to say he's no more dangerous than George Bush's pal Arnold Schwarzenegger, who wasted an army of cops in *Terminator 2*. Images of extraordinary cruelty and violence are marketed every day, many of far less artistic merit than *Cop Killer*. This is our free market of ideas and images, and it shouldn't be any less free for a black man than for other purveyors of "irresponsible" sentiments, from David Duke to Andrew Dice Clay.

Just, please, don't dignify Ice-T's contribution with the word sedition. The past masters of sedition—men like George Washington, Toussaint-Louverture, Fidel Castro or Mao Ze-dong, all of whom led and won armed insurrections—would be unimpressed by *Cop Killer* and probably saddened. They would shake their heads and mutter words like "infantile" and "adventurism." They might point out that the cops are hardly a noble target, being, for the most part, honest working stiffs who've got stuck with the job of patrolling ghettos ravaged by economic decline and official neglect.

There is a difference, the true seditionist would argue, between a revolution and a gesture of macho defiance. Gestures are cheap. They feel good; they blow off some rage. But revolutions, violent or otherwise, are made by people who have learned how to count very slowly to 10.

Questions:

1. What schemas does each rhetor assume the audience holds? To what values and what system of beliefs do Kinsley and Ehrenreich appeal?

2. Is one of the writers more persuasive than the other? How?

IV

Longer Pairs for Rhetorical Analysis

MAKING THE GRADE

Kurt Wiesenfeld

Wiesenfeld is a physicist and physics teacher at Georgia Tech in Atlanta. In this essay, he responds to his students' pleas for better grades by explaining that grades need to be earned, not given. He writes, "there's a weird innocence to the assumption that one expects (even deserves) a better grade simply by begging for it." This article originally appeared in the 17 June 1996 issue of Newsweek.

It was a rookie error. After 10 years I should have known better, but I went to my office the day after final grades were posted. There was a tentative knock on the door. "Professor Wiesenfeld? I took your Physics 2121 class? I flunked it? I wonder if there's anything I can do to improve my grade?" I thought: "Why are you asking me? Isn't it too late to worry about it? Do you dislike making declarative statements?"

After the student gave his tale of woe and left, the phone rang. "I got a D in your class. Is there any way you can change it to 'Incomplete'?" Then the e-mail assault began: "I'm shy about coming in to talk to you, but I'm not shy about asking for a better grade. Anyway, it's worth a try." The next day I had three phone messages from students asking *me* to call *them*. I didn't.

Time was, when you received a grade, that was it. You might groan and moan, but you accepted it as the outcome of your efforts or lack thereof (and, yes, sometimes a tough grader). In the last few years, however, some students have developed a disgruntled-consumer approach. If they don't like their grade, they go to the "return" counter to trade it in for something better.

What alarms me is their indifference toward grades as an indication of personal effort and performance. Many, when pressed about why they think they deserve a better grade, admit they don't deserve one but would like one anyway. Having been raised on gold stars for effort and smiley faces for self-esteem, they've learned that they can get by without hard work and real talent if they can talk the professor into giving them a break. This attitude is beyond cynicism. There's a weird innocence to the assumption that one expects (even deserves) a better grade simply by begging for it. With that outlook, I guess I shouldn't be as flabbergasted as I was that 12 students asked me to change their grades *after* final grades were posted.

That's 10 percent of my class who let three months of midterms, quizzes and lab reports slide until long past remedy. My graduate student calls it hyperrational thinking: if effort and intelligence don't matter, why should deadlines? What matters is getting a better grade through an unearned bonus, the academic equivalent of a freebie T-shirt or toaster giveaway. Rewards are disconnected from the quality of one's work. An act and its consequences are unrelated, random events.

Their arguments for wheedling better grades often ignore academic performance. Perhaps they feel it's not relevant. "If my grade isn't raised to a D I'll lose my scholarship." "If you don't give me a C, I'll flunk out." One sincerely overwrought student pleaded, "If I don't pass, my life is over." This is tough stuff to deal with. Apparently, I'm responsible for someone's losing a scholarship, flunking out or deciding whether life has meaning. Perhaps these students see me as a commodities broker with something they want—a grade. Though intrinsically worthless, grades, if properly manipulated, can be traded for what has value: a degree, which means a job, which means money. The one thing college actually offers—a chance to learn—is considered irrelevant, even less than worthless, because of the long hours and hard work required.

In a society saturated with surface values, love of knowledge for its own sake does sound eccentric. The benefits of fame and wealth are more obvious. So is it right to blame students for reflecting the superficial values saturating our society?

Yes, of course it's right. These guys had better take themselves seriously now, because our country will be forced to take them seriously later, when the stakes are much higher. They must recognize that their attitude is not only self-destructive, but socially destructive. The erosion of quality control—giving appropriate grades for actual accomplishments—is a major concern in my department. One colleague noted that a physics major could obtain a degree without ever answering a written exam question completely. How? By pulling in enough partial credit and extra credit. And by getting breaks on grades.

But what happens once she or he graduates and gets a job? That's when the misfortunes of eroding academic standards multiply. We lament that school children get "kicked upstairs" until they graduate from high school despite being illiterate and mathematically inept, but we seem unconcerned with college graduates whose less blatant deficiencies are far more harmful if their accreditation exceeds their qualifications.

cause   consequence

Most of my students are science and engineering majors. If they're good at getting partial credit but not at getting the answer right, then the new bridge breaks or the new drug doesn't work. One finds examples here in Atlanta. Last year a light tower in the Olympic Stadium collapsed, killing a worker. It collapsed because an engineer miscalculated how much weight it could hold. A new 12-story dormitory could develop dangerous cracks due to a foundation that's uneven by more than six inches. The error resulted from incorrect data being fed into a computer. I drive past that dorm daily on my way to work, wondering if a foundation crushed under kilotons of weight is repairable or if this structure will have to be demolished. Two 10,000-pound steel beams at the new natatorium collapsed in March, crashing into the student athletic complex. (Should we give partial credit since no one was hurt?) Those are real-world consequences of errors and lack of expertise.

But the lesson is lost on the grade-grousing 10 percent. Say that you won't (not can't, but won't) change the grade they deserve to what they want, and they're frequently bewildered or angry. They don't think it's fair that they're judged according to their performance, not their desires or "potential." They don't think it's fair that they should jeopardize their scholarships or be in danger of flunking out simply because they could not or did not do their work. But it's more than fair; it's necessary to help preserve a minimum standard of quality that our society needs to maintain safety and integrity. I don't know if the 13th-hour students will learn that lesson, but I've learned mine. From now on, after final grades are posted, I'll lie low until the next quarter starts.

A LIBERATING CURRICULUM

Roberta F. Borkat

Roberta Borkat is an English and Comparative Literature professor at San Diego State University, and she originally published this essay in Newsweek *magazine on 12 April 1993. Borkat's argument, in which she calls for the unilateral distribution of A's to students in the second week of the semester, is a classic example of a satire. As you read, look for evidence of her sarcastic tone and clues to her "real" argument.*

A blessed change has come over me. Events of recent months have revealed to me that I have been laboring as a university professor for more than 20 years under a misguided theory of teaching. I humbly regret that during all those years I have caused distress and inconvenience to thousands of students while providing some amusement to my more practical colleagues. Enlightenment came to me in a sublime moment of clarity while I was being verbally attacked by a student whose paper I had just proved to have been plagiarized from "The Norton Anthology of English Literature." Suddenly, I understood the true purpose of my profession, and I devised a plan to embody that revelation. Every moment since then has been filled with delight about the advantages to students, professors and universities from my Plan to Increase Student Happiness.

The plan is simplicity itself: at the end of the second week of the semester, all students enrolled in each course will receive a final grade of A. Then their minds will be relieved of anxiety, and they will be free to do whatever they want for the rest of the term.

The benefits are immediately evident. Students will be assured of high grade-point averages and an absence of obstacles in their march toward graduation. Professors will be relieved of useless burdens and will have time to pursue their real interests. Universities will have achieved the long-desired goal of molding individual professors into interchangeable parts of a smoothly operating machine. Even the environment will be improved because education will no longer consume vast quantities of paper for books, compositions and examinations.

Although this scheme will instantly solve countless problems that have plagued education, a few people may raise trivial objections and even urge universities not to adopt it. Some of my colleagues may protest that we have an obligation to uphold the integrity of our profession. Poor fools, I understand their delusion, for I formerly shared it. To them, I say: "Hey, lighten up! Why make life difficult?"

Those who believe that we have a duty to increase the knowledge of our students may also object. I, too, used to think that knowledge was important and that we should encourage hard work and perseverance. Now I realize that the concept of rewards for merit is elitist and, therefore, wrong in a society that aims for equality in all things. We are a democracy. What could be more democratic than to give exactly the same grade to every single student?

One or two forlorn colleagues may even protest that we have a responsibility to significant works of the past because the writings of such authors as Chaucer, Shakespeare, Milton and Swift are intrinsically valuable. I can empathize with these misguided souls, for I once labored under the illusion that I was giving my students a precious gift by introducing them to works by great poets, playwrights and satirists. Now I recognize the error of my ways. The writings of such authors may have seemed meaningful to our ancestors, who had nothing better to do, but we are living in a time of wonderful improvements. The writers of bygone eras have been made irrelevant, replaced by MTV and *People* magazine. After all, their bodies are dead. Why shouldn't their ideas be dead, too?

Joyous Smiles

If any colleagues persist in protesting that we should try to convey knowledge to students and preserve our cultural heritage, I offer this suggestion; honestly consider what students really want. As one young man graciously explained to me, he had no desire to take my course but had enrolled in it merely to fulfill a requirement that he resented. His job schedule made it impossible for him to attend at least 30 percent of my class sessions, and he wouldn't have time to do much of the reading. Nevertheless, he wanted a good grade. Another student consulted me after the first exam, upset because she had not studied and had earned only 14 points out of a possible 100. I told her that, if she studied hard and attended class more regularly, she could do well enough on the remaining tests to pass the course. This encouragement did not satisfy her. What she wanted was an assurance that she would receive at least a B. Under my plan both students would be guaranteed an A. Why not? They have good looks and self-esteem. What more could anyone ever need in life?

I do not ask for thanks from the many people who will benefit. I'm grateful to my colleagues who for decades have tried to help me realize that seriousness about teaching is not the path to professorial prestige, rapid promotion and frequent sabbaticals. Alas, I was stubborn. Not until I heard the illuminating explanation of the student who had plagiarized from the anthology's introduction to Jonathan Swift did I fully grasp the wisdom that others had been generously offering to me for years—learning is just too hard. Now, with a light heart, I await the plan's adoption. In my mind's eye, I can see the happy faces of university administrators and professors, released at last from the irksome chore of dealing with students. I can imagine the joyous smiles of thousands of students, all with straight-A averages and plenty of free time.

My only regret is that I wasted so much time. For nearly 30 years, I threw away numerous hours annually on trivia: writing, grading and explaining examinations; grading hundreds of papers a semester; holding private conferences with students; reading countless books; buying extra materials to give students a feeling for the music, art and clothing of past centuries; endlessly worrying about how to improve my teaching. At last I see the folly of grubbing away in meaningless efforts. I wish that I had faced facts earlier and had not lost years because of old-fashioned notions. But such are the penalties for those who do not understand the true purpose of education.

IMAGEBUSTERS

Todd Gitlin

> *Todd Gitlin is the author of many books, including* The Sixties: Years of
> Hope, Days of Rage *(1987) and* The Twilight of Common Dreams
> *(1995). This essay originally appeared in* The American Prospect *in
> the Winter of 1994. Gitlin is a professor at New York University where
> he teaches courses on culture, journalism, and sociology.*

I have denounced movie violence for more than two decades, all the way back to *The Wild Bunch* and *The Godfather*. I consider Hollywood's slashes, splatters, chain saws, and car crashes a disgrace, a degradation of culture, and a wound to the souls of producers and consumers alike.

But I also think liberals are making a serious mistake by pursuing their vigorous campaign against violence in the media. However morally and aesthetically reprehensible today's screen violence, the crusades of Senator Paul Simon and Attorney General Janet Reno against television violence are cheap shots. There are indeed reasons to attribute violence to the media, but the links are weaker than recent headlines would have one believe. The attempt to demonize the media distracts attention from the real causes of—and the serious remedies for—the epidemic of violence.

The sheer volume of alarm can't be explained by the actual violence generated by the media's awful images. Rather, Simon and Reno—not to mention Dan Quayle and the Reverend Donald Wildmon—have signed up for a traditional American pastime. The campaign against the devil's images threads through the history of middle class reform movements. For a nation that styles itself practical, at least in technical pursuits, the United States has always been remarkably quick to become a playground of moral prohibitions and symbolic crusades.

If today's censorious forces smell smoke, it is not in the absence of fire. In recent years, market forces have driven screen violence to an amazing pitch. But the question the liberal crusaders fail to address is not whether these violent screen images are wholesome but just how much real-world violence can be blamed on the media. Assume, for the sake of argument, that *every* copycat crime reported in the media can be plausibly traced to television and movies. Let us make an exceedingly high estimate that the resulting carnage results in 100 deaths per year that would not otherwise have taken place. These would amount to 0.28 percent of the total of 36,000 murders, accidents, and suicides committed by gunshot in the United States in 1992.

That media violence contributes to a climate in which violence is legitimate—and there can be no doubt of this—does not make it an urgent social problem. Violence on the screens, however loathsome, does not make a significant contribution to violence on the streets. Images don't spill blood. Rage, equipped with guns, does. Desperation does. Revenge does. As liberals say, the drug trade does; poverty does; unemployment does. It seems likely that a given percent increase in decently paying jobs will save thousands of times more lives than the same percent decrease in media bang-bang.

Now, I also give conservative arguments about the sources of violence their due. A culture that despises and disrespects authority is disposed to aggression, so people look to violence to resolve conflict. The absence of legitimate parental authority also feeds a culture of aggression. But aggression per se, however unpleasant, is not the decisive murderous element. A child who shoves another child after watching a fist-fight on television is not committing a drive-by shooting. Violence plays on big screens around the world without generating epidemics of carnage. The necessary condition permitting a culture of aggression to flare into a culture of violence is access to lethal weapons.

It's dark out there in the world of real violence, hopelessness, drugs, and guns. There is little political will for a war on poverty, guns, or family breakdown. Here, under the light, we are offered instead a crusade against media violence. This is large-ly a feel-good exercise, a moral panic substituting for practicality. It appeals to an American propensity that sociologist Philip Slater called the Toilet Assumption: Once the appearance of a social problem is swept out of sight, so is the problem. And the crusade costs nothing.

There is, for some liberals, an additional attraction. By campaigning against media violence, they hope to seize "family values" from conservatives. But the mantle of antiviolence they wrap themselves in is threadbare, and they are showing off new clothes that will not stop bullets.

The symbolic crusade against media violence is a confession of despair. Those who embrace it are saying, in effect, that they either do not know how, or do not dare, to do anything serious about American violence. They are tilting at images. If Janet Reno cites the American Psychological Association's recently published report, *Violence and Youth*, to indict television, she also should take note of the following state-ments within it: "Many social science disciplines, in addition to psychology, have firmly established that poverty and its contextual life circumstances are major deter-minants of violence. . . . It is very likely that socioeconomic inequality—not race—facilitates higher rates of violence among ethnic minority groups. . . . There is considerable evidence that the alarming rise in youth homicides is related to the avail-ability of firearms." The phrase "major determinant" does not appear whenever the report turns to the subject of media violence.

The question for reformers, then, is one of proportion and focus. If there were nothing else to do about deadly violence in America, then the passionate crusade against TV violence might be more justifiable, even though First Amendment abso-lutists would still have strong counter arguments. But the imagebusting campaign permits politicians to fulminate photogenically without having to take on the Nation-al Rifle Association or, for that matter, the drug epidemic, the crisis of the family, or the shortage of serious jobs.

So let a thousand criticisms bloom. Let reformers flood the networks and cable companies and, yes, advertisers, with protests against the gross overabundance of the stupid, the tawdry, and the ugly.

But not least, let the reformers not only turn off the set, but also criticize the form of life that has led so many to turn, and keep, it on.

NIGHTMARES OF DEPRAVITY

Robert Dole

> *Bob Dole, former Republican Majority Leader, U.S. Senator for Kansas, and ex-Presidential candidate, delivered these remarks to a live audience in Los Angeles, California on 31 May 1995, during his presidential campaign.*

I want to talk about a specific matter tonight. I may not win an Oscar, but I'll talk about it anyway. I want to talk to you tonight about the future of America—about issues of moral importance, matters of social consequence.

Last month, during my announcement tour, I gave voice to concerns held across this country about what is happening to our popular culture. I made what I thought was an obvious point, a point that worries countless American parents: that one of the greatest threats to American family values is the way our popular culture ridicules them. Our music, movies, television and advertising regularly push the limits of decency, bombarding our children with destructive messages of casual violence and even more casual sex. And I concluded that we must hold Hollywood and the entire entertainment industry accountable for putting profit ahead of common decency.

So here I am in California—the home of the entertainment industry and to many of the people who shape our popular culture. And I'm asking for their help. I believe our country is crying out for leaders who will call us as a people to our better nature, not to profit from our weaknesses; who will bring back our confidence in the good, not play on our fears of life's dark corners. This is true for those of us who seek public office. And it is true for those who are blessed with the talent to lead America's vaunted entertainment industry.

Actors and producers, writers and directors, people of talent around the world dream of coming to Hollywood. Because if you are the best, this is where you are. Americans were pioneers in film, and dominate world-wide competition today. The American entertainment industry is at the cutting edge of creative excellence, but also too often the leading edge of a culture becoming dangerously coarse.

I have two goals tonight. One is to make crystal clear to you the effect this industry has on America's children, in the hope that it will rise to their defense. And the other is to speak more broadly to America about the corporate executives who hide behind the lofty language of free speech in order to profit from the debasing of America.

There is often heard in Hollywood a kind of "aw shucks" response to attempts to link societal effects with causes in the culture. It's the "we just make movies people want" response. I'll take that up in a minute. But when they go to work tomorrow, when they sift through competing proposals for their time and their money, when they consider how badly they need the next job, I want the leaders of the entertainment industry to think about the influence they have on America's children.

Let there be no mistake: televisions and movie screens, boomboxes and headsets are windows on the world for our children. If you are too old, or too sophisticated, or too close to the problem, just ask a parent. What to some is art, to our children is a nightly news report on the world outside their limited experience. What to some is make-believe, to them is the "real skinny" on the adult world they are so eager to experience. Kids know first hand what they see in their families, their schools, their immediate communities. But our popular culture shapes their view of the "real world." Our children believe those paintings in celluloid are reflections of reality. But I don't recognize America in much of what I see.

My voice and the rising voices of millions of other Americans who share this view represent more than the codgy old attempt of one generation to steal the fun of another. A line has been crossed—not just of taste, but of human dignity and decency. It is crossed every time sexual violence is given a catchy tune. When teen suicide is set to an appealing beat. When Hollywood's dream factories turn out nightmares of depravity.

You know what I mean. I mean *Natural Born Killers. True Romance.* Films that revel in mindless violence and loveless sex. I'm talking about groups like Cannibal Corpse, Geto Boys and 2 Live Crew. About a culture business that makes money from "music" extolling the pleasures of raping, torturing and mutilating women; from "songs" about killing policemen and rejecting law. The mainstreaming of deviancy must come to an end, but it will only stop when the leaders of the entertainment industry recognize and shoulder their responsibility.

But let me be very clear: I am not saying that our growing social problems are entirely Hollywood's fault. They are not. People are responsible for their actions. Movies and music do not make children into murderers. But a numbing exposure to graphic violence and immorality does steal away innocence, smothering our instinct for outrage. And I think we have reached the point where our popular culture threatens to undermine our character as a nation.

Which brings me to my second point tonight. Our freedom is precious. I have risked my life to defend it, and would do so again. We must always be proud that in America we have the freedom to speak without Big Brother's permission. Our freedom to reap the rewards of our capitalist system has raised the standard of living around the world. The profit motive is the engine of that system, and is honorable. But those who cultivate moral confusion for profit should understand this: we will name their names and shame them as they deserve to be shamed. We will contest them for the heart and soul of every child, in every neighborhood. For we who are outraged also have the freedom to speak. If we refuse to condemn evil, it is not tolerance but surrender. And we will never surrender.

Let me be specific. One of the companies on the leading edge of coarseness and violence is Time Warner. It is a symbol of how much we have lost. In the 1930s its corporate predecessor, Warner Brothers, made a series of movies, including *G-Men*, for the purpose of restoring "dignity and public confidence in the police." It made movies to help the war effort in the early 1940s. Its company slogan, put on a billboard across from the studio, was "Combining Good Citizenship with Good Picture Making."

Today Time Warner owns a company called Interscope Records which columnist John Leo called the "cultural equivalent of owning half the world's mustard gas factories." Ice-T of "Cop Killer" fame is one of Time Warner's "stars." I cannot bring myself to repeat the lyrics of some of the "music" Time Warner promotes. But our children do. There is a difference between the description of evil through art, and the marketing of evil through commerce. I would like to ask the executives of Time

Warner a question: Is this what you intended to accomplish with your careers? Must you debase our nation and threaten our children for the sake of corporate profits?

And please don't answer that you are simply responding to the market. Because that is not true. In the movie business, as Michael Medved points out, the most profitable films are the ones most friendly to the family. Last year, the top five grossing films were the block busters *The Lion King, Forrest Gump, True Lies, The Santa Clause* and *The Flintstones*. To put it in perspective, it has been reported that *The Lion King* made six times as much money as *Natural Born Killers*.

The corporate executives who dismiss my criticism should not misunderstand. Mine is not the objection of some tiny group of zealots or an ideological fringe. From inner-city mothers to suburban mothers to families in rural America—parents are afraid, and growing angry. There once was a time when parents felt the community of adults was on their side. Now they feel surrounded by forces assaulting their children and their code of values.

This is not a partisan matter. I am a conservative Republican, but I am joined in this fight by moderates, independents and liberal Democrats. Senator Bill Bradley has spoken eloquently on this subject, as has Senator Paul Simon, who talks of our nation's "crisis of glamorized violence." And leaders of the entertainment industry are beginning to speak up, as well.

Mark Canton, the president of Universal Pictures, said, "Any smart business person can see what we must do—make more 'PG'-rated films." He said, "Together . . . we can make the needed changes. If we don't, this decade will be noted in the history books as the embarrassing legacy of what began as a great art form. We will be labeled, 'the decline of an empire.'"

Change is possible—in Hollywood, and across the entertainment industry. There are few national priorities more urgent. I know that good and caring people work in this industry. If they are deaf to the concerns I have raised tonight, it must be because they do not fully understand what is at stake. But we must make them understand. We must make it clear that tolerance does not mean neutrality between love and cruelty, between peace and violence, between right and wrong. Ours is not a crusade for censorship, it is a call for good citizenship.

When I announced I was running for president, I said that my mission is to rein in our government, to reconnect the powerful with the values which have made America strong and to reassert America's place as a great nation in the world. Tonight I am speaking beyond this room to some of the most powerful arbiters of our values. Tonight my challenge to the entertainment industry is to accept a calling above and beyond the bottom line—to fulfill a duty to the society which provides its profits. Help our nation maintain the innocence of its children. Prove to us that courage and conscience are alive and well in Hollywood.

"REEL" VS. REAL VIOLENCE

John Russo

John Russo was the producer of Night of the Living Dead, *the movie that many believe changed the American conception of horror movies. Russo co-produced a new version of the movie in 1990.*

One day I switched on the evening news just in time to see a Pennsylvania politician waving around a .357 magnum, warning reporters to back off so they wouldn't get hurt, then sticking the gun in his mouth and . . .

Mercifully, the station I was watching didn't show him pulling the trigger, but I learned later that another Pittsburgh station showed the whole suicide unedited. What I saw was enough to make me ill. My stomach was in a knot, and I couldn't get the incident out of my mind. I still can't, even though three years have gone by.

I have a special reason for wondering and worrying about blood and violence on TV and movie screens. I write, produce and direct horror movies. I co-authored "Night of the Living Dead," the so-called "granddaddy of the splatter flicks." And since then I've made a string of movies depicting murder and mayhem.

I can watch these kinds of movies when they've been made by other people, and I can even help create the bloody effects in my own movies without getting a knot in my stomach. Yet I still retain my capacity to be shocked, horrified and saddened when something like this happens in real life.

So there must be a difference between real violence and "reel" violence. And if I didn't feel that this is true, I'd stop making the kinds of movies that I make. What are those differences?

My movies are scary and unsettling, but they are also cautionary tales. They might show witches at work, doing horrible things or carrying out nefarious schemes, but in doing so they convey a warning against superstition and the dementia it can spawn. They might show people under extreme duress, set upon by human or inhuman creatures, but in doing so they teach people how duress can be handled and blind, ignorant fear can be confronted and conquered. My purpose hasn't been to glorify or encourage murder and mayhem, but to give horror fans the vicarious chills and thrills they crave.

The most powerful and consequently financially successful horror movies—"Night of the Living Dead," "The Texas Chainsaw Massacre," "Halloween" and "Friday The 13th"—feature a small cast in a confined situation that is made terrifying by the presence of a monster/madman/murderer. Usually the victims are young, beautiful women. Often the murders are filmed from the point of view of the murderer. For all these reasons, we filmmakers have been accused of hating women and portraying them as objects to be punished for being sexually desirable. Horror fans have been accused of identifying with the psychopathic killers portrayed in these movies and deriving vicarious enjoyment from watching the killers act out the fans' dark fantasies.

But there are two simple, pragmatic reasons why the victims are often filmed from the point of view of the killer. First, it's an effective technique for not revealing who the killer is, thus preserving an aura of suspense. Second, it affords dramatically explicit angles for showing the victim's terror—and the horror of what the killer is doing.

These films *are* horrifying because they reflect—but do not create—a frightful trend in our society. Murders, assaults and rapes are being committed with more frequency and with increasing brutality. Serial killers and mass murderers are constantly making headlines. Most of these killers are men, often sexually warped men, and they most often kill women. So we filmmakers have stuck to the facts in our portrayal of them. That's why our movies are so scary. Too many of our fellow citizens are turning into monsters, and contemporary horror movies have seized upon this fear and personified it. So now we have Jason, Michael and Freddy instead of Dracula and Frankenstein. Our old-time movie monsters used to be creatures of fantasy. But today, unfortunately, they are extensions of reality.

Recently, at a horror convention in Albany, I was autographing videocassettes of a show I had hosted, entitled "Witches, Vampires & Zombies," and a young man asked me if the tape showed actual human sacrifices. He was disappointed when I informed him that the ceremonies on the tape were fictional depictions. He was looking for "snuff movies"—the kind that actually show people dying.

Unfortunately, tapes showing real death are widely available nowadays. A video of the Pennsylvania politician blowing his brains out went on sale just a few weeks after the incident was broadcast. But I don't think that the people who are morbidly fixated on this sort of thing are the same people who are in love with the horror-movie genre.

I'm afraid that the young man I met in Albany has a serious personality disorder. And I don't think he's really a horror fan. He didn't buy my tape, but he would have bought it if the human sacrifices had been real. "Reel" violence didn't interest him. He didn't care about the niceties of theme, plot or character development. He just wanted to see people die.

I haven't seen any snuff movies for sale at the horror conventions I've attended. True horror fans aren't interested. They don't go to the movies just to see artificial blood and gore, either. The films that gratuitously deliver those kinds of effects usually are box-office flops. The hit horror films have a lot more to offer. While scaring us and entertaining us, they teach us how to deal with our deepest fears, dreads and anxieties.

But modern horror movies aren't to blame for these fears, dreads and anxieties. They didn't create our real-life Jasons, Michaels and Freddys any more than the gangster movies of the 1920s and 1930s created Al Capone and Dutch Schultz. If the movies reflect, with disturbing accuracy, the psychic terrain of the world we live in, then it's up to us to change that world and make it a safer place.

A DESENSITIZED SOCIETY DRENCHED IN SLEAZE

Jeff Jacoby

> *Jeff Jacoby is a regular columnist for the* Boston Globe, *where this essay originally appeared.*

I was seventeen years old when I first saw an X-rated movie. It was Thanksgiving in Washington, D.C. My college dorm had all but emptied out for the holiday weekend. With no classes, no tests, and nobody around, I decided to scratch an itch that had long been tormenting me.

I used to see these movies advertised in the old *Washington Star*, and—like any seventeen-year-old boy whose sex life is mostly theoretical—I burned with curiosity. I wondered what such films might be like, what awful, thrilling secrets they might expose.

And so that weekend I took myself to see one. Full of anticipation, nervous and embarrassed, I walked to the Casino Royale at 14th Street and New York Avenue. At the top of a long flight of stairs, a cashier sat behind a cage. "Five dollars," he demanded—steep for my budget, especially since a ticket to the movies in the late seventies usually cost $3.50. But I'd come this far and couldn't turn back. I paid, I entered, I watched.

For about 20 minutes. The movie, I still remember, was called *Cry for Cindy*, and what I saw on the screen I'd never seen—I'd never even imagined—before. A man and a woman, oral sex, extreme close-ups. The sheer gynecological explicitness of it jolted me. Was *this* the forbidden delight hinted at by those ads? This wasn't arousing, it was repellent. I was shocked. More than that: I was ashamed.

I literally couldn't take it. I bolted the theater and tumbled down the steps. My heart was pounding and my face was burning. I felt dirty. Guilty. I was conscience-stricken.

All that—over a dirty movie.

Well, I was an innocent at seventeen. I was naïve and inexperienced, shy with girls, the product of a parochial-school education and a strict upbringing. Explicit sex—in the movies, music, my social life—was foreign to me. Coming from such an environment, who *wouldn't* recoil from *Cry for Cindy* or feel repelled by what it put up on that screen?

But here's the rub: Dirty movies don't have that effect on me anymore. I don't make a practice of seeking out skin flicks or films with explicit nudity, but in the years since I was seventeen, I've certainly seen my share. Today another sex scene is just another sex scene. Not shocking, not appalling, nothing I feel ashamed to look at. Writhing bodies on the screen? Raunchy lyrics in a song? They may entertain me or they may bore me, but one thing they no longer do is make me blush.

I've become jaded. And if a decade and a half of being exposed to this stuff can leave *me* jaded—with my background, my religious schooling, my disciplined origins—what impact does it have on kids and young adults who have never been sheltered from anything? What impact does it have on a generation growing up amid dysfunctional families, broken-down schools, and a culture of values-free secularism?

If sex- and violence-drenched entertainment can desensitize me, it can desensitize anyone. It can desensitize a whole society. It can drag us to the point where nothing is revolting. Where nothing makes us blush.

And what happens to an unblushing society? Why, everything. Central Park joggers get raped and beaten into comas. Sixth-graders sleep around. Los Angeles rioters burn down their neighborhood and murder dozens of their neighbors. The Menendez boys blow off their parents' heads. Lorena Bobbitt mutilates her husband in his sleep. "Artists" sell photographs of crucifixes dunked in urine. Pro-life fanatics open fire on abortion clinics. Daytime TV fills up with deviants. The U.S. Naval Academy fills up with cheaters. The teen suicide rate goes through the roof.

And we get used to all of it. We don't blush.

The point isn't that moviegoers walk out of Oliver Stone's latest grotesquerie primed to kill. Or that Geto Boys' sociopathic lyrics ("Leavin' out her house, grabbed the bitch by her mouth/Drug her back in, slam her down on the couch./Whipped out my knife, said, 'If you scream I'm cutting,'/Open her legs and . . .") cause rape. The point is that when blood and mayhem and sleazy sex drench our popular culture, we get accustomed to blood and mayhem and sleazy sex. We grow jaded. Depravity becomes more and more tolerable because less and less scandalizes us.

Of course, the entertainment industry accepts no responsibility for any of this. Time Warner and Hollywood indignantly reject the criticisms heaped on them in recent days. We don't cause society's ills, they say, we only reflect them. "If an artist wants to deal with violence or sexuality or images of darkness and horror," said film director Clive Barker, "those are legitimate subjects for artists."

They are, true. Artists have dealt with violence and sexuality and horror since time immemorial. But debauchery is not art. There is nothing ennobling about a two-hour paean to bloodlust. To suggest that Snoop Doggy Dogg's barbaric gang-rape fantasies somehow follow in the tradition of Sophocles' tragic drama, Chaucer's romantic poetry, or Solzhenitsyn's moral testimony is to suggest that there is no difference between meaning and meaninglessness.

For Hollywood and Time Warner, perhaps there no longer is. The question before the house is, what about the rest of us?

THE DEATH PENALTY IS JUSTICE

Edward I. Koch

Though currently known as the feisty judge on the syndicated People's Court, *Democrat Edward Koch has a more serious past, having served as mayor of New York City for twelve years from 1978 to 1990. While in office, he established a no-nonsense reputation as a dauntless leader. The essay which follows was originally published in* The New Republic *in 1985 and presents Koch's position in favor of capital punishment as the only just response to murder. Koch is also the author of* Mayor: An Autobiography *(1984), which he wrote in collaboration with William Rauch.*

Last December a man named Robert Lee Willie, who had been convicted of raping and murdering an 18-year-old woman, was executed in the Louisiana state prison. In a statement issued several minutes before his death, Mr. Willie said, "Killing people is wrong. . . . It makes no difference whether it's citizens, countries, or governments. Killing is wrong." Two weeks later in South Carolina, an admitted killer named Joseph Carl Shaw was put to death for murdering two teenagers. In an appeal to the governor for clemency, Mr. Shaw wrote: "Killing is wrong when I did it. Killing is wrong when you do it. I hope you have the courage and moral strength to stop the killing."

It is a curiosity of modern life that we find ourselves being lectured on morality by cold-blooded killers. Mr. Willie previously had been convicted of aggravated rape, aggravated kidnapping, and the murders of a Louisiana deputy and a man from Missouri. Mr. Shaw committed another murder a week before the two for which he was executed, and admitted mutilating the body of the 14-year-old girl he killed. I can't help wondering what prompted these murderers to speak out against killing as they entered the deathhouse door. Did their newfound reverence for life stem from the realization that they were about to lose their own?

Life is indeed precious, and I believe the death penalty helps to affirm this fact. Had the death penalty been a real possibility in the minds of these murderers, they might well have stayed their hand. They might have shown moral awareness before their victims died, and not after. Consider the tragic death of Rosa Velez, who happened to be home when a man named Luis Vera burglarized her apartment in Brooklyn. "Yeah, I shot her," Vera admitted. "She knew me, and I knew I wouldn't go to the chair."

During my twenty-two years in public service, I have heard the pros and cons of capital punishment expressed with special intensity. As a district leader, councilman, congressman, and mayor, I have represented constituencies generally thought of as liberal. Because I support the death penalty for heinous crimes of murder, I have sometimes been the subject of emotional and outraged attacks by voters who find my position reprehensible or worse. I have listened to their ideas. I have weighed their objections carefully. I still support the death penalty. The reasons I maintain my position can be best understood by examining the arguments most frequently heard in opposition.

1. The death penalty is "barbaric."

Sometimes opponents of capital punishment horrify with tales of lingering death on the gallows, of faulty electric chairs, or of agony in the gas chamber. Partly in response to such protests, several states such as North Carolina and Texas switched to execution by lethal injection. The condemned person is put to death painlessly, without ropes, voltage, bullets, or gas. Did this answer the objections of death penalty opponents? Of course not. On June 22, 1984, the *New York Times* published an editorial that sarcastically attacked the new "hygienic" method of death by injection, and stated that "execution can never be made humane through science." So it's not the method that really troubles opponents. It's the death itself they consider barbaric.

Admittedly, capital punishment is not a pleasant topic. However, one does not have to like the death penalty in order to support it any more than one must like radical surgery, radiation, or chemotherapy in order to find necessary these attempts at curing cancer. Ultimately we may learn how to cure cancer with a simple pill. Unfortunately, that day has not yet arrived. Today we are faced with the choice of letting the cancer spread or trying to cure it with the methods available, methods that one day will almost certainly be considered barbaric. But to give up and do nothing would be far more barbaric and would certainly delay the discovery of an eventual cure. The analogy between cancer and murder is imperfect, because murder is not the "disease" we are trying to cure. The disease is injustice. We may not like the death penalty, but it must be available to punish crimes of cold-blooded murder, cases in which any other form of punishment would be inadequate and, therefore, unjust. If we create a society in which injustice is not tolerated, incidents of murder—the most flagrant form of injustice—will diminish.

2. No other major democracy uses the death penalty.

No other major democracy—in fact, few other countries of any description—are plagued by a murder rate such as that in the United States. Fewer and fewer Americans can remember the days when unlocked doors were the norm and murder was a rare and terrible offense. In America the murder rate climbed 122 percent between 1963 and 1980. During that same period, the murder rate in New York City increased by almost 400 percent, and the statistics are even worse in many other cities. A study at M.I.T. showed that based on 1970 homicide rates a person who lived in a large American city ran a greater risk of being murdered than an American soldier in World War II ran of being killed in combat. It is not surprising that the laws of each country differ according to differing conditions and traditions. If other countries had our murder problem, the cry for capital punishment would be just as loud as it is here. And I daresay that any other major democracy where 75 percent of the people supported the death penalty would soon enact it into law.

3. An innocent person might be executed by mistake.

Consider the work of Hugo Adam Bedau, one of the most implacable foes of capital punishment in this country. According to Mr. Bedau, it is "false sentimentality to argue that the death penalty should be abolished because of the abstract possibility that an innocent person might be executed." He cites a study of the 7,000 executions in this country from 1893 to 1971, and concludes that the record fails to show that such cases occur. The main point, however, is this. If government functioned only when the possibility of error didn't exist, government wouldn't function at all. Human life deserves special protection, and one of the best ways to guarantee that protection is to assure that convicted murderers do not kill again. Only the death penalty can accomplish this end. In a recent case in New Jersey, a man named Richard Biegenwald was freed from prison after serving 18 years for murder; since his release he has been convicted of committing four murders. A prisoner named Lemuel Smith, who, while serving four life sentences for murder (plus two life sentences for kidnapping and robbery) in New York's Green Haven Prison, lured a woman corrections officer into the chaplain's office and strangled her. He then mutilated and dismembered her body. An additional life sentence for Smith is meaningless. Because New York has no death penalty statute, Smith has effectively been given a license to kill.

But the problem of multiple murder is not confined to the nation's penitentiaries. In 1981, 91 police officers were killed in the line of duty in this country. Seven percent of those arrested in the cases that have been solved had a previous arrest for murder. In New York City in 1976 and 1977, 85 persons arrested for homicide had a previous arrest for murder. Six of these individuals had two previous arrests for murder, and one had four previous murder arrests. During those two years the New York police were arresting for murder persons with a previous arrest for murder on the average of one every 8.5 days. This is not surprising when we learn that in 1975, for example, the median time served in Massachusetts for homicide was less than two and a half years. In 1976 a study sponsored by the Twentieth Century Fund found that the average time served may be considerably lower.

4. *Capital punishment cheapens the value of human life.*

On the contrary, it can be easily demonstrated that the death penalty strengthens the value of human life. If the penalty for rape were lowered, clearly it would signal a lessened regard for the victim's suffering, humiliation, and personal integrity. It would cheapen their horrible experience, and expose them to an increased danger of recurrence. When we lower the penalty for murder, it signals a lessened regard for the value of the victim's life. Some critics of capital punishment, such as columnist Jimmy Breslin, have suggested that a life sentence is actually a harsher penalty for murder than death. This is sophistic nonsense. A few killers may decide not to appeal a death sentence, but the overwhelming majority make every effort to stay alive. It is by exacting the highest penalty for the taking of human life that we affirm the highest value of human life.

5. *The death penalty is applied in a discriminatory manner.*

This factor no longer seems to be the problem it once was. The appeals process for a condemned prisoner is lengthy and painstaking. Every effort is made to see that the verdict and sentence were fairly arrived at. However, assertions of discrimination are not an argument for ending the death penalty but for extending it. It is not justice to exclude everyone from the penalty of the law if a few are found to be so favored. Justice requires that the law be applied equally to all.

6. *Thou Shalt Not Kill.*

The Bible is our greatest source of moral inspiration. Opponents of the death penalty frequently cite the sixth of the Ten Commandments in an attempt to prove that capital punishment is divinely proscribed. In the original Hebrew, however, the Sixth Commandment reads "Thou Shalt Not Commit Murder," and the Torah specifies capital punishment for a variety of offenses. The biblical viewpoint has been upheld by philosophers throughout history. The greatest thinkers of the 19th century—Kant, Locke, Hobbes, Rousseau, Montesquieu, and Mill—agreed that natural law properly authorizes the sovereign to take life in order to vindicate justice. Only Jeremy Bentham was ambivalent. Washington, Jefferson, and Franklin endorsed it. Abraham Lincoln authorized executions for deserters in wartime. Alexis de Tocqueville, who expressed profound respect for American institutions, believed that the death penalty was indispensable to the support of social order. The United States Constitution, widely admired as one of the seminal achievements in the history of humanity, condemns cruel and inhuman punishment, but does not condemn capital punishment.

The death penalty is state-sanctioned murder. This is the defense with which Messrs. Willie and Shaw hoped to soften the resolve of those who sentenced them to death. By saying in effect, "You're no better than I am," the murderer seeks to bring his accusers down to his own level. It is also a popular argument among opponents of capital punishment; but a transparently false one. Simply put, the state has rights that the private individual does not. In democracy, those rights are given to the state by the electorate. The execution of a lawfully condemned killer is no more an act of murder than is legal imprisonment an act of kidnapping. If an individual forces his neighbor to pay him money under threat of punishment, it's called extortion. If the state does it it's called taxation. Rights and responsibilities surrendered by the invidual are what give the state its power to govern. This contract is the foundation of civilization itself.

Everyone wants his or her rights, and will defend them jealously. Not everyone, however, wants responsibilities, especially the painful responsibilities that come with law enforcement. Twenty-one years ago a woman named Kitty Genovese was assaulted and murdered on a street in New York. Dozens of neighbors heard her cries for help but did nothing to assist her. They didn't even call the police. In such a climate the criminal understandably grows bolder. In the presence of moral cowardice, he lectures us on our supposed failings and tries to equate his crimes with our quest for justice.

The death of anyone—even a convicted killer—diminishes us all. But we are diminished even more by a justice system that fails to function. It is illusion to let ourselves believe that doing away with capital punishment removes the murderer's deed from our conscience. The rights of society are paramount. When we protect guilty lives, we give up innocent lives in exchange. When opponents of capital punishment say to the state, "I will not let you kill in my name," they are also saying to murderers: "You can kill in your *own* name as long as I have an excuse for not getting involved."

It is hard to imagine anything worse than being murdered while neighbors do nothing. But something worse exists. When those same neighbors shrink back from justly punishing the murderer, the victim dies twice.

NO DEATH PENALTY

David Bruck

> *David Bruck is a lawyer in the South Carolina Office of Appellate Defense. Susan Smith, accused and convicted of drowning her two young sons, was one of Bruck's most notable clients. Many of Bruck's defendants are prisoners on death row. This article was published just one month after Koch's in the March 1985 issue of* The New Republic.

Mayor Ed Koch contends that the death penalty "affirms life." By failing to execute murderers, he says, we "signal a lessened regard for the value of the victim's life." Koch suggests that people who oppose the death penalty are like Kitty Genovese's neighbors, who heard her cries for help but did nothing while an attacker stabbed her to death.

This is the standard "moral" defense of death as punishment: even if executions don't deter violent crime any more effectively than imprisonment, they are still required as the only means we have of doing justice in response to the worst of crimes.

Until recently, this "moral" argument had to be considered in the abstract, since no one was being executed in the United States. But the death penalty is back now, at least in the southern states, where every one of the more than 30 executions carried out over the last two years have taken place. Those of us who live in those states are getting to see the difference between the death penalty in theory, and what happens when you actually try to use it.

South Carolina resumed executing prisoners in January with the electrocution of Joseph Carl Shaw. Shaw was condemned to death for helping to murder two teenagers while he was serving as a military policeman at Fort Dickson, South Carolina. His crime, propelled by mental illness and PCP, was one of terrible brutality. It is Shaw's last words ("Killing was wrong when I did it. It is wrong when you do it. . . .") that so outraged Mayor Koch: he finds it "a curiosity of modern life that we are being lectured on morality by cold-blooded killers." And so it is.

But it was not "modern life" that brought this curiosity into being. It was capital punishment. The electric chair was J. C. Shaw's platform. (The mayor mistakenly writes that Shaw's statement came in the form of a plea to the governor for clemency: actually Shaw made it only seconds before his death, as he waited, shaved and strapped into the chair, for the switch to be thrown.) It was the chair that provided Shaw with celebrity and an opportunity to lecture us on right and wrong. What made this weird moral reversal even worse is that J. C. Shaw faced his own death with undeniable dignity and courage. And while Shaw died, the TV crews recorded another "curiosity" of the death penalty—the crowd gathered outside the deathhouse to cheer on the executioner. Whoops of elation greeted the announcement of Shaw's death. Waiting at the penitentiary gates for the appearance of the hearse bearing Shaw's remains, one demonstrator started yelling, "Where's the beef?"

For those who had to see the execution of J. C. Shaw, it wasn't easy to keep in mind that the purpose of the whole spectacle was to affirm life. It will be harder still when Florida executes a cop-killer named Alvin Ford. Ford has lost his mind during his years of death-row confinement, and now spends his days trembling, rocking back and forth, and muttering unintelligible prayers. This had led to litigation over whether Ford meets a centuries-old legal standard for mental competency. Since the Middle Ages, the Anglo-American legal system has generally prohibited the execution of anyone who is too mentally ill to understand what is about to be done to him and why. If Florida wins its case, it will have earned the right to electrocute Ford in his present condition. If it loses, he will not be executed until the state has first nursed him back to some semblance of mental health.

We can at least be thankful that this demoralizing spectacle involves a prisoner who is actually guilty of murder. But this may not always be so. The ordeal of Lenell Jeter—the young black engineer who recently served more than a year of a life sentence for a Texas armed robbery that he didn't commit—should remind us that the system is quite capable of making the very worst sort of mistake. That Jeter was eventually cleared is a fluke. If the robbery had occurred at 7 P.M. rather than 3 P.M., he'd have had no alibi, and would still be in prison today. And if someone had been killed in that robbery, Jeter probably would have been sentenced to death. We'd have seen the usual execution-day interviews with state officials and the victim's relatives, all complaining that Jeter's appeals took too long. And Jeter's last words from the gurney would have taken their place among the growing literature of death-house oration that so irritates the mayor.

Koch quotes Hugo Adam Bedau, a prominent abolitionist, to the effect that the record fails to establish that innocent defendants have been executed in the past. But this doesn't mean, as Koch implies, that it hasn't happened. All Bedau was saying was that doubts concerning executed prisoners' guilt are almost never resolved. Bedau is at work now on an effort to determine how many wrongful death sentences may have been imposed: his list of murder convictions since 1900 in which the state eventually *admitted* error is some 400 cases long. Of course, very few of these cases involved actual executions; the mistakes that Bedau documents were uncovered precisely because the prisoner was alive and able to fight for his vindication. The cases where someone is executed are the very cases in which we're least likely to learn that we got the wrong man.

I don't claim that executions of entirely innocent people will occur very often. But they will occur. And other sorts of mistakes already have. Roosevelt Green was executed in Georgia two days before J. C. Shaw. Green and an accomplice kidnapped a young woman. Green swore that his companion shot her to death after Green had left, and that he knew nothing about the murder. Green's claim was supported by a statement that his accomplice made to a witness after the crime. The jury never resolved whether Green was telling the truth, and when he tried to take a polygraph examination a few days before his scheduled execution, the state of Georgia refused to allow the examiner into the prison. As the pressure for symbolic retribution mounts, the courts, like the public, are losing patience with such details. Green was electrocuted on January 9, while members of the Ku Klux Klan rallied outside the prison.

Then there is another sort of arbitrariness that happens all the time. Last October, Louisiana executed a man named Ernest Knighton. Knighton had killed a gas station owner during a robbery. Like any murder, this was a terrible crime. But it was not premeditated, and is the sort of crime that very rarely results in a death sentence. Why was Knighton electrocuted when almost everyone else who committed the same offense was not? Was it because he was black? Was it because his victim and all 12 members of the jury that sentenced him were white? Was it because Knighton's court-appointed lawyer presented no evidence on his behalf at his sentencing hearing? Or maybe there's no reason except bad luck. One thing is clear: Ernest Knighton was picked out to die the way a fisherman takes a cricket out of a bait jar. No one cares which cricket gets impaled on the hook.

Not every prisoner executed recently was chosen that randomly. But many were. And having selected these men so casually, so blindly, the death penalty system asks us to accept that the purpose of killing each of them is to affirm the sanctity of human life.

The death penalty states are also learning that the death penalty is easier to advocate than it is to administer. In Florida, where executions have become almost routine, the governor reports that nearly a third of his time is spent reviewing the clemency requests of condemned prisoners. The Florida Supreme Court is hopelessly backlogged with death cases. Some have taken five years to decide, and the rest of the Court's work waits in line behind the death appeals. Florida's death row currently holds more than 230 prisoners. State officials are reportedly considering building a special "death prison" dedicated entirely to the isolation and electrocution of the condemned. The state is also considering the creation of a special public defender unit that will do nothing else but handle death penalty appeals. The death penalty, in short, is spawning death agencies.

And what is Florida getting for all of this? The state went through almost all of 1983 without executing anyone: its rate of intentional homicide declined by 17 percent. Last year Florida executed eight people—the most of any state, and the sixth highest total for any year since Florida started electrocuting people back in 1924. Elsewhere in the U.S. last year, the homicide rate continued to decline. But in Florida, it actually rose by 5.1 percent.

But these are just the tiresome facts. The electric chair has been a center piece of each of Koch's recent political campaigns, and he knows better than anyone how little the facts have to do with the public's support for capital punishment. What really fuels the death penalty is the justifiable frustration and rage of people who see that the government is not coping with violent crime. So what if the death penalty doesn't work? At least it gives us the satisfaction of knowing that we got one or two of the sons of bitches.

Perhaps we want retribution on the flesh and bone of a handful of convicted murderers so badly that we're willing to close our eyes to all of the demoralization and danger that come with it. A lot of politicians think so, and they may be right. But if they are, then let's at least look honestly at what we're doing. This lottery of death both comes from and encourages an attitude toward human life that is not reverent, but reckless.

And that is why the mayor is dead wrong when he confuses such fury with justice. He suggests that we trivialize murder unless we kill murderers. By that logic, we also trivialize rape unless we sodomize rapists. The sin of Kitty Genovese's neighbors wasn't that they failed to stab her attacker to death. Justice does demand that murderers be punished. And common sense demands that society be protected from them. But neither justice nor self-preservation demands that we kill men who we have already imprisoned.

The electric chair in which J. C. Shaw died earlier this year was built in 1912 at the suggestion of South Carolina's governor at the time, Cole Blease. Governor Blease's other criminal justice initiative was an impassioned crusade in favor of lynch law. Any lesser response, the governor insisted, trivialized the loathsome crimes of interracial rape and murder. In 1912 a lot of people agreed with Governor Blease that a proper regard for justice required both lynching and the electric chair. Eventually we are going to learn that justice requires neither.

Questions:

1. What does Koch argue is the reason for supporting capital punishment? What does Bruck argue?

2. In the fourth paragraph, Koch claims to support the death penalty for cases of "heinous crimes of murder." Is he making a distinction between different kinds of murder? If so, how does he distinguish one type from another?

3. Bruck takes Koch's previous essay as the point of departure for his argument, focusing on refuting Koch's position as morally dangerous. To what extent is this an effective strategy for presenting his own argument, given his audience?

4. Koch admittedly builds his case by refuting the seven arguments most frequently advanced to oppose the death penalty. Does this establish your confidence in him? Do you think this strategy established the confidence of *The New Republic* readers? Which argument is most successfully refuted? Which is weakly refuted?

5. Compare the account of J. C. Shaw's crime as presented by both Koch and Bruck. How does Bruck's inclusion of the details and circumstances surrounding the case strengthen his argument? How does it weaken Koch's?

6. How does the extrinsic ethos of both rhetors affect your perceptions of the credibility of the arguments themselves?

7. How do you think Koch would respond to Bruck's argument about racial inequities in the criminal justice system? In what ways does his revelation of this issue increase his credibility?

8. Label both arguments according to their presentation of intrinsic ethos, logos, and pathos. Which are the most effective examples given the audience?

9. How would you describe the tone of both arguments?

10. Suppose you were a judge presiding over a debate in which the death penalty were being considered. Having heard the arguments as presented by both Koch and Bruck, who would you argue had won the debate and why?

UNIT THREE

Mapping a Debate

INTRODUCTION

When preparing to enter a public debate, one must first become conversant with the various parties engaged in the discussion and the positions held by each. Such a task requires that one move beyond the central opposition within a debate to explore other relevant disagreements. Thus, an exploration of the issues surrounding the death penalty would reveal that within the positions labeled broadly as "for" or "against" the death penalty there are also distinct positions on the questions of the death penalty's effectiveness as a deterrent, the fairness of its application, the social and moral consequences of state sanctioned executions, as well as many others. Analyzing these many points of disagreement will not only reveal the levels of contention between the key opposing parties, but it will also reveal that even parties that concur on their general position may clash over other questions raised in the debate. For example, one may find that some proponents of the death penalty defend its use by asserting that it is a deterrent, while other supporters may reject the deterrence argument while supporting the death penalty on moral grounds.

Inevitably, the more research one does on a topic, the more complex one finds that topic to be. To contend with the complexity of their subject, a writer will need to organize or "map" the debate. Writing an overview is a way to do just that. The purpose of an overview is to clearly present a debate, identifying the key issues, positions, and parties involved. Most overviews attempt to present various perspectives on an issue without passing judgement on them, thus allowing the writer to appear "objective" and avoid alienating readers that may not have agreed with the writer's positions or opinions on the debate. In the process of researching and writing an overview, a writer will increase their knowledge of the subject and his or her depth of understanding of the issues raised in the debate.

The following three articles are overviews. Consider, as you read, how each writer has chosen to organize or "map" their respective debate. What issues does each writer highlight? Is the presentation of the parties and positions balanced? Or does it reveal the writer's biases?

Matthew Elliot

I

Overview Articles

A ROOM OF THEIR OWN

LynNell Hancock and Claudia Kalb

Who can forget the pubescent pain of junior high? Boys sprout pimples, girls sprout attitude and both genders goad each other into a state of sexual confusion. Teachers in Manassas, Va., figured that all these colliding hormones were distracting students from their academic tasks. So officials at Marsteller Middle School decided to try something old: dividing girls and boys into separate academic classes. Eighth-grade girls say they prefer doing physics experiments without boys around to hog the equipment. Boys say they'd rather recite Shakespeare without girls around to make them feel "like geeks." An eerie return to the turn of the century, when boys and girls marched into public schools through separate doors? Yes, say education researchers. But will it work—and is it legal?

In districts across the country, public schools are experimenting with sexual segregation, in the name of school reform. There is no precise tally, in part because schools are wary of drawing attention to classes that may violate gender-bias laws. But, researchers say, in more than a dozen states—including Texas, Colorado, Michigan and Georgia—coed schools are creating single-sex classes. Some, like Marsteller, believe that separating the sexes will eliminate distractions. Others, like Robert Coleman Elementary in Baltimore, made the move primarily to get boys to work harder and tighten up discipline.

The great majority of the experiments are designed to boost girls' math and science scores. The stimulus for these efforts was a report four years ago from the American Association of University Women, which argued that girls were being shortchanged in public-school classrooms—particularly in math and science. The single-sex classroom, however, is not what the gender-equity researchers involved with AAUW had in mind as a remedy. Their report was meant to help improve coeducation, not dismantle it. Research shows single-sex schools tend to produce girls with more confidence and higher grades. But single-sex classrooms within coed schools? There are no long-term studies that approach, only a smattering of skeptics and true believers. "It's a plan that misses two boats," charges David Sadker, coauthor of "Failing at Fairness"—the education of boys, and the reality that children need to learn how to cope in a coed world. In short, says University of Michigan researcher Valerie Lee, "these classes are a bogus answer to a complex problem."

Critics worry that segregated classes will set back the cause of gender equity just when girls are finally being integrated into all-male academics. Half a century ago, boys in advanced science classes learned, for example, that mold is used for penicillin while girls in home economics learned that mold is the gunk on the shower curtain. "It's not an era we're eager to return to," says Norma Cantu of the U.S. Office of Civil Rights.

Miracles happen: As a general principle, federal law doesn't permit segregation by sex in public schools. (Exceptions can be made for singing groups, contact sports and human-sexuality and remedial classes.) Some schools have survived legal challenges by claiming that their all-girl classes fill remedial needs. A middle school in Ventura, Calif., faced down a challenge by changing the name of its all-girl math class to Math PLUS (Power Learning for Underrepresented Students). Enrollment is open to boys, though none has registered yet.

Despite the skeptics, single-sex experiments continue to spread. Teachers and students believe they work. At the high school in Presque Isle, Maine, members of the popular all-girl algebra class go on to tackle the sciences. University of Maine professor Bonnie Wood found that girls who take the algebra course are twice as likely to enroll in advanced chemistry and college physics than their coed counterparts. Michigan's Rochester High School turns away 70 students every year from its girls-only science and engineering class. Marsteller boys raised their collective average in language arts by one grade after a single term. Girls boosted their science average by .4 of a point.

For the teachers involved, the progress is no mystery. Sheryl Quinlan, who teaches science at Marsteller, knows single-sex classes let her kids think with something besides their hormones. Impressing the opposite sex is a 14-year-old's reason for being. Take away that pressure, and miracles happen. Quinlan recalls the girl who took a "zero" on her oral report rather than deliver it in front of her boyfriend. Those days are over. Now, says Amanda Drobney, 14, "you can mess up in front of girls, and it's OK." We've come a long way, babies—or have we?

Questions:

1. What do Hancock and Kalb suggest are the key questions at issue in this debate?

2. What groups and individuals do Hancock and Kalb use as representative of the various positions within the debate? What other voices may be relevant to this discussion? If you were exploring this topic, where might you direct your research to locate these voices?

3. To what extent do Hancock and Kalb remain "objective"? Are the key opposing positions addressed in a balanced manner? Does the concluding question suggest the authors' position?

BABIES IN LIMBO: LAWS OUTPACED BY FERTILITY ADVANCES

Multiple Parties to Conception Muddle Issues of Parentage

Rick Weiss

Miscarriages are always tragic, but some people couldn't help privately expressing relief when Tracy Veloff's pregnancy failed in December.

Veloff was a paid surrogate mother, and the child she was carrying had been made from the egg of a woman who had been dead for a year. It was the world's first case of posthumous maternity, a precedent that many found troubling.

Lawyers were already haggling over who would be the child's parents. The biological mother, Julie Garber, was buried in December, 1996, after freezing a few hastily produced embryos. Veloff, the surrogate mother, had no intention of raising the child she was paid to carry. Neither did the anonymous sperm donor who fertilized those eggs.

Even Garber's parents, who had arranged the pregnancy, did not plan to raise the child themselves. They had inherited the embryos along with their daughter's furniture and other possessions, they said—a concept some legal authorities found disconcerting—and it was their prerogative to grow them into grandchildren.

The Garber case is just one of an increasing number of ethical predicaments to emerge in recent years as a dizzying array of reproductive technologies has redefined the meaning of "parent" and "child" in ways wholly unfamiliar to American society and its legal system. Of the many areas of science that today are giving rise to bioethical quandaries, this one more than any other strikes at the heart of society's most cherished institution: the family.

Today's ethical crisis in reproductive medicine is the product of converging social, economic and scientific factors. Many women in the work force have delayed childbearing to the point where technological intervention now offers their only hope of becoming biological mothers; a lack of financial support from the federal government has pushed the $2 billion-a-year fertility industry onto an aggressively entrepreneurial track; and recent advances in egg freezing, embryo manipulation and other techniques have shattered many of the biological barriers to parenthood.

The result of this convergence has been a large, uncontrolled experiment in novel methods of family making. It has been, by some measures, a highly successful experiment—one that has brought the joys of parenthood to thousands of women who otherwise would have remained childless. In 1995 alone, 11,315 women gave birth to children conceived by some form of assisted reproductive technology, according to the American Society for Reproductive Medicine.

At the same time it has generated ethical, legal and social conundrums. New treatments are being rushed into use before they are fully proven to be safe or effective, potentially putting some women and children at heightened risk of physical and psychological harm. In some cases, women are not fully aware that they, their eggs or the resulting embryos are the subject of research, experts said.

As a result, a growing number of people are calling for new laws to regulate assisted reproductive medicine. The field today is largely free of federal or state oversight.

In the continued absence of such regulation, critics say, more and more people—particularly children—could be harmed.

"This field is screaming for oversight, regulation and control," said Arthur Caplan, director of the Center for Bioethics at the University of Pennsylvania. "If you are going to make babies in new and novel ways, you have to be sure it's in the interest of the baby."

The ethical and legal confusion surrounding high-tech family building extends beyond the questions of embryo inheritance and parentage raised by the Garber case. Courts are also finding themselves embroiled in debates over fertility clinic record-keeping practices, which in some cases appear to have led to the loss of women's frozen embryos. And they are having to settle questions of who should bear responsibility when a woman's egg is inadvertently inseminated by diseased sperm.

In one far-reaching case, a Pennsylvania jury may soon decide the difficult question of whether fertility clinics are more than "baby marts" and have a responsibility to ensure that their clients are prepared for the challenges of child-rearing. The case came about after a 26-year-old bachelor paid a clinic $30,000 to have a child made for him, then murdered the child within six weeks of bringing him home.

"Every so often you have to step back and say, 'What are we trying to do here?'" said Barbara Katz Rothman, a sociology professor at Baruch College in New York. "Most of us don't have a really clear sense" of how the fertility industry should be run, Rothman said. "But I'm fairly certain that we shouldn't just be turning this over to the forces of the market."

Given the lack of uniform standards and the confused state of the law, an American Bar Association panel is preparing a landmark legal analysis that it hopes will be translated into uniform legislation to be adopted by individual states. The proposal is scheduled to be unveiled this summer.

Meanwhile, some experts are saying that at a minimum, fertility doctors should provide written warnings to their clients about the legal and ethical entanglements they may face—especially when donated eggs, sperm or embryos are involved.

"The standard care for assisted reproductive medicine should be that you advise people not only of the medical risks but also the legal and social risks," said R. Alta Charo, a professor of law and bioethics at the University of Wisconsin at Madison.

What Defines a Parent?

Of all the legal and social complications wrought by modern fertility techniques, perhaps the most significant are those involving embryo ownership and parentage. The courts have not been enthusiastic in their new role as arbiters of parenthood. In the words of one New York court, these "are intensely personal and essentially private matters which are appropriately resolved by the prospective parents rather than the courts."

But with baby making now being done in so many ways, with so many different participants, the question of who an embryo or child belongs to can be difficult to answer. A recent analysis by Nanette R. Elster of the Chicago-Kent College of Law found that several fertility techniques in use today allow seven or eight people to have parental claims on a single newborn. In some situations using the newest technologies, as many as 10 people could claim a piece of the parental pie.

"We've now broken up the components of parenthood into so many pieces," said Wisconsin's Charo, "we can find ourselves in a situation where nobody has presumptive parental status."

That's what happened to Jaycee Buzzanca. The infertile couple who arranged for her creation, John and Luanne Buzzanca of Orange County, Calif., hired a married woman, Pamela Snell, to carry a child to term for them—a child made from the sperm and egg of anonymous, unrelated donors.

The situation became complicated when, in March 1995, one month before Jaycee was born, John filed for divorce—an act he claims relieved him of parental responsibilities, including child support. According to California law, fatherhood is defined by biological parentage or by marriage to the child's birth mother. Since John Buzzanca fits neither definition, he claims he has no fatherly obligations.

Luanne Buzzanca wanted to be Jaycee's legal mother but was neither her biological mother nor her birth mother. The surrogate mother didn't qualify either, having signed a contract relinquishing her maternal rights after birth. And the egg and sperm donors, who sold their genes with no intention of becoming active parents, remain anonymous.

So it was that Orange County Superior Court Judge Robert D. Monarch ruled in September that Jaycee has no legal parents. Period.

Lawyers familiar with the case said they presume that Jaycee, now living with Luanne, will not spend her entire life a legal orphan. Late last month, a court of appeals heard arguments in the case and is expected to assign a parent soon. But the case is emblematic of the kinds of quandaries arising as novel baby-making techniques emerge.

"The medical technologies are racing away, creating all sorts of kids," said Susan Crocklin, a Massachusetts attorney specializing in reproductive technology. "Now we need the role of the law to define and protect those families."

What If a Donor Dies?

Matters become even more confusing when the most obvious parent is long dead. Julie Garber was 28 and single when she died of leukemia in December 1996. Before embarking on a course of chemotherapy and radiation that would make her infertile, she arranged with a sperm bank to have a dozen of her eggs fertilized and the resulting embryos frozen. Her hope was to have them implanted in her uterus after her recovery.

When Garber died, her parents hired a surrogate mother to bring their daughter's ungestated offspring to term—an act they said fulfilled one of her last wishes. The plan was to give away any resulting offspring to their other daughter, Garber's sister.

After three tries, the adventure ended in December when the last of Julie Garber's embryos were rejected by the surrogate mother's body a few weeks into pregnancy.

The American Society for Reproductive Medicine recommends "caution" when posthumous reproduction is being considered, although the organization allows that the practice is not inherently wrong when the deceased has left express permission, as Julie Garber did.

Yet courts have been hostile to the idea that frozen embryos can be inherited like furniture or other property. "A man's sperm or a woman's ova or a couple's embryos are not the same as a quarter of land, a cache of cash, or a favorite limousine," a California court of appeals declared in November 1996.

Moreover, little is known about the psychological downside for a child who eventually learns that one or both parents were dead long before that child's own gestation began. Some experts have begun to complain that in the modern conception industry, the rights and privileges of potential parents—even dead ones—are gaining precedence over the welfare of the children being produced.

Lori Andrews, a professor of law and bioethics at Chicago-Kent College of Law, said she has been amazed at some of the things she has heard from people who support Julie Garber's right to reproduce after death. "One surrogate who applied to carry the Garber embryos said, 'I loved [being a mother] so much, I think Julie has the right to be a mother too,'" Andrews said. "Well, I'm sorry, but Julie is dead."

In addition, Andrews said, most sperm donors probably assume that their sperm will be used to create a child with a living mother and may object to fathering a motherless child.

Similar problems arise with dead sperm donors. Not long ago, Andrews said, a man from Milwaukee deposited some of his sperm in a sperm bank before undergoing cancer therapy, with the intention of using them to have children later. The man died, and when the hospital called his mother to see what they should do with the sperm, she decided to take out advertisements offering his semen to women in need.

"She was quoted as saying she wanted to have as many grandchildren as possible," Andrews said. "Well, I'm a real big believer in consent before reproduction. I can't believe this man wanted his sperm spread all over Milwaukee. He donated thinking he would be a father to his children."

Who Takes Responsibility?

There is at least one advantage to posthumous paternity: A dead father cannot harm his child. Consider the case of young Jonathan Austin, who was killed by his 26-year-old father, James Alan Austin, three years ago last month.

The father, a Pennsylvania bank analyst, paid $30,000 to the Infertility Center of America in Indianapolis to inseminate a woman with his sperm. Less than two months after he took his son home, he beat and shook the baby to death. Now he's serving 12-1/2 to 25 years in prison.

Child abuse is by no means a problem unique to the fertility business, but the Austin case has led some to question whether just anyone with a bank account should be allowed to order a baby.

On the one hand, said Caplan, the Pennsylvania ethicist, no one would propose placing limits on people's right to procreate naturally. "Isn't every knucklehead free to do whatever they want in the bedroom?" he asked.

At the same time, Caplan said, higher standards traditionally have applied in the baby brokering business. "Would [James Austin] have been able to adopt?" he asked. "Not without some kind of checks."

"Some clinics do psychological counseling and investigate into people's backgrounds, but this clinic did not," said Jane Lessner, a Philadelphia attorney representing Jonathan Austin's biological mother in a civil suit against the clinic. No law requires that fertility clinics subject their clients to psychological screening for parental potential, but Lessner argues that clinics have that responsibility. "They are in the business," she said. "They are the people that should know best about potential problems and therefore have special responsibilities to the people involved."

The Indianapolis clinic has been sold, and no spokesman for the former owners could be reached for comment. The case is headed for trial in Northampton County's Court of Common Pleas.

How Is Quality Maintained?

Even if fertility clinics have no special responsibility for assuring the parental skills of their clients, generic laws regarding good business practices suggest they at least have a responsibility to keep track of and protect the eggs, sperm and embryos left in their care. Yet quality control standards for fertility clinic laboratories differ widely from lab to lab and from state to state. And the history of in vitro fertilization in this country is littered with tales of lost, damaged or misappropriated sperm, eggs and embryos.

In the most famous case, doctors at a clinic in Irvine, Calif., implanted dozens of embryos into the wrong women in the early 1990s. That clinic is now closed and Ricardo Asch, the physician who headed it, has left the country. But a stream of less well-publicized cases has followed—each highlighting a different shortcoming in record-keeping or some other aspect of quality control.

In Rhode Island, for example, Carol and David Frisina are in the midst of a lawsuit against Women & Infants Hospital for the mysterious disappearance of six of the nine embryos they had frozen there. The Providence clinic is also defending itself against a suit brought by Vickie and Robert Lamontagne, who allege that a 1995 error led to the disappearance of three of their embryos. Doctors first informed Vickie Lamontagne of the loss while she was on her back in the hospital, ready to have the embryos implanted into her uterus.

In both cases, attorney David J. Oliveira said, incomplete records raise the discomfiting possibility that, as in the Irvine scandal, some of the embryos have been transferred to other women.

"We really don't know what happened to them. The trail is very sparse, and that's part of the problem," Oliveira said. "We've learned from these cases and on a national basis that the [reproductive] technology has far surpassed the development of adequate record-keeping procedures. Quality assurance has been cobbled together on an *ad hoc* basis as problems have arisen."

Hospital officials said in a statement they could not address specific allegations. However, they said, "we affirm our adherence to accepted standards of laboratory and clinical practice." They noted that a state health department investigation, while critical of the hospital's record-keeping, found no evidence that the embryos had been given to other women.

Record-keeping standards are also at issue in the case of Brittany Johnson, an 8-year-old Los Angeles girl who in 1995 learned she had polycystic kidney disease. Records suggest she inherited the genetic condition from a man known only as "Donor 276," whose sperm allowed Brittany's mother to become pregnant with her.

According to court documents filed by Brittany's parents, a Los Angeles sperm bank provided those sperm to them—and to an unknown number of other infertile couples—despite a signed statement from the donor suggesting he might have a family history of kidney disease. The sperm bank has denied negligence or blame for Brittany's kidney disease—a condition that for now is having little effect on her life but could eventually lead to a lifetime of dialysis or the need for a kidney transplant.

Who Regulates the Field?

No single regulatory body can address the array of complications resulting from the revolution in reproduction—least of all the federal government, which abdicated much of its responsibility over the field years ago when it slowed and then stopped all federal funding for embryo research.

In place of federal oversight, a hodgepodge of state regulations has emerged. For example, about half of all states now insist that donated sperm be tested for the human immunodeficiency virus (HIV), which causes AIDS. A similar number of states require a husband's permission before a married woman can accept donor sperm. Almost every state has laws to clarify who the legal father is when donor sperm are used. Five states have laws regulating egg donation.

Different states' laws deal differently (and some not at all) with such issues as whether embryos may be bought and sold, genetically tested or used in research. And there is enormous variation from state to state when it comes to the regulation of surrogacy arrangements. Some states ban such contracts outright. Others ban payments to intermediaries or "baby brokers." Others limit the use of surrogacy to infertile couples. At least 15 other types of limitations on surrogacy have been passed by one or more states.

To address that confusion, a committee of the American Bar Association has been working for more than a year to create what amounts to model legislation for states to consider. It's a difficult task.

"The field is moving so quickly, you can't easily anticipate the next twist," said Ami Jaeger, co-chairman of the ABA committee and principal at the BioLaw Group in Santa Fe, which provides legal and consulting services in genetics and assisted reproduction.

But there are several basic principles that the panel hopes the ABA will back at its annual meeting this summer: that a doctor is responsible for informing fertility patients of the potential for legal and ethical complications. That posthumous reproduction may in some circumstances be inappropriate. That only a limited number of unrelated "third party" individuals should be allowed to have a hand in creating a baby.

Overall, the aim will be to ensure that anyone seeking fertility treatment knows in advance about the possible legal pitfalls. And most important, Jaeger and others said, to assert that in all matters of assisted reproduction, the baby-to-be's interests don't get lost along the way.

"The principle I want to get in is that you must have a connection to the kid. It must be your sperm or your egg, or you're going to carry" the fetus, said Crockin, the Massachusetts attorney, who has worked with the ABA panel. "Designer embryos where you pick a sperm and you pick an egg and you pick a woman to carry the child ... I question the ethics of providing that kind of service."

It remains unclear whether that traditional view will hold up against the tide of new reproductive technology.

Questions:

1. Explore the various definitions of "parent" and "child" at issue in this discussion. How can, on the one hand, "as many as 10 people" claim to be the parent of a single child, while, on the other, a child may have "no legal parents"? What do different parties see as the cause of this crisis? What solutions are offered?

2. Weiss includes discussions of several specific cases, such as that of Julie Garber as well as Jaycee Buzzanca. Does Weiss' use of these cases help to clarify the complex issues raised by the advances in reproductive technology? How?

3. Under what various jurisdictions do questions raised in Weiss' essay fall? What, for example, are the legal ramifications for the "revolution of reproduction"? What are the medical implications? the ethical?

MARATHONS GAIN
NEW FACES, SLOWER PACES

Amy Shipley

The story goes like this. There are two women at the start line of a five-kilometer race. One remarks that her next race will be a marathon. The other flashes a look of disbelief. The first woman shakes her head, explains. "It's not like it used to be," she says. "You can walk them now."

The exchange, overheard this summer by Road Runners Club of America Vice President Freddi Carlip, provides a peek inside the so-called second running boom that has pushed marathoning out of the domain of the running-obsessed and into the health-conscious mainstream. The rules haven't changed—marathons still require the traversal of 26.2 miles—but the average runner has. And controversy has followed.

Many in the new wave of marathoners alternate stretches of running with walking. Overall times have slowed significantly even while participation has soared. Some hard-core runners say the so-called second running boom differs so drastically from the first one in the 1970s that it's not helping the sport—and not fit to be labeled any sort of "running" boom at all.

"The challenge of the marathon is that it's an awful long way to run," said running coach Bob Glover, co-author of *The Runner's Handbook*. "You can't knock someone for reaching a goal, but my main thing is, if someone doesn't train properly to run all the way, then they shouldn't say they have 'run' a marathon."

That type of attitude raises the ire of second boomers and their supporters, who point out that 26.2 miles is a long haul no matter how one covers the distance. They say longtime runners should be welcoming newcomers, not kicking them out of their playground. Since 1980, the number of marathoners in the United States has nearly quadrupled. About 400,000 crossed marathon finish lines last year, up from 120,000 finishers 18 years ago.

"The division in the running movement now between runners and run-walkers just breaks my heart," said Susan Kalish, executive director of the American Running and Fitness Association in Bethesda. "Now, there are three categories: It's us, slower than us, and them. It just makes no sense to me at all. The people who run-walk are doing it for health."

Men averaged 3 hours 32 minutes to finish marathons in 1980; women averaged 4 hours 4 minutes. In the USA Track and Field Road Runner Information Center's most recent study in 1995, men finished 23 minutes later on average (3:55) and women, 11 minutes later (4:15). Center researcher Ryan Lamppa said the downward trend is believed to have continued.

Substantial increases in women, the middle-aged and novice runners who compete for charitable foundations have contributed to the overall growth and slower marathon times. Last year, the average marathoner was 40 years old and women composed 30 percent of the total, according to the Road Running Information Center.

Frank Shorter, who won the 1972 Olympic marathon gold medal, remembers when the stereotypical marathon racer was male, skinny as chopsticks, taut with muscle fiber, and often a fringe character in American society. Said Shorter: "These guys had long hair, they ate strange food, they walked around with an aura that said, 'I can do something you can't do.'"

That is no longer the case. The new generation runner is often the most ordinary guy on the block. Former musician John Bingham has completed 13 marathons in the last six years. His best time is 4 hours 35 minutes. In running circles, he is The Penguin, a moniker he uses in his monthly column in Runner's World magazine. He walks about a minute for every mile he runs. "I was a lifetime smoker, an overeater," said Bingham, 49. "My interest in the act of running really began as a personal odyssey . . . Once [I] crossed that finish line, with the exception of the birth of my first son, nothing changed me emotionally like that."

Just about every other sport, from football to figure skating, separates its elite from its beginners. But not road racing. From the world's fastest Kenyans who complete races in just over two hours to the first-time marathoner who strives to beat five, all compete on the same course. Only the Boston Marathon and the Olympic trials require qualifying times—the other U.S. races are open to anybody who gets the application in early enough.

The diversity hasn't always bred compatibility.

Charity organizations have both capitalized on and contributed to the second running boom—and they've faced a sizable dose of skepticism. Charities have raised millions in recent years by offering all-expenses-paid trips to races to those who run for the cause. An estimated 19,000 people compete in about 30 marathons annually for the Leukemia Society's Team in Training—the most well-known group of charity runners. Team in Training members represented about one in 20 marathoners (five percent) last year.

The charity organizations, which also include the Joints in Motion team for the Arthritis Foundation and the local AIDS Marathon Training Program to benefit the Whitman Walker Clinic, draw many novice marathoners. Runners prepare for six to eight months in local training groups. They often are led by volunteer coaches who teach run-walk approaches. Team in Training, which is about 60 percent female, raised a whopping $36 million for cancer research in the last year—50 percent of the total Leukemia Society funds. About 2,000 charity runners will compete in the Marine Corps Marathon's field of about 18,300 Sunday, race director Rick Nealis said.

Yet charity groups have contributed to the latest running controversy almost as much as they have pumped money into worthy causes.

"In the late '70s during the first running boom, people were probably racing and training in excess," Glover said. "This time, the bulk of the people seem to be doing the other extreme, probably too little. I just don't believe that we should be promoting that anybody can do it, and here's how to do it with as little [effort] as possible."

Even Carlip, who says "we have to welcome both sides" to running, acknowledges the confusion ushered in by the changing times. In the '70s, she said, "it was almost sacrilegious to even think of walking in a race. No one would ever want to." Now, walking is an essential part of many running programs.

"I think this is actually more healthy and well-rounded than what happened in the '70s," said former U.S. running star Alberto Salazar, who is now a spokesman for

Joints in Motion. "It was like everyone was trying to run the same intensity as the athletes who devoted their careers to running . . . I don't know if it's hard-core runners who somehow feel their turf has been invaded . . . [but] I think it's kind of snooty for people to say: 'They're not runners because they're not as fast as us.'"

Back-of-the-pack runners maintain that merely moving forward for five or six straight hours, even at a slow pace, is an exhausting exercise. The run-walk approach—for years advocated by former world-class runner Jeff Galloway—is designed to get people to the finish line in good spirits and without great discomfort. Hard-core marathoners have for years battled the "wall," the excruciating slap of fatigue that often strikes at about the 20th mile. Run-walking is supposed to eradicate the dreaded wall.

As Bingham put it: "It's a little different than people out there just trying not to puke."

Even those who have no philosophical objection to run-walkers say they present some tangible problems on race courses. Groups of runners who stop simultaneously for a walk break can be frustrating—or hazardous—to those running immediately behind. The masses of casual runners, some say, cause marathon fields to close early, thereby stealing participation slots from more serious participants. In fact, the Marine Corps Marathon closed earlier this year than ever: June 17. Last year, the race closed Aug. 28. Before that, the race always had accepted applicants until the very last minute.

Dissenting runners also ask: Are all of these first-time runners, especially those introduced to marathons through charity groups, staying in the sport? There are no statistics to say for sure.

Not since the 1970s and early '80s when U.S. runners Salazar, Joan Benoit, Bill Rodgers and Shorter achieved superstar status, has the United States been a leading figure in international long-distance running. Some runners say the new boomers are not merely leaving the problem unremedied, but in a way they are exacerbating it. They say the slow-down philosophy sets a poor standard for young runners, who have little to aspire to and few U.S. stars to emulate in the long-distance running field.

They say the enormous influx of new-generation marathoners has made it unnecessary for race directors to increase appearance fees or prize money to lure top runners (this year's New York City Marathon will pay the winner $50,000 plus a car), making it difficult for professionals to make a living. Why worry about attracting stars to your racing field when the field will be full regardless?

While world-class racers have lost their "luster" in the United States, Rodgers said, road races themselves have sunk from "sport" to merely "event." He suggested that charity groups funnel some of their proceeds back into running, either on road races themselves or youth development. Others agree.

"We're more concerned about raising money [for charities] than running competitively," said Tom Fleming, who coaches the Adidas Running Room team in Bloomfield, N.J. "Why can't a road race be held to make money for road racing? How's that for a different concept? The cancer society is making more money and our sport is still in the toilet."

The response of the other side? Simple.

The charity groups "came up with a great idea," Shorter said. "You come up with your own great idea."

To the second boomers, success is not dictated by a stopwatch or a mileage log. The sport is about fitness, camaraderie and seeking spiritual well-being along the arduous path of a marathon course. For many newcomers to marathoning, their goals are so personal they seem genuinely perplexed as to what the fuss is about. They also seem annoyed. The racing business is booming. Where would it be without them? And what business are their personal fitness choices to anyone else, anyway?

Bingham runs a handful of marathons annually, often leading pacing groups sponsored by *Runner's World* magazine. For those under Bingham's charge, the real goal is always within reach: Having fun. During one race, a pair of participants ducked into a convenience store for cold drinks.

"When I am having fun, I slow down because I don't want it to end," Bingham said. "The biggest complainers [about run-walkers and charity runners] are sort of sub-elites who are frustrated about their own running careers. Those people are grumpy in general.

"They sometimes forget our priorities are very different. They should come run in the back with us. They would find out we are doing it for very different reasons. What we are after is not as tangible as PRs [personal records], medals or trophies."

Questions:

1. Shipley quotes championship runner Bill Rodgers as saying that "road races have sunk from 'sport' to merely 'event.'" What are the implications of this shift in definition? What does Rodgers and other traditional marathoners see as the cause of this shift?

2. How do proponents of "run-walking" reply to the criticism that they are ruining the Marathon?

3. How do you define the act of "running" a marathon? How would you respond to the opposing arguments?

II

Identifying Positions in Opinion Pieces

In January, 1999 the use of the word "niggardly" by David Howard, an aide to DC Mayor Anthony Williams, and Howard's subsequent resignation, triggered a firestorm of rhetoric locally, nationally, and even internationally. In the ensuing debates, blame was placed on everything and everyone from Howard, to Williams, to the term itself, to "political correctness." The following three columns appeared in the Washington Post *within days of the controversy. Consider these articles in relationship to each other. How does each contextualize the controversy? What issues are emphasized in their distinct positions? The fourth article is an overview of the debates that appeared in* Newsweek. *After having read three articles on the topic, consider whether the overview reflects the debate as presented by the* Post *columnists. Does this overview remain objective? Or does it enter into the debate?*

MUCH ADO ABOUT AN N-WORD

Colbert I. King

The writer is a member of the editorial page staff.

Ignorance scored a big victory this week in the District of Columbia. Cowardice did all right for itself, too. The losers are residents who still cling to the hope of living in a city where leaders don't succumb to cheap racial manipulation and merit trumps race. The case of David Howard shows we're not there yet.

Once upon a time, David Howard was a prized catch for Mayor Anthony Williams—the kind of loyal, can-do staff person a leader loves having around. Howard was so valuable that the new mayor named him public advocate and placed him in charge of the constituent services office. Today, Howard is voluntarily off the public payroll. The reason is almost too embarrassing to mention.

In a recent conversation with a couple of workers about the need to be thrifty, Howard used the word—be still, my heart—"niggardly."

NIGGARDLY. Say it slowly: nig-gard-ly. Now faster: niggardly, niggardly, niggardly. Say it any way you want—at the top of your voice, under your breath, in the shower or in the park. It matters not. Niggardly is not the nasty N-word; it never has been. Look it up. (If there's any saving grace in this whole sorry episode, it is that maybe more people will open their dictionaries.)

Unfortunately, the offended employee, a Williams campaign staffer named Marshall Brown—whose real claim to fame is a life of faithful service to ex-mayor Marion Barry—never cracked his Webster's. Race became the convenient proxy for pressuring the mayor to move Howard out of a coveted position.

Challenged, Williams wilted. Instead of tearing Howard's resignation into shreds, ordering him back to work—and handing Marshall Brown a New World dictionary— Williams accepted Howard's decision to quit, accusing him of having exercised bad judgment.

Get this: A few weeks ago, U.S. District Judge Harold H. Greene, excoriating the Navy for failing to obey a federal order to remedy discrimination against an African American employee, told Navy lawyers, "Do something that rectifies the discrimination. That's what I want you to do, that's what the EEOC wants them to do, instead of being niggardly and parsimonious about this whole thing and giving him the job that has the least potential for advancement and has the least supervisory authority."

Pray tell, Mr. Mayor, was that a judicial exercise in "bad judgment"? When did niggardly become a racial slur? Before the Howard story broke, "niggardly" had appeared in the *Washington Post* 65 times during the past several years. It has been used by reporters in practically every section of this newspaper, by prominent nationally syndicated columnists and the U.S. Supreme Court's most liberal justice.

Methinks Anthony Williams has a bad case of jitters brought on by the belittling rhetoric of a handful of blacker-than-thou critics who live to make the racially insecure cower. (They have been ably assisted by a few arrogant white people—including some in the press—who fancy themselves free from prejudice but who are really obsessed with the "blackness" of prominent African Americans to the point of pathology.) Not that Williams wasn't warned there'd be days like this. (See "Welcome, Mayor Williams," op-ed, Nov. 7, 1998). "Kick them out of your office," I wrote. Instead, the mayor let them in. Now they've gotten next to him.

Get a grip, Mr. Mayor. Don't panic and start handing your detractors a victory they couldn't win at the polls. It's plain to see. Some of them want to intimidate you into governing the city by their set of self-serving, racially tinged rules. Fall for that, start catering to them for approval, and it's Sharon Pratt Kelly all over again. Besides, if you start running, they'll keep chasing. You know better. Stand your ground.

That said, let's deal upfront with something else.

There's talk that Howard, a white guy, was not suited for the advocate's job since the work involved dealing with mostly African American constituents. Whatever you do, Mr. Mayor, don't buy into that notion. Decades of civil rights gains are at stake.

Accept the idea that a leader's race should match the race of those being led—or that a public servant should only serve or work with members of his or her own race—and you're saying that the president was wrong to appoint Ron Brown as commerce secretary, that Isiah Leggett should never have been elevated to chairman of the Montgomery County Council and that Franklin Raines should not head Fannie Mae. That logic could have been used against Colin Powell's appointment as chairman of the Joint Chiefs. Follow it and Ann Fudge would not be the president of Maxwell House Coffee and Post Cereals, and Jackie Robinson would never have worn a Dodgers uniform.

For the past few weeks, I've been on a soapbox about white separatists who preach their group's supremacy. They fervently believe it would be better for America if the races went their own ways: lived in separate neighborhoods, had separate recreation facilities, attended separate schools, worked and socialized apart. Separatists would drool at the notion of your excluding David Howard from a job because he's "not one of our own." And why? Because they know that kind of scheming cuts both ways—and works to their advantage.

For those of us who can only make it if the playing field is level and the rules are the same for all, racially designated jobs are, in the long run, limiting and self-defeating. Allow race to trump merit in this city, or anywhere and we are the losers. Let's face it, the D.C. government ain't big enough to hire us all.

P.S.: Since the Harvard story broke, two readers have called to say Marshall Brown told friends that David Howard had used the n-word and not "niggardly." Contacted on Thursday about those reports and his role in the incident, Marshall Brown repeatedly declined comment."

Puh-leeze!

SOME WORDS JUST TASTE UNPLEASANT ON THE TONGUE

Courtland Milloy

As a personal matter, I prefer the word "stingy," and a distinct unpleasantness registers in my mind upon hearing and seeing the word "niggardly," even though I know that the dictionary says they mean the same thing. But that's just me. I don't like the sound.

In recent conversations with white colleagues, I have found myself somewhat on edge in anticipation of their pronouncing it.

"What do you think about what happened to David Howard?" asked an editor, who is white. She was referring to a white aide to D.C. Mayor Anthony A. Williams, who recently resigned in a controversy over his supposed use of "niggardly."

"What do you think?" I asked back, not so much to hear what she thought but to test my own reaction to how she would say the word. Would she curl a lip, inadvertently bare a tooth, overemphasize the "nig" part, smirk or give any other indication that she was unaware or deliberately dismissive of the historic offensiveness of the sound?

Suffice it to say that I have a lot of undigested racial bile, and I am actually grateful for these little brouhahas that help me gently flush it out.

"It's not a word that I would ordinarily use," the editor began with a disarming preface. "But . . ."

Then she said it. Oddly, I discerned no lip movement whatsoever, as if she had used some ventriloquist trick to bring it lightly out of nowhere, at once acknowledging my peculiar sensibilities while staying true to her beliefs.

Heard that way, I might even buy into the textbook meaning.

But the fact remains that, in the back of my mind, I still question any white person who says "niggardly" to me when they could have said "miserly." Of course, such thinking is no more rational than the concept of race itself, which is America's greatest ongoing fiction. But the effects of racism is real and, for me, mostly subliminal, operating below the level of consciousness, constituting responses and patterns of interaction between blacks and whites that have been inculcated over centuries.

When the subject of race is at hand, I say, the only dictionary that counts is the one that gives meaning to human experience. That would be the heart, not the one by Webster, which, by the way, has also claimed that the word "nigger" is just another name for black people.

On the day after the Howard story broke last week, I arrived at the office to learn that a number of colleagues had already been to a top editor to make the case for expanded coverage of the perceived injustice. E-mail protests and telephone calls were coming in from all over the country.

My first thought was: Isn't it amazing how white people respond when one of their own gets shafted, especially by a black? What was essentially a local personnel management mix-up by a neophyte politician had become a national referendum on the ignorance and hypersensitivity of black people.

I would wake up the next morning to Katie Couric on the "Today Show" wrongly telling the nation that Howard had been handed a "pink slip," in effect, had been fired because of some illiterate black person in the District, and for a moment, I felt like I was watching a political attack ad for Sen. Jesse Helms (R-N.C.).

When Williams, as the District's chief financial officer, fired 165 black people last year without due process, just called them incompetent and gave them one day to pack up and leave, the response was nothing like this. The fact that Senate Majority Leader Trent Lott (R-Miss.) and Rep. Robert L. Barr Jr. (R-Ga.) have ties to a group that is an outgrowth of the Ku Klux Klan barely draws a yawn.

But this one hits a nerve.

"Sometimes news makes it all the way to Texas . . . if it is sufficiently amazing," came an e-mail from Bill Wood in Fort Worth. "The recent firing of David Howard by the mayor of Washington, D.C. made the grade. The mayor's action was absolutely racist and I hope the Post takes an appropriate editorial posture."

The writer would no doubt consider appropriate the posture taken on The Post's Op-Ed page yesterday by columnist Colbert I. King:

"NIGGARDLY. Say it slowly: nig-gard-ly," King wrote. "Now faster: niggardly, niggardly, niggardly. Say it anyway you want—at the top of your voice, under your breath, in the shower, in the park. It matters not. Niggardly is not the nasty N-word; it never has been. Look it up."

I'm actually impressed that King, who is black, is so comfortable with the word.

On the other hand, I am concerned about a disturbing tendency among us to detoxify offensive sounds by embracing them. There is the self-application of the term "niggaz," for instance, to say nothing of "black," which has the worst collection of meanings of any word in the English language.

Another Post colleague has noted that there are many words that have the potential to offend but get used all the time without an uproar. I don't think so. I say take a word like "fagot," which the dictionary says means a bundle of sticks, twigs or branches. Spelled with one g, it has nothing to do with a slur against homosexuals. But if I wanted to start a fire, I'd never call for wood that way.

USE THE RIGHT WORD FOR THE TIMES

Jonathan Yardley

It is a pity that "niggardly," a perfectly good if dated word that means "meanly, parsimonious, close-fisted, stingy," is the phonetic near-term of one of the vilest—if not *the* vilest—words in the English language. The two have absolutely no relationship to each other beyond the way they sound and look, but it's easy to confuse them, which is reason enough to consign "niggardly" (along with all other variations on "niggard") to the trash pile.

To say this is not political correctness, no matter what Rush Limbaugh and other guardians of the nation may tell you, but a decent regard for the feelings of others. To persist in using dated words or phrases ("blackguard," "black eye," "black as the ace of spades") when there are other perfectly good ones that mean exactly the same thing is not some form of linguistic purism but perverse, self-congratulatory anachronism. The language changes all the time, for better and for worse, for good reasons and for bad; confusion that leads to unnecessarily hurt feelings is among the good reasons for change.

This is not to suggest that David Howard, the District of Columbia official who used "niggardly" in an entirely legitimate context, spoke improperly; it is not to endorse the subordinate who insisted on interpreting this as a racial slur even after the definition was explained to him; it most certainly is not to applaud the haste with which Mayor Anthony Williams accepted Howard's resignation or the stubbornness with which he insisted thereafter that, in the words of one of his own subordinates, "in this environment it may have been poor judgment for someone in [Howard's] position to use that word."

Howard by all accounts is a decent man, free of prejudice, devoted to public service in the administration of the mayor who returned his loyalty so shabbily; he discovered "niggardly," he says, while studying for the SAT in high school, yet further evidence that this test does at least as much harm as good. Marshall Brown, who took such offense at Howard's use of the word, may well have been spoiling for a fight, which is all too common on all sides in our exaggeratedly sensitive racial climate. As for the newly inaugurated mayor, he, too, seems to be a decent man, but he obviously needs more seasoning in the tricky business of making one's way through this city's racial and social land mines.

There's nothing nice to be said about the knock-the-chip-off-my-shoulder animosity with which so many Americans of different races, ethnic backgrounds and sexual preferences confront each other. The revolution of rising expectations (to borrow Adlai Stevenson's phrase) of the postwar years is now in its mature phase, bringing ever-increasing rights and material blessings to those previously denied them, but it has also brought a rising awareness of the difference among us, since it is on the basis of those differences that rights and material blessings are withheld and demanded. A lot of people spend too much time looking around to take offense, and when they find it—whether it's real or imagined makes absolutely no difference—they're almost always too quick to overreact.

Yet what needs to be understood is that, however overheated the climate may be, however puerile and foolish so many people appear as they dash around looking for reasons to insult each other, it's the real world. It's all well and good to lock oneself in a radio studio, as Limbaugh does, and pitch camp in an 18th-century never-never land, but this merely evades reality, which is that in the process of trying to live up to all the promises in the Declaration of Independence and the Constitution, we've come to live in a world unimaginably different from the one in which those great documents were written.

In the 18th century Benjamin Franklin could write, "By the niggardly treatment of good masters they have been driven out of the school," and people would know exactly what he meant. Now those words are reprinted in the Oxford English Dictionary as examples of usage, but all too few of us know what they mean. One can take this as a comment on the prevailing level of education (as I do), but it is also a reflection, in miniature, of the changes that have taken place since the days when Mother England was mother of us all.

As one who traces his blood to the sceptered isle, I am occasionally susceptible to nostalgia for days of yore, but it passes quickly. The world we have now strikes me as on the whole rather good, as does the challenge of learning how to live in it as comfortably and prudently as possible. My life has been enriched beyond measure by people whose blood, skin color, ancestral country and language are utterly different from my own. I would far rather make peace than war with them, and if excising a few marginal words from the language of my distant forebears is one way of doing this, so be it.

What could be more "niggardly," i.e., closefisted and stingy, than to cling stubbornly and belligerently to words we no longer need? The English language is huge—the OED runs to 20 immense volumes and doubtless will be far larger in its next incarnation—and it offers an abundance of synonyms. The next time you're about to say, as David Howard did, "I will have to be niggardly with this fund," hold your tongue a moment. "Stingy" will do just fine. It won't hurt anyone else, and it won't hurt you.

THE SLUR THAT WASN'T

D.C.'s mayor draws fire in a war over words.

Lynette Clemetson

Washington phones were ringing off the hook. Two weeks ago word spread through-out the capital that one of the newly elected Mayor Anthony Williams's top aides—a white man—had flown off the handle and said something like "Why are all these n——s calling me?" City workers were aghast. But in fact, it didn't happen like that at all. David Howard, the openly gay head of the mayor's constituent-services office, had used the word *"niggardly"* in reference to his department's funds. A black staffer mis-took the adjective, which means "stingy" or "miserly," for the similar-sounding racial slur. Seeing the shocked look on his colleague's face, Howard apologized for the unin-tended offense. But by then it was already too late.

The buzz over the incident grew so intense that Howard last week offered to quit, telling *The New York Times* that "I used bad judgment in using the word." Williams accepted his resignation, and now the Washington mayor is being denounced by blacks, whites and gay leaders for sacrificing a trusted aide to political correctness. Local and national papers jumped in to ridicule the semantic confusion; the mayor's office was flooded with phone calls. Even NAACP chairman Julian Bond commented on the ridiculousness of the affair, saying he thought Williams had been *"niggardly"* in his judgment. In the face of such criticism, Williams is backpedaling. Pending an investigation, he says he may invite Howard back into the fold in another position.

How did Williams get into this mess? As so often happens in D.C. politics, the matter came down to race. Williams gained the support of the Washington establish-ment three years ago after stabilizing the district's tangled finances as chief financial officer. He won the election with a promise to take control of Washington's bloated and corrupt government, but Wiliams's coziness with the powers that be provoked suspicion from some in the black community. When he appointed senior advisers, residents of the predominantly black Southeast neighborhood—who had supported Williams—complained about the conspicuous absence of anyone from their com-munity. Anger over the mayor's choice of aides may have played a role in the Howard incident. There is some speculation that the black aide who spread word of the sup-posed slur had hoped to get Howard's job. The final straw seemed to come in mid-January, the same weekend the *"niggardly"* rumor began circulating. *The Washington Post* ran a lengthy opinion piece by a black resident questioning whether the mayor was "black enough" to run the city.

The criticism stung. Williams acknowledged as much in a statement after Howard stepped down: "While I'm troubled by recent news stories concerning race—questions about whether I'm black enough or have too many advisers who are not—I understand they reflect a great hurt within our city." The mayor thought that by accepting Howard's resignation he would help mend the racial divide. But he's learn-ing that when it comes to race, politics and symbolism, there are no easy answers.

III

Contextualizing an Article within a Debate

PORNOGRAPHY HURTS WOMEN

Susan Brownmiller

> *Susan Brownmiller is the founder of Women Against Pornography and a frequent contributor to the* New York Times Magazine *and* Book Review, Esquire, Vogue, *and* Mademoiselle. *She is the author of several books, including* Femininity, *1984. This essay is drawn from* Against Our Will, *1975.*

Pornography has been so thickly glossed over with the patina of chic these days in the name of verbal freedom and sophistication that important distinctions between freedom of political expression (a democratic necessity), honest sex education for children (a societal good) and ugly smut (the deliberate devaluation of the role of women through obscene, distorted depictions) have been hopelessly confused. Part of the problem is that those who traditionally have been the most vigorous opponents of porn are often those same people who shudder at the explicit mention of any sexual subject. Under their watchful, vigilante eyes, frank and free dissemination of educational materials relating to abortion, contraception, the act of birth, and female biology in general is also dangerous, subversive and dirty. (I am not unmindful that frank and free discussion of rape, "the unspeakable crime," might well give these righteous vigilantes further cause to shudder.) Because the battle lines were falsely drawn a long time ago, before there was a vocal women's movement, the antipornography forces appear to be, for the most part, religious, Southern, conservative and right-wing, while the pro-porn forces are identified as Eastern, atheistic and liberal.

Exigence

[But a woman's perspective demands a totally new alignment, or at least a fresh appraisal.] The majority report of the President's Commission on Obscenity and Pornography (1970), a report that argued strongly for the removal of all legal restrictions on pornography, soft and hard, made plain that 90 percent of all pornographic materials is geared to the male heterosexual market (the other 10 percent is geared to the male homosexual taste), that buyers of porn are "predominantly white, middle-class, middle-aged married males" and that the graphic depictions, the meat and potatoes of porn, are of the naked female body and of the multiplicity of acts done to that body.

Discussing the content of stag films, "a familiar and firmly established part of the American scene," the commission report dutifully, if easily explained, "Because pornography historically has been thought to be primarily a masculine interest, the emphasis in stag films seems to represent the preferences of the middle-class American male. Thus male homosexuality and bestiality are relatively rare, while lesbianism is rather common."

The commissioners in this instance had merely verified what purveyors of porn have always known: hard-core pornography is not a celebration of sexual freedom; it is a cynical exploitation of female sexual activity through the device of making all such activity, and consequently all females, "dirty." Heterosexual male consumers of pornography are frankly turned on by watching lesbians in action (although never in the final scenes, but always as a curtain raiser); they are turned off with the sudden swiftness of a water faucet by watching naked men act upon each other. One study quoted in the commission report came to the unastounding conclusion that "seeing a stag film in the presence of male peers bolsters masculine esteem." Indeed. The men in groups who watch the films, it is important to note, are *not* naked.

When male response to pornography is compared to female response, a pronounced difference in attitude emerges. According to the commission, "Males report being more highly aroused by depictions of nude females, and show more interest in depictions of nude females than [do] females." Quoting the figures of Alfred Kinsey, the commission noted that a majority of males (77 percent) were "aroused" by visual depictions of explicit sex while a majority of females (68 percent) were not aroused. Further, "females more often than males reported 'disgust' and 'offense.'"

From whence comes this female disgust and offense? Are females sexually backward or more conservative by nature? The gut distaste that a majority of women feel when we look at pornography, a distaste that, incredibly, is no longer fashionable to admit, comes, I think, from the gut knowledge that we and our bodies are being stripped, exposed and contorted for the purpose of ridicule to bolster that "masculine esteem" which gets its kick and sense of power from viewing females as anonymous, panting playthings, adult toys, dehumanized objects to be used, abused, broken and discarded.

This, of course, is also the philosophy of rape. It is no accident (for what else could be its purpose?) that females in the pornographic genre are depicted in two cleanly delineated roles: as virgins who are caught and "banged" or as nymphomaniacs who are never sated. The most popular and prevalent pornographic fantasy combines the two: an innocent, untutored female is raped and "subjected to unnatural practices" that turn her into a raving, slobbering nymphomaniac, a dependent sexual slave who can never get enough of the big, male cock.

There can be no "equality" in porn, no female equivalent, no turning of the tables in the name of bawdy fun. Pornography, like rape, is a male invention, designed to dehumanize women to reduce the female to an object of sexual access, not to free sensuality from moralistic or parental inhibition. The staple of porn will always be the naked female body, breasts and genitals exposed, because as man devised it, her naked body is the female's "shame," her private parts the private property of man, while his are the ancient, holy, universal, patriarchal instrument of his power, his rule by force over *her*.

Pornography is the undiluted essence of anti-female propaganda. Yet the very same liberals who were so quick to understand the method and purpose behind the mighty propaganda machine of Hitler's Third Reich, the consciously spewed-out anti-Semitic caricatures and obscenities that gave an ideological base to the Holocaust and the Final Solution, the very same liberals who, enlightened by blacks, searched their own conscience and came to understand that their tolerance of "nigger" jokes and portrayals of shuffling, rolling-eyed servants in movies perpetuated the degrading myths of black inferiority and gave an ideological base to the continuation of black oppression—these very same liberals now fervidly maintain that the hatred and contempt for women that find expression in four-letter words used as expletives and in what are quaintly called "adult" or "erotic" books and movies are a valid extension of freedom of speech that must be preserved as a Constitutional right.

To defend the right of a lone, crazed American Nazi to grind out propaganda calling for the extermination of all Jews, as the ACLU has done in the name of free speech, is, after all, a self-righteous and not particularly courageous stand, for American Jewry is not currently threatened by storm troopers, concentration camps and imminent extermination but I wonder if the ACLU's position might change if, come tomorrow morning, the bookstores and movie theaters lining Forty-second Street in New York City were devoted not to the humiliation of women by rape and torture, as they currently are, but in a systematized, commercially successful propaganda machine depicting the sadistic pleasures of gassing Jews or lynching blacks?

Is this analogy extreme? Not if you are a woman who is conscious of the ever-present threat of rape and the proliferation of a cultural ideology that makes it sound like "liberated" fun. The majority report of the President's Commission on Obscenity and Pornography tried to pooh-pooh the opinion of law enforcement agencies around the country that claimed their own concrete experience with offenders who were caught with the stuff led to conclude that pornographic material is a causative factor in crimes of sexual violence. The commission maintained that it was not possible at this time to scientifically prove or disprove such a connection.

But does one need scientific methodology in order to conclude that the anti-female propaganda that permeates our nation's cultural output promotes a climate in which acts of sexual hostility directed against women are not only tolerated but ideologically encouraged? A similar debate has raged for many years over whether or not the extensive glorification of violence (the gangster as hero; the loving treatment accorded bloody shoot-'em-ups in movies, books and on TV) has a causal effect, a direct relationship to the rising rate of crime, particularly among youth. Interestingly enough, in this area—nonsexual and not specifically related to abuses against women—public opinion seems to be swinging to the position that explicit violence in the entertainment media does have a deleterious effect; it makes violence commonplace, numbingly routine and no longer morally shocking.

More to the point, those who call for a curtailment of scenes of violence in movies and on television in the name of sensitivity, good taste and what's best for our children are not accused of being pro-censorship or against freedom of speech. Similarly, minority group organizations, black, Hispanic, Japanese, Italian, Jewish, or American Indian, that campaign against ethnic slurs and demeaning portrayals in movies, on television shows and in commercials are perceived as waging a just political fight, for if a minority group claims to be offended by a specific portrayal, be it Little Black Sambo or the Frito Bandido, and relates it to a history of ridicule and oppression, few liberals would dare to trot out a Constitutional argument in theoretical opposition, not if they wish to maintain their liberal credentials. Yet when it comes to the treatment of women, the liberal consciousness remains fiercely obdurate, refusing to be budged, for the sin of appearing square or prissy in the age of the so-called sexual revolution has become the worst offense of all.

Exigence

GROUP EXERCISE

Panel Discussion on Pornography

Exercise Created by Keely McCarthy

Imagine some council members of Prince George's County, MD are trying to ban the making, selling, buying and viewing of pornography in their community. Susan Brownmiller is heading the committee promoting this law. She has allies in the religious community but is opposed by other feminists who argue that pornography can be used by women as an expression of their sexuality and by other liberals who argue that banning pornography would violate free speech.

1. Divide into 3 groups. One group will represent the religious community that wants to ban pornography on moral grounds; one group will represent feminists who see pornography as a legitimate form of sexual expression; and one group will represent liberals who argue that pornography must be allowed in order to uphold the freedom of speech.

2. Each group must make their primary argument using the stases provided below. Then build up your argument supporting points which come from stases. Write your conclusions below in your group's section. Finally choose a name for your group and a spokesperson to argue your position to the class.

3. Each representative presents their group's case to the class.

4. After all sides have presented their cases the groups will respond to each other and to Ms. Brownmiller. Group #1, the religious community, will respond to group #3; Group #2, the feminists who support pornography, will respond to group #1; and Group #3, those dedicated to free speech, will respond to Ms. Brownmiller. Respond by constructing an argument that challenges the other group's main argument.

5. Finally, each group makes their rebuttal and tells us what stases their rebuttal falls under.

Primary argument & stasis: _____

Other stases used:
1. _____
2. _____
3. _____

Group #1—the religious community:
Primary stasis: Value
Argument: _____

Definitional argument: _____
Value-based argument: _____
Causal argument: _____
Action/Policy: _____

rebuttal to group #3 _____

Group #2—feminists for pornography
Primary stasis: Definition
Argument: _____

Jurisdiction argument: _____
Value-based argument: _____
Causal argument: _____
Action/Policy: _____

rebuttal to group #1 _____

Group #3—Liberals for free speech
Primary stasis: Jurisdiction
Argument: Freedom of Expression / Freedom of Press

Factual/Definitional argument: Constitution - Freedom of speech + Press
Value-based argument: personal ~~defines~~ choice to watch or not
Causal argument: Domino effect
Action/Policy: nothing should be left alone as long as it doesnt
      violate any human rights.
rebuttal to Susan Brownmiller its these persons rights to make
    these videos and if you don't like it don't watch it.

UNIT FOUR

Definition

INTRODUCTION: WHY DEFINE?

Definition is integral to argument and persuasion. If you get to say what something is or you take it upon yourself to do so, you have or you seize the opportunity to wield a powerful rhetorical tool. Definition is powerful because it can control an argument and its direction and even, in some instances, its conclusion. As one of the first or foundational stases, definition sets the course for subsequent propositions or assertions about a situation's cause, value, and action.

Definitions can be highly effective rhetorically because they can function implicitly as full arguments in miniature. Take, for example, the anti-abortion slogan of the right to life groups in America: "abortion is murder." The familiar slogan is a definition that essentially contains the three other stases: since homicides result in (cause) the deaths of citizen victims undeserving of the crime perpetrated against them and murder is considered by society at large as inherently bad (quality) it stands to reason that the nation must interdict and ban (action) the killing of "citizens." The characterization of abortion as the equivalent of murder implicitly contains an argument that extends beyond a definition of what abortion is.

Defining is an act of categorization. If you posit a thing as belonging to a particular category, then that thing inherits other aspects and qualities that pertain to that category. In the case above, placing abortion in the murder domain means that the former potentially inherits all that is associated with the notion of murder, including that society considers it both an abhorrent and an illegal act. If by defining you place an X within a new category, then your audience may begin to see X anew, that is, relative to a changed or substituted category. Getting people to look at the familiar or same-old in a novel, not-previously-considered way can be the critical first step to move them to reconsider an entire situation or controversy.

Definition, in its characterization of what constitutes a thing, also can imply, by default, what the thing is not. This, too, makes definition a powerful weapon in a rhetor's arsenal. In more ways than one, definition can call the argumentative shots or, if not that, at least influence the initial course of a given argument's trajectory.

Patricia A. Lissner

I

Cartoons as Definitions

The three cartoons that follow show how defining a thing in a new or different way can create diverse rhetorical effects.

Can you describe how a definition can alter our everyday, usually unchallenged ways of thinking about a person, an event, and an activity? Explain what one cartoon's new categorization means or makes allowance for, or what it fosters in the way of a person's actions. Consider the promotional hype that emerges via re-categorizing clothing definitions that *Cathy* depicts. Can you think of other advertisers which use definition either to re-categorize their product or the purchaser of their product?

SPEED BUMP DAVE COVERLY

NON SEQUITUR WILEY

CATHY CATHY GUISEWITE

II

Defining the Seemingly Prosaic

YOU CALL THESE CLOTHES?

Below is a letter sent to the editors of the Washington Post *in October, 1998, by one of its readers. The letter writer complains about and takes issue with the coverage of recent fashions in the newspaper's Style section. The photographs reproduce two pictures from earlier articles reporting on the latest offerings from the fashion houses of Europe.*

Enough already!

How many more days, how much more ink, how many more pages of news print will you spend on those ghastly fashion reports from Europe in the Style section?

Does anyone not planning a Halloween costume care?

The so-called fashion designers seem to have made a mockery of the clothing industry. I may be considered a dowdy old fuddy-duddy, but I wouldn't be buried in a shroud that looks anything like what your pages have inflicted on us lately. Who is kidding whom? Grunge was bad enough, but post-grunge is beyond belief.

Could we return to wearable fashions, please?

—**Marion Corddry**

"Michiko Koshino #123" from the fall 1997 collection.
Copyright © 1997 FirstVIEW. Reprinted with permission.

Questions:

In the opinion of Marion Corddry, the *Post* fashion editor's assessment of what constitutes clothes needs to be rethought. Corddry disputes the characterization of at least one designer's fall offerings as clothes. In her opinion the fashion pages should be reserved for "wearable fashions" and not "costumes" or "shrouds," which is how she perceives the apparel modeled in the photographs. For her, the catwalk models wear something more accurately and better defined as "grunge" or, worse yet, "post-grunge."

Along the reverse-it-to-sell-it lines of the Cathy cartoon, perhaps the fashion promoters might advertise their grunge as the new anti-grunge. Can you think of other ways to counter argue Corddry's position that what the models are dressed in does not constitute fashion or, at least, "wearable fashion"? Would you define these garments as costumes? What are the distinctions, if any, between fashions, costumes, garments, apparel, garb, raiment, attire,

"Ghost #21" from the fall 1998 collection. Copyright © 1998 FirstVIEW. Reprinted with permission.

ensembles, and clothes? Does the use of these words reveal certain socio-economic qualities about the user or mark the user as more sophisticated or more clothes savvy? Does one or more of these semi-synonymous words represent sub-categories of larger categories? Explain.

Related to this topic you will find below a poem on a very commonplace clothing item: a shirt. The poem, composed by American's reigning poet laureate Robert Pinsky and entitled "Shirt," is replete with tactics of definition. These are discussed in your Introduction to Academic Writing *text. One tactic poignantly deployed by Pinsky is that of social context. Pinsky brings in the terrible Triangle Factory conflagration in which over 150 young seamstresses and garment workers perished, contemporary sweat shop clothing manufacture, and the dependence on slave labor in antebellum America to cultivate, harvest, process, and make the material goods for the production of cotton fabrics and apparel.*

"SHIRT"

by Robert Pinsky

> *(Pinsky's poem appears in* The Figured Wheel: New and Collected Poems, 1966-1996)

The back, the yoke, the yardage. Lapped seams,
The nearly invisible stitches along the collar
Turned in a sweatshop by Koreans or Malaysians

Gossiping over tea and noodles on their break
Or talking money or politics while one fitted
This armpiece with its overseam to the band

Of cuff I button at my wrist. The pressure, the cutter,
The wringer, the mangle. The needle, the union,
The treadle, the bobbin. The code. The infamous blaze

At the Triangle Factory in nineteen-eleven.
One hundred and forty-six died in the flames
On the ninth floor, no hydrants, no fire escapes—

The witness in a building across the street
Who watched how a young man helped a girl to step
Up to the windowsill, then held her out

Away from the masonry wall and let her drop.
And then another. As if he were helping them up
To enter a streetcar, and not eternity.

A third before he dropped her put her arms
Around his neck and kissed him. Then he held
Her into space, and dropped her. Almost at once

He stepped to the sill himself, his jacket flared
And fluttered up from his shirt as he came down,
Air filling up the legs of his gray trousers—

Like Hart Crane's Bedlamite, "shrill shirt ballooning."
Wonderful how the pattern matches perfectly
Across the placket and over the twin bar-tacked

Corners of both pockets, like a strict rhyme
Or a major chord. Prints, plaids, checks,
Houndstooth, Tattersall, Madras. The clan tartans

Invented by mill-owners inspired by the hoax of Ossian,
To control their savage Scottish workers, tamed
By a fabricated heraldry: MacGregor,

Bailey, MacMartin. The kilt, devised for workers
To wear among the dusty clattering looms.
Weavers, carders, spinners. The loader,

The docker, the navvy. The planter, the picker, the sorter
Sweating at her machine in a litter of cotton
As slaves in calico headrags sweated in fields:

George Herbert, your descendant is a Black
Lady in South Carolina, her name is Irma
And she inspected my shirt. Its color and fit

And feel and its clean smell have satisfied
Both her and me. We have culled its cost and quality
Down to the buttons of simulated bone,

The buttonholes, the sizing, the facing, the characters
Printed in black on neckband and tail. The shape,
The label, the labor, the color, the shade. The shirt.

Question:

Write an essay in which you discuss why Pinsky's definition of a shirt is so much fuller and richer than a standard dictionary definition. In writing your definition assignment for English 101 you will need to think outside the dictionary box, that is, the usual, but the stricter dictionary type of definition. Robert Pinsky certainly achieves this outside-the-box thinking in his poem. In the course of your essay discussion, explain how he utilizes at least five tactics of definition to open up and broaden our understanding of a shirt.

PROLOGUE FROM *THE HAND*

Frank R. Wilson

The hand is so ordinary and common it hardly seems to warrant a definition. And yet that is exactly what the author of a recent, fascinating monograph has done. Dr. Frank R. Wilson is a neurologist and medical director of the Peter F. Ostwald Health Program for Performing Artists at the University of California School of Medicine, San Francisco. He has authored another book, Tone Deaf and All Thumbs?*

In the excerpt we have from his highly acclaimed and current work, Wilson commences his investigation into how the hand shapes cognition, emotion, language, psychology, and culture by defining the human hand. His definition goes far beyond any dictionary approach.

Early this morning, even before you were out of bed, your hands and arms came to life, goading your weak and helpless body into the new day. . . .

After tugging at the covers and sheets and rolling yourself in a more comfortable position, you realized that you really did have to get out of bed. Next came the whole circus routine of noisy bathroom antics: the twisting of faucet handles, opening and closing of cabinet and shower doors, putting the toilet seat back where it belongs. There were slippery things to play with: soap, brushes, tubes, and little jars with caps and lids to twist or flip open. If you shaved, there was a razor to steer around the nose and over the chin; if you put on makeup, there were pencils, brushes, and tubes to bring color to eyelids, cheeks, and lips.

Each morning begins with a ritual dash through our own private obstacle course—objects to be opened or closed, lifted or pushed, twisted or turned, pulled twiddled, or tied, and some sort of breakfast to be peeled or unwrapped, toasted, brewed, boiled, or fried. The hands move so ably over this terrain that we think nothing of the accomplishment. Whatever your own particular early-morning routine happens to be, it is nothing short of a virtuoso display of highly choreographed manual skill.

Where would we be without our hands? Our lives are so full of commonplace experience in which the hands are so skillfully and silently involved that we rarely consider how dependent upon them we actually are. We notice our hands when we are washing them, when our fingernails need to be trimmed, or when little brown spots and wrinkles crop up and begin to annoy us. We also pay attention to a hand that hurts or has been injured. . . .

It is not possible to understand the hand as a dynamic part of the body, or to safely tackle broader issues concerning the hand in relation to brain function or human development, without at least a minimal grasp of the fundamentals of its physical structure and function. But what do we mean by "the hand?" Should we define it on the basis of its visible physical boundaries? From the perspective of classical *surface* anatomy, the hand extends from the wrist to the fingertips. But under the skin this boundary is just an abstraction, a pencil line drawn by mapmakers, giving no clue as to what the hand is or how it actually works.

On both sides of the wrist, under a thin layer of skin and connective tissue, pale white, cordlike tendons and nerves pass from the hand into the forearm. Are the tendons above the wrist—that is, in the forearm—part of the hand? After all, we are able to hammer nails or use a pencil only because of the pull of tendons and muscles near the elbow. From the perspective of *biomechanical* anatomy, the hand is an integral part of the entire arm, in effect a specialized termination of a cranelike structure suspended from the neck and the upper chest. Should we agree that the hand must be conceptualized in biomechanical terms, we invite further complexities of definition. We would know very little about the living actions of the hand except for observations of the effects of injury on its function; such observations are well documented from the time of ancient Greece, when it was known that muscles could be permanently paralyzed by cutting a thin white cord that somehow activates the muscle. Such cords are called nerves, and physicians and anatomists in ancient Alexandria already knew that nerves originated in the spinal cord. What are we to do with this fact? Are the nerves controlling the muscles and tendons that cause the hand to move also part of the hand?

Another set of observations, beginning a little over a century ago, has made it clear that the hand can be rendered useless by damage to the brain from injury (a fall or a gunshot wound) or as the result of a disease process (stroke, multiple sclerosis, or Parkinsonism, for example). Pathological change associated with specific diseases or injuries, when confined to different parts of the brain, can have quite different and distinctive effects on hand function. Should those parts of the brain that regulate hand function be considered part of the hand? The perspective of *physiological or functional* anatomy suggests that the answer is yes. We need go no further than this to realize that a precise definition of the hand is beyond us. Although we understand what is meant conventionally by the simple anatomic term, we can no longer say with certainty where the hand itself, or its control or influence, begins or ends in the body.

The problem of understanding what the hand is becomes infinitely more complicated, and the inquiry far more difficult to contain, if we try to account for differences in the way people use their hands, or if we try to understand how individuals acquire skill in the use of their hands. When we connect the hands to real life, in other words, we confront the open-ended and overlapping worlds of sensorimotor and cognitive function and the endless combinations of speed, strength, and dexterity seen in individual human skill and performance.

Question:

Dr. Frank Wilson draws on tactics of definition to explain what a hand is. Identify three of these. In his Prologue to *The Hand*, what kinds of persuasive means does Wilson use to start to answer the question he poses: "[W]hat do we mean by 'the hand?'" Wilson begins the Prologue using "you" and "your," but quickly switches to "we" and "our." Why do you think he does this? What does he gain, if anything, by these pronouns and by his subtle move from second person to first person pronouns?

III

Not the Meaning, but the Meanings

For the definition assignment for English 101 you will be asked to select a word that requires an expanded definition beyond that which a dictionary supplies. In the article that follows, you will read about a black novelist and essayist who years earlier came face to face with a word with very large definitional implications. Gloria Naylor movingly describes how as a child she struggled to understand the meaning of the word "nigger." Naylor thought she knew the meaning until one day in school she found herself feeling the term as verbally assaulting. Naylor's article considers a complicated word with a complicated pedigree. It is a word that resists a simple gloss and defies a single definitive explanation; thus, the "meanings" in her article's title. Nonetheless, Naylor delves into the word's nuances and offers insight into the profound, life-impacting issues that surround this culturally, socially, racially, and psychologically charged word.

THE MEANINGS OF A WORD

Gloria Naylor

An American novelist and essayist, Gloria Naylor was born in 1950 in New York City. She served as a missionary for Jehovah's Witnesses from 1967 to 1975 and then worked as a hotel telephone operator until 1981. That year she graduated from Brooklyn College of the City of New York with a B.A. and went on to do graduate work in Afro-American studies at Yale University. Since receiving an M.A. from Yale, Naylor has published three novels dealing with the varied histories and life-styles often lumped together as "the black experience": The Women of Brewster Place *(1982), about the lives of eight black women, which won the American Book Award for fiction and was made into a television movie;* Linden Hills *(1985), about a black middle-class neighborhood; and* Mama Day *(1988), about a Georgian woman with visionary powers. In 1989 Naylor became one of the four judges of the Book-of-the-Month Club.*

From an experience as a third-grader, Naylor develops an essay that not only defines a word but also explores how words acquire their meanings. The essay first appeared in The New York Times *in 1986.*

Language is the subject. It is the written form with which I've managed to keep the wolf away from the door and, in diaries, to keep my sanity. In spite of this, I consider the written word inferior to the spoken, and much of the frustration experienced by novelists is the awareness that whatever we manage to capture in even the most transcendent passages falls far short of the richness of life. Dialogue achieves its power in the dynamics of a fleeting moment of sight, sound, smell, and touch.

I'm not going to enter the debate here about whether it is language that shapes reality or vice versa. That battle is doomed to be waged whenever we seek intermittent reprieve from the chicken and egg dispute. I will simply take the position that the spoken word, like the written word, amounts to a nonsensical arrangement of sounds or letters without a consensus that assigns "meaning." And building from the meanings of what we hear, we order reality. Words themselves are innocuous; it is the consensus that gives them true power.

*   *   *

I remember the first time I heard the word *nigger.* In my third-grade class, our math tests were being passed down the rows, and as I handed the papers to a little boy in back of me, I remarked that once again he had received a much lower mark than I did. He snatched his test from me and spit out that word. Had he called me a nymphomaniac or a necrophiliac, I couldn't have been more puzzled. I didn't know what a nigger was, but I knew that whatever it meant, it was something he shouldn't have called me. This was verified when I raised my hand, and in a loud voice repeated what he had said and watched the teacher scold him for using a "bad" word. I was later to go home and ask the inevitable question that every black parent must face—"Mommy, what does *nigger* mean?"

And what exactly did it mean? Thinking back, I realize that this could not have been the first time the word was used in my presence. I was part of a large extended family that had migrated from the rural South after World War II and formed a close-knit network that gravitated around my maternal grandparents. Their ground-floor apartment in one of the buildings they owned in Harlem was a weekend mecca for my immediately family, along with countless aunts, uncles, and cousins who brought assorted friends. It was a bustling and open house with assorted neighbors and tenants popping in and out to exchange bits of gossip, pick up an old quarrel, or referee the ongoing checkers game in which my grandmother cheated shamelessly. They were all there to let down their hair and put up their feet after a week of labor in the factories, laundries, and shipyards of New York.

Amid the clamor, which could reach deafening proportions—two or three conversations going on simultaneously, punctuated by the sound of a baby's crying somewhere in the back rooms or out on the street—there was still a rigid set of rules about what was said and how. Older children were sent out of the living room when it was time to get into the juicy details about "you-know-who" up on the third floor had gone and gotten herself "p-r-e-g-n-a-n-t!" But my parents, knowing that I could spell well beyond my years, always demanded that I follow the others out to play. Beyond sexual misconduct and death, everything else was considered harmless for our young ears. And so among the anecdotes of the triumphs and disappointments in the various workings of their lives, the word *nigger* was used in my presence, but it was set within contexts and inflections that caused it to register in my mind as something else.

In the singular, the word was always applied to a man who had distinguished himself in some situation that brought their approval for his strength, intelligence, or drive:

"Did Johnny *really* do that?"

"I'm telling you, that nigger pulled in $6,000 of overtime last year. Said he got enough for a down payment on a house."

When used with a possessive adjective by a woman—"my nigger"—it became a term of endearment for her husband or boyfriend. But it could be more than just a term applied to a man. In their mouths it became the pure essence of manhood—a disembodied force that channeled their past history of struggle and present survival against the odds into a victorious statement of being: "Yeah, that old foreman found out quick enough—you don't mess with a nigger."

In the plural, it became a description of some group within the community that had overstepped the bounds of decency as my family defined it. Parents who neglected their children, a drunken couple who fought in public, people who simply refused to look for work, those with excessively dirty mouths or unkempt households were all "trifling niggers." This particular circle could forgive hard times, unemployment, the occasional bout of depression—they had gone through all of that themselves—but the unforgivable sin was a lack of self-respect.

A woman could never be a "nigger" in the singular, with its connotation of confirming worth. The noun *girl* was its closest equivalent in that sense, but only when used in direct address and regardless of the gender doing the addressing. *Girl* was a token of respect for a woman. The one-syllable word was drawn out to sound like three in recognition of the extra ounce of wit, nerve, or daring that the woman had shown in the situation under discussion.

"G-i-r-l, stop. You mean you said that to his face?"

But if the word was used in a third-person reference or shortened so that it almost snapped out of the mouth, it always involved some element of communal disapproval. And age became an important factor in these exchanges. It was only between individuals of the same generation, or from any older person to a younger (but never the other way around), that *girl* would be considered a compliment.

* * *

I don't agree with the argument that use of the word *nigger* at this social stratum of the black community was an internalization of racism. The dynamics were the exact opposite: the people in my grandmother's living room took a word that whites used to signify worthlessness or degradation and rendered it impotent. Gathering there together, they transformed *nigger* to signify the varied and complex human beings they knew themselves to be. If the word was to disappear totally from the mouths of even the most liberal of white society, no one in that room was naïve enough to believe it would disappear from white minds. Meeting the word head-on, they proved it had absolutely nothing to do with the way they were determined to live their lives.

So there must have been dozens of times that *nigger* was spoken in front of me before I reached the third grade. But I didn't "hear" it until it was said by a small pair of lips that had already learned it could be a way to humiliate me. That was the word I went home and asked my mother about. And since she knew that I had to grow up in America, she took me in her lap and explained.

Questions:

This article demonstrates that a word can have different meanings depending on who uses the word and for what purpose. Naylor proposes that users of a word play an important part in what a word means and, thus, what a thing is. Do you agree with this proposition? If so, can you think of other words whose meanings shift depending on who speaks or writes the word, or depending on the context in which the word is used? Can you think of instances when advertisers or politicians co-opt a word for their promotion of product or self?

In conjunction with Naylor's article you may want to or you may be asked to read the provocative column by Leonard Pitts that appeared in the Washington Post. *Pitts, like Naylor, examines the word "nigger." He explores how a word's meaning and its application can change.*

YOU CAN'T LIFT EVERY VOICE UNTIL YOU'VE CHANGED YOUR TUNE

Leonard Pitts Jr.

Leonard Pitts is a columnist for the Miami Herald. *He lives in the Maryland suburbs of Washington.*

As Richard Pryor told it years ago, he was sitting in a hotel lobby on a trip to Africa when he heard a voice within. "What do you see?" it asked. "Look around."

"I looked around and I saw people of all colors and shapes. And the voice said, 'Do you see any niggers?' I said, 'No.' It said, 'Do you know why? There aren't any.'"

Pryor told an audience that he started crying then. The comedian, whose speech had always been peppered with that ugly word, abruptly realized that it had not passed his lips in the three weeks he'd spent among the blacks of Africa. Pryor subsequently renounced the word altogether: The most profane man in America decided that here was a term too profane even for him.

I mention this only because there is, in case you hadn't noticed, a renewed struggle underway over the use and abuse of the N-word. And it's left me a little ticked off at the blatant hypocrisy. Of black people.

I'm sorry, but I just don't get it. Over recent months, black activists have battled the people who put out the Merriam-Webster dictionary, a black educator has challenged Mark Twain's "Huckleberry Finn," and Spike Lee has lambasted Quentin Tarantino, all over the use and abuse of the N-word.

But I haven't seen anybody say a damn thing about black comics who fly it like a dirty flag. Haven't heard a peep about the tiny talents of raunch rap who spill it into the ether like sewage. Haven't heard anyone say the obvious: that if we as African Americans truly abhor this word, then the protest ought to begin on our own doorstep.

Yeah, yeah, I know the rules. It's okay for us to say it, but not for whites. Except that some young blacks say it is okay for whites if those whites are honorary blacks, down with the brothers. Yet if those same whites mistakenly use the word outside their circle of black friends, they're likely to incite a riot.

I know the rules, but the rules are stupid. Contradictory. And confusing. If white people are baffled about what is and isn't allowed, I can't blame them. I blame us.

We've become entirely too casual, too gratuitous, with this instrument of disparagement. These days, one is less likely to hear the word from a white jerk with his bedsheet draped on his head than from a black one with his pants sagging off his butt. I once heard a young black colleague make a point of saying it in front of a white woman, who was properly flummoxed. The colleague explained with blithe self-satisfaction that she enjoyed dropping the word into conversation in order to observe white folks' stunned reaction.

All of which suggests to me that we as black people suffer from historical amnesia. A blindness to the suffering of ancestors. And a stubborn refusal to learn the lesson Pryor did: to grow up and leave this evil thing behind.

So the last word some beaten black man heard before gravity yanked him down and the rope bit into his neck becomes a shock tactic for a callow youth. The word that followed his torn corpse as it was dragged down dusty roads behind the bumper of a car now serves some oafish rapper who can't find anything else to rhyme with trigger.

That's grotesque. It is obscene.

And it renders just slightly hollow all these recent protests of mortal offense.

I'm supposed to be outraged that the word is used—with historical accuracy—in a classic novel that came out 114 years ago? No. Mark Twain doesn't bother me. Snoop Doggy Dogg does. Def comedy does.

Because they suggest to me that behind the facade of arrogant cool, we still hate us.

That self-loathing is slavery's hardiest legacy, Jim Crow's bastard child. And I'm impatient to see it dead. Impatient for a day when we love ourselves enough to be offended by anyone who uses this word. Moreover, love our children enough to stop teaching it to them.

Here's a new and much simpler rule for the use of the N-word:

Don't.

Questions:

In the course of his exploration of the "use and abuse of the N-word," Pitts offers that awareness of one negative denotation of a highly charged word can justify dropping this word entirely from one's vocabulary. Do you agree or not with this view? Who do you think should determine what words should be avoided? Or should this always be a personal decision? What are the potential gains to having a controversial word disappear from society's collective vocabulary, and what are the potential losses?

This last question was at the center of the storm that took place in early 1999 in Washington, D.C. over a white city administrator's use of "niggardly." Commentators, radio talk show hosts and call-in contributors, local and national officials, and common citizens rushed to weigh in on the debate. What do you think should happen to "niggardly"? Should it have a future or not? Argue your position.

The exercise that follows shows the difficulty of pinning down what factors and elements constitute a term: "courage." The exercise brings out that what is considered courageous can depend on the circumstances of an action or event, the intentionality and attitude of the potentially courageous person, and other variables. In other words, what constitutes "courage" in one situation need not in a situation that appears much the same or similar and what constitutes "courage" for one person isn't necessarily the same for another.

WHAT IS COURAGE?

Suppose you wanted to define the concept "courage." Working in groups, try to decide whether each of the following cases is an example of courage.

1. A neighbor rushes into a burning house to rescue a child from certain death and emerges, coughing and choking, with the child in her arms. Is the neighbor courageous?

2. A fireman rushes into a burning house to rescue a child from certain death and emerges with the child in his arms. The fireman is wearing protective clothing and a gas mask. When a newspaper reporter calls him courageous, he says, "Hey, this is my job. I know what to do." Is the fireman courageous?

3. A child is trapped on the second floor of a burning house. The fire marshal tells the parent to wait because there is no chance the child can be reached and saved from the first floor. The marshal wants his fire rescue team to try cutting a hole in the roof to reach the child. The parent rushes into the house anyway and is burnt to death. Was the parent courageous?

4. Are mountain climbers and parachutists courageous when they scale rock precipices or jump out of airplanes during their leisure hours?

5. Is a robber courageous in performing a daring bank robbery?

6. Mutt and Jeff are standing on a cliff high above a lake. Mutt dares Jeff to dive into the water. Jeff refuses, saying it is too dangerous. Mutt double dares Jeff, who still refuses. So Mutt dives into the water and, on surfacing, yells up to Jeff, calling him a coward and taunting him to dive. Jeff starts to dive, but then backs off and takes the trail down to the lake, feeling ashamed and silly. Was Mutt courageous? Was Jeff courageous?

After your group has determined which of the above cases are examples of courage, write a paragraph (as a group) in which you explain the definition of "courageous" which you have developed from the examples.

Question:

This exercise helps to demonstrate that relatively simple, common terms should not automatically be taken for granted. By this demonstration we can appreciate (1) the value of defining a term frequently tossed about in an argument because it is presumed to mean the same for everyone, and (2) the practicality, as well as perhaps the necessity, of defining terms that are at the crux of an argument. Can you think of other common words, like "courage," that we suppose that others take to be relatively the same thing as we do? Consider polling friends with scenarios (of the type in the courage exercise) to elicit qualities, circumstances, distinctive features, and other factors that particularize one of these words.

IV

The Process of Broadening or Narrowing; Extracting and Enumerating Characteristics; Locating Sub-Categories

The two previous articles give one serious pause about the racial deno-
tations and connotations at work within a word's definition. The three
articles that follow contribute to this discussion. The first of these, an
excerpt from The Nature of Prejudice, *is written by the American psy-*
chologist and former Harvard professor Gordon Allport. Allport's obser-
vations about prejudice and the definitional issues that surround
prejudice are as pertinent today as they were when his celebrated book
was first published in 1954. In the course of investigating prejudicial
labeling (i.e., defining or naming) practices and how they sway prejudi-
cial thinking, Allport explains how the negative semantics of the word
"black"—with its built-in, "implied value-judgment"—foster racial
misunderstanding and animosity between races. When reading the All-
port excerpt, keep in mind the arguments by Naylor and Pitts about
"nigger" and their respective recommendations for the use and non-use
of the word.

THE NATURE OF PREJUDICE

Gordon Allport

Without words we should scarcely be able to form categories at all. A dog perhaps forms rudimentary generalizations, such as small-boys-are-to-be-avoided—but this concept runs its course on the conditioned reflex level, and does not become the object of thought as such. In order to hold a generalization in mind for reflection and recall, for identification and for action, we need to fix it in words. Without words our world would be, as William James said, an "empirical sand-heap."

Nouns That Cut Slices

In the empirical world of human beings there are some [four] billion grains of sand corresponding to our category "the human race." We cannot possibly deal with so many separate entities in our thought, nor can we individualize even among the hundreds whom we encounter in our daily round. We must group them, form clusters. We welcome, therefore, the names that help us to perform the clustering.

The most important property of a noun is that it brings many grains of sand into a single pail, disregarding that fact that the same grains might have fitted just as appropriately into another pail. To state the matter technically, a noun *abstracts* from a concrete reality some one feature and assembles different concrete realities only with respect to this one feature. The very act of classifying forces us to overlook all other features, many of which might offer a sounder basis than the rubric we select. Irving Lee gives the following example:

> I knew a man who lost the use of both eyes. He was called a "blind man." He could also be called an expert typist, a conscientious worker, a good student, a careful listener, a man who wanted a job. But he couldn't get a job in the department store order room where employees sat and typed orders which came over the telephone. The personnel man was impatient to get the interview over. "But you're a blind man," he kept saying, and one could almost feel his silent assumption that somehow the incapacity in one aspect made the man incapable in every other. So blinded by the label was the interviewer that he could not be persuaded to look beyond it.

Some labels, such as "blind man," are exceedingly salient and powerful. They tend to prevent alternative classification, or even cross-classification. Ethnic labels are often of this type, particularly if they refer to some highly visible feature, e.g., Negro, Oriental. They resemble the labels that point to some outstanding incapacity—*feeble-minded, cripple, blind man.* Let us call such symbols "labels of primary potency." These symbols act like shrieking sirens, deafening us to all finer discriminations that we might otherwise perceive. Even though the blindness of one man and the darkness of pigmentation of another may be defining attributes for some purposes they are irrelevant and "noisy" for others.

Most people are unaware of this basic law of language—that every label applied to a given person refers properly only to one aspect of his nature. You may correctly say that a certain man is *human, a philanthropist, a Chinese, a physician, an athlete.* A given person may be all of these; but the chances are that *Chinese* stands out in your mind as the symbol of primary potency. Yet neither this nor any other classificatory label can refer to the whole of a man's nature. (Only his proper name can do so.)

Thus each label we use, especially those of primary potency, distracts our attention from concrete reality. The living, breathing, complex individual—the ultimate unit of human nature—is lost to sight. The label magnifies one attribute out of all proportion to its true significance, and masks other important attributes of the individual. . . .

A category, once formed with the aid of a symbol of primary potency, tends to attract more attributes than it should. The category labeled *Chinese* comes to signify not only ethnic membership but also reticence, impassivity, poverty, treachery. To be sure . . . there may be genuine ethnic-linked traits, making for a certain *probability* that the member of an ethnic stock may have these attributes. But our cognitive process is not cautious. The labeled category, as we have seen, includes indiscriminately the defining attribute, probable attributes, and wholly fanciful, nonexistent attributes.

Even proper names—which ought to invite us to look at the individual person—may act like symbols of primary potency, especially if they arouse ethnic associations. Mr. Greenberg is a person, but since his name is Jewish, it activates in the hearer his entire category of Jews-as-a-whole. An ingenious experiment performed by Razran shows this point clearly, and at the same time demonstrates how a proper name, acting like an ethnic symbol, may bring with it an avalanche of stereotypes.

> Thirty photographs of college girls were shown on a screen to 150 students. The subjects rated the girls on a scale from one to five for *beauty, intelligence, character, ambition, general likability.* Two months later the same subjects were asked to rate the same photographs (and fifteen additional ones introduced to complicate the memory factor). This time five of the original photographs were given Jewish surnames (Cohen, Kantor, etc.), five Italian (Valenti, etc.), five Irish (O'Brien, etc.); and the remaining girls were given names chosen from the signers of the Declaration of Independence and from the Social Register (Davis, Adams, Clark, etc.).
>
> When Jewish names were attached to photographs there occurred the following changes in ratings:
> decrease in liking
> decrease in character
> decrease in beauty
> increase in intelligence
> increase in ambition

For those photographs given Italian names there occurred:

> decrease in liking
> decrease in character
> decrease in beauty
> decrease in intelligence

Thus a mere proper name leads to prejudgments of personal attributes. The individual is fitted to the prejudice ethnic category, and not judged in his own right.

While the Irish names also brought about depreciated judgment, the depreciation was not as great as in the case of the Jews and Italians. The failing of likability of the "Jewish girls" was twice as great as for "Italians" and five times as great as for "Irish." We note, however, that the "Jewish" photographs caused higher ratings in *intelligence* and in *ambition*. Not all stereotypes of out-groups are unfavorable.

The anthropologist, Margaret Mead, has suggested that labels of primary potency lose some of their force when they are changed from nouns into adjectives. To speak of a Negro soldier, a Catholic teacher, or a Jewish artist calls attention to the fact that some other group classifications are just as legitimate as the racial or religious. If George Johnson is spoken of not only as a Negro but also as a *soldier*, we have at least two attributes to know him by, and two are more accurate than one. To depict him truly as an individual, of course, we should have to name many more attributes. It is a useful suggestion that we designate ethnic and religious membership where possible with *adjectives* rather than with *nouns*.

Emotionally Toned Labels

Many categories have two kinds of labels—one less emotional and one more emotional. Ask yourself how you feel, and what thoughts you have, when you read the words *school teacher*, and then *school marm*. Certainly the second phrase calls up something more strict, more ridiculous, more disagreeable than the former. Here are four innocent letters: m-a-r-m. But they make us shudder a bit, laugh a bit, and scorn a bit. They call up an image of a spare, humorless, irritable old maid. They do not tell us that she is an individual human being with sorrows and troubles of her own. They force her instantly into a rejective category.

In the ethnic sphere even plain labels such as Negro, Italian, Jew, Catholic, Irish-American, French-Canadian may have emotional tone for a reason that we shall soon explain. But they all have their higher key equivalents: nigger, wop, kike, papist, harp, canuck. When these labels are employed we can be almost certain that the speaker *intends* not only to characterize the person's membership, but also to disparage and reject him.

Quite apart from the insulting intent that lies behind the use of certain labels, there is also an inherent ("physiognomic") handicap in many terms designating ethnic membership. For example, the proper names characteristic of certain ethnic memberships strike us as absurd. (We compare them, of course, with what is familiar and therefore "right.") Chinese names are short and silly; Polish names intrinsically difficult and outlandish. Unfamiliar dialects strike us as ludicrous. Foreign dress (which, of course, is a visual ethnic symbol) seems unnecessarily queer.

But of all these "physiognomic" handicaps the reference to color, clearly implied certain symbols, is the greatest. The word Negro comes from the Latin *niger* meaning black. In point of fact, no Negro has a black complexion, but by comparison with other blonder stocks, he has come to be known as a "black man." Unfortunately *black* in the English language is a word having a preponderance of sinister connotations: the outlook is black, blackball, blackguard, blackhearted, black death, blacklist, blackmail, Black Hand. In his novel *Moby Dick*, Herman Melville considers at length the remarkably morbid connotations of black and the remarkably virtuous connotations of white.

Nor is the ominous flavor of black confined to the English language. A cross-cultural study reveals that the semantic significance of black is more or less universally the same. Among certain Siberian tribes, members of a privileged clan call themselves "white bones," and refer to all others as "black bones." Even among Uganda Negroes there is some evidence for a white god at the apex of the theocratic hierarchy; certain it is that a white cloth, signifying purity, is used to ward off evil spirit and disease.

There is thus an implied value-judgment in the very concept of *white race* and *black race*. One might also study the numerous unpleasant connotations of *yellow*, and their possible bearing on our conception of the people of the Orient.

Such reasoning should not be carried too far, since there are undoubtedly, in various contexts, pleasant associations with both black and yellow. Black velvet is agreeable; so too are chocolate and coffee. Yellow tulips are well liked; the sun and moon are radiantly yellow. Yet it is true that "color" words are used with chauvinistic overtones more than most people realize. There is certainly condescension indicated in many familiar phrases: dark as a nigger's pocket, darktown strutters, white hope (a term originated when a white contender was sought against the Negro heavyweight champion, Jack Johnson), the white man's burden, the yellow peril, black boy. Scores of everyday phrases are stamped with the flavor of prejudice, whether the user knows it or not.

We spoke of the fact that even the most proper and sedate labels for minority groups sometimes seem to exude a negative flavor. In many contexts and situations the very terms *French-Canadian, Mexican,* or *Jew,* correct and nonmalicious though they are, sound a bit opprobrious. The reason is that they are labels of social deviants. Especially in a culture where uniformity is prized, the name of *any* deviant carries with it *ipso facto* a negative value-judgment. Words like *insane, alcoholic, pervert* are presumably neutral designations of a human condition, but they are more: they are finger-pointings at deviance. Minority groups are deviants, and for this reason, from the very outset, the most innocent labels in many situations imply a shading of disrepute. When we wish to highlight the deviance and denigrate it still further we use words of a higher emotional key: crackpot, soak, pansy, greaser, Okie, nigger, harp, kike.

Members of minority groups are often understandably sensitive to names given them. Not only do they object to deliberately insulting epithets, but sometimes see evil intent where none exists. Often the word Negro is spelled with a small *n*, occasionally as a studied insult, more often from ignorance. (The term is not cognate with white, which is not capitalized, but rather with Caucasian, which is.) Terms like *mulatto* or *octoroon* cause hard feeling because of the condescension with which they have often been used in the past. Sex differentiations are objectionable, since they seem doubly to emphasize ethnic difference: why speak of Jewess and not of Protestantess, or of Negress and not of whitess? Similar overemphasis is implied in the terms like Chinaman or Scotchman; why not American man? Grounds for misunderstanding lie in the fact that minority group members are sensitive to such shadings, while majority members may employ them unthinkingly.

The Communist Label

Until we label an out-group it does not clearly exist in our minds. Take the curiously vague situation that we often meet when a person wishes to locate responsibility on the shoulders of some out-group whose nature he cannot specify. In such a case he usually employs the pronoun "they" without an antecedent. "Why don't they make these sidewalks wider?" "I hear they are going to build a factory in this town and hire a lot of foreigners." "I won't pay this tax bill; they can just whistle for their money." If asked "who?" the speaker is likely to grow confused and embarrassed. The common use of the orphaned pronoun *they* teaches us that people often want and need to designate out-groups (usually for the purpose of venting hostility) even when they have no clear conception of the out-group in question. And so long as the target of wrath remains vague and ill-defined specific prejudice cannot crystallize around it. To have enemies we need labels.

Until relatively recently—strange as it may seem—there was no agreed-upon symbol for *communist*. The word, of course, existed but it had no special emotional connotation, and did not designate a public enemy. Even when, after World War I, there was a growing feeling of economic and social menace in this country, there was no agreement as to the actual source of the menace.

A content analysis of the *Boston Herald* for the year 1920 turned up the following list of labels. Each was used in a context implying some threat. Hysteria had overspread the country, as it did after World War II. Someone must be responsible for the postwar malaise, rising prices, uncertainty. There must be a villain. But in 1920 the villain was impartially designated by reporters and editorial writers with the following symbols:

> alien, agitator, anarchist, apostle of bomb and torch, Bolshevik, communist, communist laborite, conspirator, emissary of false promise, extremist, foreigner, hyphenated-American, incendiary, IWW, parlor anarchist, parlor pink, parlor socialist, plotter, radical, red, revolutionary, Russian agitator, socialist, Soviet, syndicalist, traitor, undesirable.[1]

From this excited array we note that the *need* for an enemy (someone to serve as a focus for discontent and jitters) was considerably more apparent than the precise *identity* of the enemy. At any rate, there was no clearly agreed-upon label. Perhaps partly for this reason the hysteria abated. Since no clear category of "communism" existed there was no true focus for the hostility.

But following World War II this collection of vaguely interchangeable labels became fewer in number and more commonly agreed upon. The out-group menace came to be designated almost always as *communist* or *red*. In 1920 the threat, lacking a clear label, was vague; after 1945 both symbol and thing became more definite. Not that people knew precisely what they meant when they said "communist," but with the aid of the term they were at least able to point consistently to *something* that inspired fear. The term developed the power of signifying menace and led to various repressive measures against anyone to whom the label was rightly or wrongly attached.

Logically, the label should apply to specifiable defining attributes, such as members of the Communist Party, or people whose allegiance is with the Russian system, or followers, historically, or Karl Marx. But the label came in for more extensive use.

What seems to have happened is approximately as follows. Having suffered through a period of war and being acutely aware of devastating revolutions abroad, it is natural that most people should be upset, dreading to lose their possessions, annoyed by high taxes, seeing customary moral and religious values threatened, and dreading worse disasters to come. Seeking an explanation for this unrest, a single identifiable enemy is wanted. It is not enough to designate "Russia" or some other distant land. Nor is it satisfactory to fix blame on "changing social conditions." What is needed is a human agent near at hand: someone in Washington, someone in our schools, in our factories, in our neighborhood. If we *feel* an immediate threat, we reason, there must be a near-lying danger. It is, we conclude, communism, not only in Russia but also in America, at our doorstep, in our government, in our churches, in our colleges, in our neighborhood.

Are we saying that hostility toward communism is prejudice? Not necessarily. There are certainly phases of the dispute wherein realistic social conflict is involved. American values (e.g., respect for the person) and totalitarian values as represented in Soviet practice are intrinsically at odds. A realistic opposition in some form will occur. Prejudice enters only when the defining attributes of "communist" grow imprecise, when anyone who favors any form of social change is called a communist. People who fear social change are the ones most likely to affix the label to any persons or practices that seem to them threatening.

For them the category is undifferentiated. It includes books, movies, preachers, teachers who utter what for them are uncongenial thoughts. If evil befalls—perhaps forest fires or a factory explosion—it is due to communist saboteurs. The category becomes monopolistic, covering almost anything that is uncongenial. On the floor of the House of Representatives in 1946, Representative Rankin called James Roosevelt a communist. Congressman Outland replied with psychological acumen, "Apparently everyone who disagrees with Mr. Rankin is a communist."

When differentiated thinking is at a low ebb—as it is in times of social crises—there is a magnification of two-valued logic. Things are perceived as either inside or outside a moral order. What is outside is likely to be called "communist." Correspondingly—and here is where damage is done—whatever is called communist (however erroneously) is immediately cast outside the moral order.

This associative mechanism places enormous power in the hands of a demagogue. For several years Senator McCarthy managed to discredit many citizens who thought differently from himself by the simple device of calling them a communist. Few people were able to see through this trick and many reputations were ruined. But the famous senator has no monopoly on the device. As reported in the *Boston Herald* on November 1, 1946, Representative Joseph Martin, Republican leader in the House, ended his election campaign against his Democratic opponent by saying, "The people will vote tomorrow between chaos, confusion, bankruptcy, state socialism or communism, and the preservation of our American life, with all its freedom and its opportunities." Such an array of emotional labels placed his opponent outside the accepted moral order. Martin was re-elected. . . .

Not everyone, or course, is taken in. Demagogy, when it goes too far, meets with ridicule. Elizabeth Dilling's book, *The Red Network*, was so exaggerated in its two-valued logic that it was shrugged off by many people with a smile. One reader remarked, "Apparently if you step off the sidewalk with your left foot you're a communist." But it is not easy in times of social strain and hysteria to keep one's balance, and to resist the tendency of a verbal symbol to manufacture large and fanciful categories of prejudiced thinking.

Verbal Realism and Symbol Phobia

Most individuals rebel at being labeled, especially if the label is uncomplimentary. Very few are willing to be called *fascistic, socialistic,* or *anti-Semitic*. Unsavory labels may apply to others, but not to us.

An illustration of the craving that people have to attach favorable symbols to themselves is seen in the community where white people banded together to force out a Negro family that had moved in. They called themselves "Neighborly Endeavor" and chose as their motto the Golden Rule.[2] One of the first acts of this symbol-sanctified band was to sue the man who sold property to Negroes. They then flooded the house which another Negro couple planned to occupy. Such were the acts performed under the banner of the Golden Rule.

Studies made by Stagner and Hartmann show that a person's political attitudes may in fact entitle him to be called a fascist or a socialist, and yet he will emphatically repudiate the unsavory label, and fail to endorse any movement or candidate that overtly accepts them. In short, there is a *symbol phobia* that corresponds to *verbal realism*. We are more inclined to the former when we ourselves are concerned, though we are much less critical when epithets of "fascist," "communist," "blind man," "school marm" are applied to others.

When symbols provoke strong emotions they are sometimes regarded no longer as symbols, but as actual things. The expressions "son of a bitch" and "liar" are in our culture frequently regarded as "fighting words." Softer and more subtle expressions of contempt may be accepted. But in these particular cases, the epithet itself must be "taken back." We certainly do not change our opponent's attitude by making him take back a word, but it seems somehow important that the word itself be eradicated.

Such verbal realism may reach extreme length.

> The City Council of Cambridge, Massachusetts, unanimously passed a resolution (December, 1939) making it illegal "to possess, harbor, sequester, introduce or transport, within the city limits, any book, map, magazine, newspaper, pamphlet, handbill or circular containing the words Lenin or Leningrad."

Such naiveté in confusing language with reality is hard to comprehend unless we recall that word-magic plays an appreciable part in human thinking. The following examples, like the one preceding are taken from Hayakawa.[3]

The Malagasy soldier must eschew kidneys, because in the Malagasy language the word for kidney is the same as that for "shot"; so shot he would certainly be if he ate a kidney.

In May, 1937, a state senator of New York bitterly opposed a bill for the control of syphilis because "the innocence of children might be corrupted by a widespread use of the term . . . This particular word creates a shudder in every decent woman and decent man."

This tendency to reify words underscores the close cohesion that exists between category and symbol. Just the mention of "communist," "Negro," "Jew," "England," "Democrats," will send some people into a panic of fear or a frenzy of anger. Who can say whether it is the word or the thing that annoys them? The label is an intrinsic part of any monopolistic category. Hence to liberate a person from ethnic or political prejudice it is necessary at the same time to liberate him from *word fetishism*. This fact is well known to students of general semantics who tell us that prejudice is due in large part to verbal realism and to symbol phobia. Therefore any program for the reduction of prejudice must include a large measure of semantic therapy.

Notes

1. The IWW, or Industrial Workers of the World, was a radical labor organization that advocated violence. Syndicalism advocated that labor unions take over the government and industry.
2. "Do unto others as you would have others do unto you."
3. S. I. Hayakawa, author of *Language in Thought and Action.*

Questions:

One of the interesting premises in Allport's passage is that words themselves assist us in category formations. Words "help us to perform the clustering" or grouping of objects and events necessary to make sense of the world. For example, "a noun abstracts from a concrete reality some one feature" over a myriad of other specifiable features.

Nouns (which we understand as grammatical operators that define), including those we resort to as a means to describe others, are feature restrictive. Allport gives many instances of labels we assign people that exclude the positive "finer distinctions that we might otherwise perceive" and cause us to mistakenly perceive, misunderstand, and misjudge the "complex individual." Our author cautions that this is particularly the case when denigrating "labels of primary potency" are sorted to define a person or a group to which a person has associations.

Allport helps us appreciate that labeling or defining, which we identified in the introduction to this unit as categorical in scope, has prejudicial implications. He also helps us perceive the selective, excluding, and distractive aspects inherent in naming, labeling, categorizing, and defining. This selectivity, exclusivity, and distraction can be and are used, whether consciously or not, to persuasive and blinding advantage by rhetors.

Allport's "labels of primary potency" are nouns. What happens when adjectives are applied to these kinds of labels? Try applying a variety of adjectives to one "primary potency" label and consider the outcomes. Do you recognize or consider that there are connections between stereotyping and "primary potency" labeling?

CONCEPTUAL LESBIANISM

Dorothy Allison

> *The reading that follows is a chapter from Dorothy Allison's book* Skin:
> Talking About Sex, Class and Literature *published in 1994. Some of
> this essay first appeared in* The New York Native, *issue February 27,
> 1983, in a feature called "Is the Spirit Willing?"*

I'm not yet a lesbian, the letter began. Not yet? I passed the page over to my friend Jan. "What the hell do you think this is supposed to mean? You think maybe it's something she hasn't gotten around to, like putting henna in her hair or trimming her toenails? Or maybe she thinks of lesbianism as a trip she's always planned to take—like a day trip out to Coney Island or a really complicated expedition to the Himalayas, or maybe Montana?"

Jan gave me one of those looks that clearly expressed she knew I knew what the woman meant, all the different things she had implied. The letter, after all, had been written to accompany a review copy of the woman's book of poetry. And Jan was right. I could easily imagine the woman sitting down with a stack of magazines and newspapers, or a list out of one of the directories of writers and reviewers, wondering how she was going to get anybody interested in excerpting or reviewing her work. Maybe she had come to my name after hours of work and had been feeling both tired and silly. There had probably been different letters for different categories of reviewers, but I doubted she had sent one off to the *Guardian* that said, *I'm not yet a socialist.* Nor could I imagine such a letter from a male writer wherein he would define himself as *not yet a faggot.* Even the radical faeries and men's movement theorists don't talk about conceptual homosexuality as the goal of a heightened sensitivity. But lesbians have had to confront a world of misconceptions, from our teenage years when they tell us it's just a phase, to the last few years when magazines have prominently featured pretty young white female pairs, and suggested that we're all some variation on k.d. lang, Martina Navratilova, or Melissa Etheridge—somehow establishing a notion in the public mind that lesbians are young, healthy, middleclass jocks who can sing.

* * *

Ever since I heard the Ti-Grace Atkinson quote about feminism being the theory and lesbianism the practice, I've been uncomfortable with the odd glamour applied to the term *lesbian.* I use the word *glamour* deliberately, since I believe that what has grown up around the concept of lesbianism is not only an illusion of excitement, romance, and power, but an obscuring mystery. Or, as a nasty lady I used to adore would always joke, "When is a lesbian not a lesbian? When she's a feminist!"

In the early days of the women's movement, many women found themselves struck dumb by the accusation of lesbianism: "Ah, you're all a bunch of dykes!" Some of these women made a practical and moral decision to confront the basis of the prejudice. After the first roll of, "Oh no, we're not," they started saying, "So, what if we are?" Or at least some of them did. While parts of the women's movement did everything they could to disassociate themselves from anything remotely queer, just as they continue to do today, other feminists made a conscious and political decision to identify publicly with lesbians. In doing so they brought to question—in a way they had never intended—what it meant to be queer in this society. I am thinking not so much of the attention given to women like Kate Millett, who came out to wild press coverage and attack, but of women like Ti-Grace Atkinson and Robin Morgan. The former framed sex in social/political terms, and the latter insisted on her right to call herself a lesbian (and not a bisexual) while committed to her marriage, husband, and son.

I was in Tallahassee, Florida, in 1974, a photographer's assistant and community activist trying to be a female version of the happy homosexual I had read about. The conceptual war being fought on the issue of lesbianism had a major impact on my life, though at first all I wanted to know was who was really a lesbian and who was not. But I read Ti-Grace Atkinson, Shulamith Firestone, the Furies Collective, and countless raggedy newsletters from Radical Feminists and began to rethink who I was and what I could do as a lesbian activist. Eventually my women's group and I decided that Charlotte Bunch's statement, "No woman is free unless she is also free to be a lesbian," was the perfect way to frame women's struggle for autonomy. It did not matter then who was really queer. It only mattered that we all challenge the boundaries of what was acceptable behavior and what was perverse.

Right.

*   *   *

Unfortunately there seemed to be a discrepancy between my personal life and my politics. I discovered, painfully, that this blurring of the definition of lesbianism led to a few problems: regardless of how hard we tried to pretend that there was no difference between women who slept with men and women who slept with women, there did seem to be differences. For one thing, I noticed that although there were lots of lesbians working to get the childcare center established at Florida State University, there were no heterosexuals working to get the same university to recognize the lesbian peer counseling group. Nor were we supposed to identify ourselves as lesbians when we applied for funding for the women's center itself. Very quickly, in fact, *feminist* seemed to become a code word for *lesbian*, at least as far as the heterosexual population of Tallahassee was concerned. At the same time, saying you were a feminist at the local gay bar made many of the older lesbians nervous. "Yeah, but are you a lesbian?" I was asked, and began to suspect that something more than semantics was being confused.

Then I fell in love. Well, it might have been lust. I never got it all sorted out because the passion of the moment ran aground pretty quickly. Joanna was older than I was, served on the board of the women's center and the local land co-op, raised honey bees and goats, and drove a VW van with a sleeping bag perpetually unrolled in the back. She had long hair but wore it tied back all the time and was never seen in anything but blue jeans, high-topped canvas sneakers, and T-shirts. I found her tremendously sexy and tried to tell her so one night after we'd finished putting tile down on the floor of the newly funded daycare center.

"Hnnnn," Joanna's mouth gaped open and her face flushed a dark rose color. She looked away from me and started picking at the frayed cotton threads on the knees of her jeans. I told myself she was shy and sat quietly, waiting for her to get over it.

"I do like you," she said finally, but her voice was uncertain and strained. We both waited. There's no telling how long we might have sat there if my friend Flo hadn't walked in. Joanna jumped up and announced that she had to go feed her goats. Flo looked at me curiously.

"What's wrong with her?" she asked, once Joanna was gone.

I didn't know. For a few weeks I suffered all the miseries of an early Ann Bannon heroine, mooning over Joanna while she avoided me. She must be in love with some-one else, I told myself, and she was: a myopic, shaggy-haired guy out at the land co-op who had the plot of land next to Joanna's.

"I'd marry him, except he don't believe in marriage," Joanna told me finally, months after I had stopped tensing up every time she entered the room. "And I do like you," she said again. For the first time I understood the awkward emphasis on the *do*. We were eating pizza and sipping beer at one of the local student hangouts, sur-rounded by noisy fraternity boys and the celebrating members of the women's vol-leyball league. Joanna rubbed at her eyebrows with both hands and peered at me nervously. "Thing is, I just couldn't get myself around to doing anything with you. I mean, I can't even think about it without giggling." She promptly giggled. "I mean, I know I should be able to love you as easily as Charlie, make love to you, I mean." I watched that familiar blush creep up from her neck to her eyebrows. "But it just ain't happening. You know?"

I nodded. I was feeling almost as embarrassed as she was. I had never slept with a straight woman in my life, and the thought made my stomach flutter. All I could say to Joanna was that the whole thing had been a misunderstanding. I didn't want to tell her that she looked like a dyke; I didn't know how she'd take that, and I didn't want any of my friends to think I had been pursuing her. Maybe if we had done something about it, the idea wouldn't seem so disconcerting to me, but the notion that my ten-tative flirting had made Joanna's stomach feel the way mine did at that moment—that was simply awful. I watched Joanna take another sip of beer and lean forward.

"But you know something?" she said. "It certainly got Charlie going. He's been just major enthusiastic since I told him."

I felt my own cheeks flame. "You told him about me?"

"No, no." Joanna looked indignant. "I didn't say who. I just kind of told him there was a woman interested in me. He ain't got no business knowing who." I felt a little better at that, but she didn't stop. "But he did like the idea. Only I think he likes it more that I didn't do it than if I had. You know?"

Right.

* * *

At Sagaris, the feminist institute held in Vermont in 1975, I ran into a number of women who labeled themselves "political lesbians." They didn't actually have sex with women, or at least not with any great enthusiasm. None of them seemed to think that sex was a priority. They loved women and felt like men were pretty hopeless—at least until after the revolution. In fact, one of them told me, maybe all sex is just too problematic right now. She was pretty much celibate, although she felt that she should still call herself a lesbian. Didn't I agree?

I didn't. I was starting to have serious doubts about this whole concept. All right, in 1975 it was painfully obvious that there were tactical advantages to having all these woman-identified women running around. It seemed to ease the passage of some women through the coming out process, as well as providing a measure of safety for those lesbians who could not afford to be publicly out. It also gave a major theoretical boost to making lesbian rights an issue for organizations like NOW. I liked the theory of the woman-identified woman, liked watching women make other women the priority in organizing for civil rights, liked that even heterosexual women were beginning to see, on a day-to-day level, that treating other women badly was no longer socially acceptable. I knew that the issues were connected, but it still made me uncomfortable. All that talk about the woman-identified woman was taking the sexual edge off lesbianism, and I was sure I didn't like that.

Political lesbians made the concepts of lust, sexual need, and passionate desire more and more detached from the definition of lesbian. The notion that lesbians might actually be invested in having orgasms with other lesbians, that lesbians might like to fuck and suck and screw around as much as gay men or heterosexuals, became anathema.

By the late seventies, I was tracking the progress of the spiritual lesbian, a close cousin of the political lesbian, perfectly woman-identified and adamant about what was and was not acceptable practice for the rest of us. She wasn't goal-oriented (didn't really care if she came, just liked to cuddle), didn't objectify other women (never squeezed her lover's ass and breathed, "God, I'd love to get my hands in your pants"), and didn't lie awake nights mourning her inability to find true love or her constant obsession with sex and the lack of it in her life. The spiritual lesbian was a theoretical creature and a lesson to us all, not about what we were but what we must not be.

This stuff gets confusing. I remember going to political gatherings—right now I'm thinking of the matriarchy conference in New York City in 1979—where lesbians were accorded a kind of rarified status for their detachment from males, and male-identified precepts, which seemed roughly equivalent to a state of grace. But much like the state of grace I was taught about in Baptist Sunday school, the one ascribed to lesbians was pretty ephemeral and unsubstantial. It evaporated as soon as one displayed any actual sexual desire, since lust seemed to be evidence of male-identification. At that same conference, I watched one of the speakers become extremely indignant at a lesbian who raised questions from the floor, a young woman whose main affront appeared to be the fact that she was wearing a buttondown shirt and a tie.

"I think we're in trouble," I told a friend standing with me after the woman with the tie walked out followed by half a dozen women easily recognizable to me as not-at-all theoretical lesbians, but she just smiled. "When are we not?" she joked, and she was right.

The theoretical lesbian was everywhere all through the eighties, and a lot of times I could have sworn she was straight. Speaking on college campuses, identifying myself as a feminist and a lesbian but not an antipornography activist, I kept running into young women who knew who the lesbian was. The lesbian was the advanced feminist, that rare and special being endowed with social insight and political grace. I argued that there was a gap between their theory and my reality—that there were lots of lesbians who fucked around, read pornography, voted Republican (a few anyway), and didn't give a damn about the National Organization for Women. The lesbian you're talking about, I would try to explain, is the rage of all women, perhaps, but the lust of few. Real lesbians are not theoretical constructs. We have our own history, our own issues and agendas, and complicated sex lives, completely separate from heterosexuality, and just as embattled and difficult for straight society to accept as they ever were.

* * *

I do not believe that identity is conceptual. I am a lesbian and a feminist. I am not a paragon of political virtue, not endowed with an innate sense of feminist principles. My political convictions are hard-won and completely rooted in my everyday life. I can't sing. My hand and eye coordination is terrible; I'm legally blind for driving purposes. I am way past young, not very healthy, born working-poor and fighting hard to acquire a middle-class patina, but seem unable to change any of my working-class attitudes and convictions. I have never been monogamous, except in a de facto fashion these last few years when I just don't have the time and energy for any serious flirting. Contrary to rumor and assumption, I don't hate men. I have never found them sexually interesting, though. I cannot imagine falling in love with a man. Nor do I believe that sexual orientation is something one can construct, that people can just decide to be lesbians or decide not to be—for political, religious, or philosophical reasons—no matter how powerful. I don't know if sexual preference and identity is genetic or socially constructed. I suspect it's partly both, but I do believe that there are people who are queer and people who are not, and that forcing someone to change their innate orientation is a crime—whether that orientation is homosexuality, lesbianism, bisexuality, or heterosexuality. I believe that sexual desire is a powerful emotion and a healthy one. I'm pretty sure that when anyone acknowledges and acts on their desire, it does us all some good—even if only by giving other people permission to act on their desire—that it is sexual repression that warps desire and hurts people.

All of these statements sound very simple, almost trivial, but it is a simple fact that telling the truth, making simple statements of fact about your identity and beliefs—particularly when they don't match up with existing social prejudices—can get people attacked, maligned, or murdered.

Questions:

One of the most interesting formal aspects of this selection is that in contrast to many others provided here this author's defining seeks and argues for a narrower definition of her term. Allison dismisses the notion of political, spiritual, theoretical, and advanced feminist lesbians. She takes the position that one thing alone is defining of lesbianism: sexual persuasion or, as Allison might prefer to specify it, sexual lust. Narrowing a term may make life simpler in certain respects, but it necessarily has exclusionary consequences. Can you explain the motivation of others, not to narrow this particular term? Are there social advantages for different groups to collect under the "lesbian" defining umbrella? Explain.

A HUMBLE PROPOSAL

Hanns Ebensten

The next reading was authored by Hanns Ebensten, a contributor of articles and book reviews to a variety of publications. Ebensten claims that the word "gay will not do."

I am becoming increasingly anti-gay.

I did not understand why this appellation was applied to homosexual men when I first heard it used about fifty years ago, and since then I like it less and less. It is a nauseating word which brings to mind *The Gay Hussar*, one of the most cloying, vapid pieces of music ever composed, and conjures up sickening visions of painfully gay peasants with bells and ribbons around their ankles dancing in the square of some village in Mittel-Europa.[1] I am not gay, I have never been gay in my life, not even at some disastrous New Year's Eve parties in my youth with a mask on my face and dressed as a harlequin or as Nijinsky in *L'Après midi d'un Faune.*[2] To be condemned to go through life being gay seems to me to be a very sad and dismal prospect—how loathsome to be constantly merry, joyous, bright, and lively, happy even at a funeral, blithe in adversity. Does this describe me, or most of us? Are we merely brilliantly flashy, flaunting, gaudy, showy buffoons without a sensible thought in our heads?

No, I am not gay; and I believe that opposition to the concept of accepting homosexuals in the U.S. military is due, to a large extent, to this unfortunate name, which damns us with a total lack of seriousness and purpose.

Who wants a light-hearted, licentiously "gay dog," a hilarious man given only to social life and pleasures, to be beside him in the assault on the enemy beach and in the parachute attack?

No, gay will not do: We must find another and more appealing name for ourselves.

When I was a boy, homosexuality was not a fit subject for discussion. I overheard my parents, their lips primly pursed, acknowledge that Uncle Max was "a confirmed bachelor" and my mother smirked when she confided to the ladies at her coffee parties that her male hairdresser was "quite a lady." It was explained of an unmarried general who was invariably accompanied in public by a handsome young *aide-de-camp* that he "had never met the right woman"; and some actors were rumored to be *so.* Later, at school and in the army, I listened with fascination when the boys talked about weird, mythical creatures of whose existence they had heard but whom none had ever encountered—"queers," men who were "bent," "bum-rushers" and, most distasteful of all, "brown hatters," named thus for the same reason that men who demeaned themselves to their teachers or officers to seek favors were said to have "a brown nose."

Such talk was restricted to all-male environments. When this unpleasant subject was mentioned in mixed company, and in my home, which was seldom, and oblique references had to be made to someone who suffered from this affliction, the wretch was said to be *tapette*, conveniently breaking into French—the word means a chatterbox—as was customary when anything disagreeable was being discussed while servants were in the room.

In Cockney rhyming slang, in England, queer is equated with "ginger beer," so that some people I knew in London would say of an obviously effeminate man that "he's a bit ginger!" Queer was more often, and more aptly, applied to someone who was ill, specifically ill in the head, demented, rather dotty, or irregular in his or her bowel movements. "Mum got taken all queer," they said. Queer, meaning odd, strange, whimsical, suspicious, spurious, cross, crotchety, and erratic, but which is for an inexplicable reason now being used by homosexuals to denigrate themselves, is offensive in any sense of the word. To queer someone's pitch is not doing him a kindness. Bent, meaning crooked, curved, hooked, or deflected in one's purpose, was the favorite term used by "straight" soldiers and sailors who traditionally accommodated any gentleman who paid for their beer and gave them a gratuity for sexual favors— but these men were hardly quite "straight" and their patrons were only occasionally bent with age and knew quite well what they were doing.

When I came to America, I learned that a gay or queer gentleman who had just left the room is called a faggot, which is a bundle of sticks, twigs, or tree branches. In England, where it must not be confused with a "fag," it used to be applied to a shrivelled old woman. A fag, in England's great public (meaning private) schools, is a young boy who has to serve a senior student and is mistreated and abused in order to teach him that life is invariably unfair; but a fag is not necessarily a faggot.

Before we all became very bold and open-minded and outspoken and permissive, if one met a man whom one liked and with whom after several subsequent meetings, such as taking nature hikes or visiting the zoological gardens or the opera, one felt a certain rapport, one then hesitatingly, daringly asked him: "Do you like the color *green*?" or "Are you"—a pregnant pause for effect—"*musical*?" But not everyone who liked the color green was musical, so this circumspect questioning could and not infrequently did lead to embarrassment and confusion. To be "warm" was also occasionally heard, though I never understood why, and Germans still speak, with approbation or derision, according to their sentiments, of a "warmer Bruder," which sounds like something very nice and cozy to have beside one in bed on a cold night.

So there we have our choices: Do we really want to be gay, queer, bent, faggots, brown hatters, or even warm brothers? There are other collective appellations, but we are not all pederasts, catamites, sodomites, perverts, or onanists. The only other name which is neither condescending nor derogatory is long, awkward on the tongue, a dirty ten-letter word which contains those dread letters *s-e-x*, but at least it is correct.

Homosexual women are fortunate. They name themselves and are named after the island of Lesbos in Greece, the birth-place of Sappho, antiquity's greatest lyrical poet who lived there with her female lovers in the 6th Century B.C. It is a sensible and dignified name, devoid of any unpleasant traits and associations.

I suggest that homosexual men also look back to the classical Greek and Roman period for a suitable and honorable name. The ancient Greeks believed (and proved in battles) that troops composed of pairs of lovers were superior in valor to other soldiers. The city states of Sparta and Thebes employed such troops of lovers, and it is tempting for male homosexuals to name themselves Spartans or Thebans; but these names are, on reflection, not suitable—by no means all homosexual men are fighters; few of us today lead what is generally now understood to be a Spartan[3] existence; and the most famous of the ancients' troops of lovers, the Theban Sacred Band which consisted of 150 pairs of lovers, of which Plutarch wrote: "A band that is held together by erotic love is indissoluble and unbreakable," was finally defeated, though by overwhelmingly large numbers of Macedonians.

So, instead of taking our new name from the battlefield, let us consider the most famous, accepted, and documented male homosexual relationship of antiquity, that between the Emperor Hadrian and Antinous, a youth who was born in the Kingdom of Bithynia, in what is now northern Turkey. They met in 124 A.D. and remained inseparable, traveling constantly, until Antinous's death. He was broad-shouldered and exceptionally beautiful, with curly hair, as is attested by more than five hundred statues of him which survive, many of them portraits taken from life, not idealized, three of the finest being in the museums of Delphi, Olympia, and the Vatican. Eighteen centuries after his death, gazing at the statue of Antinous in the British Museum, the Poet Laureate Lord Tennyson exclaimed: "Ah—this is the inscrutable Bithynian. If we knew what he knew, we should understand the ancient world."

Antinous died on October 30, 130 A.D., by drowning in the river Nile. The inquest continues—was it an accident, murder, or suicide? The distraught Emperor founded a city there in memory of his lover and ordered statues to be raised all over the Roman Empire to his "beloved Bithynian" so that he could be worshipped as a god. There is no better, no more romantic, no more uplifting example of a fine love between two men; and I propose that homosexual men everywhere call themselves Bithynians.

It is an unfamiliar word, and few of us have an affinity with a long-forgotten minor Kingdom on the north coast of Turkey; but after a year or more of general, wide-spread use, this name will seem no more strange than does lesbian—and who, after all, apart from lesbians themselves, knows that this is the name for the natives of a Greek island in the Aegean Sea?

Heads of the U.S. Armed Forces, who are averse to having those wanton, frivolous, erratic gays in the military, will, I believe, have fewer reservations about accepting stalwart, courageous, athletic Bithynians.

Shall we start to call ourselves Bithynians?

Who will begin?

Notes

1. *Mittel-Europa:* Central Europe.

2. *Nijinsky:* Vaslav Nijinsky (1889–1950), the great Russian dancer, choreographed and performed the avant-garde ballet *L'Après midi d'un Faune (The Afternoon of a Faun).*

3. *Spartan:* Characterized by self-discipline or restraint.

Questions:

What exactly do you think Ebensten is arguing for in this article? What stasis do you think the argument is in?

TIME FOR A NEW TITLE

Karen C. Craft

> *"Time for a New Title" appears below. The title to which the author, Karen C. Craft, has reference is intended for women who stay at home with their children, women who are not employed outside their homes. This article appeared in* The Washington Post *on October 30, 1997.*

Mothers of America who are home with their kids have got to come up with a better job title. Where were we when they came up with "stay-at-home mom" to describe what we do? Who sold us this? Is there anyone out there who actually utters the job description "stay-at-home mom" with pride? Of course, you may take pride in what you do. But in that description?

Try this: Think back a few years and tell me what you would have said if someone had asked you to use the phrase "stay-at-home" in a sentence. Your answer would have been something like this: "Why won't you ever come out with us? You're just an old stay-at-home." A stick-in-the-mud. Dull. Boring.

Describing oneself as a "stay-at-home" mom does not produce a positive image. An attorney, an accountant, a doctor, a nurse, a veterinarian—these are positive job descriptions. But with a turn of the phrase, these, too, can be made negative. A sit-at-a-desk (attorney), a number-adder-and-subtracter (accountant), a teller-of-bad-news (doctor), a bed-pan-changer (nurse), an animal-caretaker (veterinarian). Any job can be boiled down to its most mundane aspect and be made to sound unenviable.

We must come up with a better title. I like full-time mother. What's wrong with that? Yes, of course you are still a mother if you give birth to a child and then go to an office every day for most of the daylight hours, but you are not *working* as a mother while you're there.

Mothers who work in offices during the day get to be called "working mothers." They even have a four-color, glossy magazine devoted to them. I have to say, though, I've never heard a mother who works in an office describe herself as a "working mother." What they usually say is, "I work full time." Now, I know when they say this they don't mean to imply that mothers who are home with their kids *don't* work full time. But it has that effect.

Let's face it, we all take our cues from the media, which take their cues from industry, which has a stake in making sure our capitalist economy remains so. A mother who earns a salary is a more valuable commodity in our society than one who doesn't. A mother with money spends money. A capitalist society must be constantly fueled and its messengers (the media) must send the message, "Hey, get out there and get a job!" It's a credit to their excellence that they've managed, in just one short generation, to create and perpetrate the impression that more women with children work outside the home for money than don't. And that this is the norm. And that we troglodytes who are taking care of our own kids during the day are somehow abnormal.

Sometimes full-time mothers are their own worst enemies. I actually heard a friend of mine, a mother with three young kids, say (in response to the question, "Do you work?)," "No, I don't work right now. I'm a stay-at-home mom."

* * *

It would be wonderful if we could all perform a little language adjustment. The next time you hear a mother who works outside the home for pay say, to distinguish herself from you, "I work full time," pipe up. Say, "So do I," or "I work full time, too." If someone asks you, "Do you work?" say, "Yes, I do." If asked to further explain, you say, "I'm a full-time mother," or "I work at home, as a full-time mother." Trust me, after just a short while, it will come naturally.

The media also perpetuates the phrase, "soccer mom." I have a feeling they think I am one, but I don't even know what it is. Do you? I guess it's a mother who does nothing all day but get her kid(s) ready for soccer, to soccer practice, to soccer games. Both of my kids play soccer, but I couldn't possibly stretch it out to fill my every day.

So all you stay-at-homes, since working mother is already taken, we need to come up with something different. Will it be full-time mother? Career mom? Professional mother?

And when we've decided that, the next step is to unionize.

Questions:

The titles that the author comes up with don't seem all that appealing. Can you think of something catchy and glitzy and descriptive? What do you think of "all-time mom"? What fallout might there be to this label? Does Craft do anything to bring in truce to the "Mommy Wars," the discord, blame-gaming, and name-throwing between mothers who are paid workers and those who are not?

FRIENDS, GOOD FRIENDS—AND SUCH GOOD FRIENDS

Judith Viorst

> *The next reading is by a prolific American writer, Judith Viorst. Author of*
> *numerous nonfiction books and magazine contributions, Viorst takes a*
> *light-hearted and entertaining approach to the topic of friendship. Her for-*
> *merly narrow definition of what a friend is or should be has, with time,*
> *broadened. Subsequently she recognizes several categories of friends which,*
> *when put all together, add up to what friendship has come to mean for her.*
> *This article below first appeared in* Redbook *magazine in the 1970s.*

Women are friends, I once would have said, when they totally love and support and trust each other, and bare to each other the secrets of their souls, and run—no questions asked—to help each other, and tell harsh truths to each other (no, you can't wear that dress unless you lose ten pounds first) when harsh truths must be told.

Women are friends, I once would have said, when they share the same affection for Ingmar Bergman, plus train rides, cats, warm rain, charades, Camus, and hate with equal ardor Newark and Brussels sprouts and Lawrence Welk and camping.

In other words, I once would have said that a friend is a friend all the way, but now I believe that's a narrow point of view. For the friendships I have and the friendships I see are conducted at many levels of intensity, serve many different functions, meet different needs and range from those as all-the-way as the friendship of the soul sisters mentioned above to that of the most nonchalant and casual playmates.

Consider these varieties of friendship:

1. **Convenience friends.**   These are women with whom, if our paths weren't crossing all the time, we'd have no particular reason to be friends: a next-door neighbor, a woman in our car pool, the mother of one of our children's closest friends or maybe some mommy with whom we serve juice and cookies each week at the Glenwood Co-op Nursery.

Convenience friends are convenient indeed. They'll lend us their cups and silverware for a party. They'll drive our kids to soccer when we're sick. They'll take us to pick up our car when we need a lift to the garage. They'll even take our cats when we go on vacation. As we will for them.

But we don't, with convenience friends, ever come too close or tell too much; we maintain our public face and emotional distance. "Which means," says Elaine, "that I'll talk about being overweight but not about being depressed. Which means I'll admit being mad but not blind with rage. Which means that I might say that we're pinched this month but never that I'm worried sick over money."

But which doesn't mean that there isn't sufficient value to be found in these friendships of mutual aid, in convenience friends.

2. **Special-interest friends.**   These friendships aren't intimate, and they needn't involve kids or silverware or cats. Their value lies in some interest jointly shared. And

so we may have an office friend or a yoga friend or a tennis friend or a friend from the Women's Democratic Club.

"I've got one woman friend," says Joyce, "who likes, as I do, to take psychology courses. Which makes it nice for me—and nice for her. It's fun to go with someone you know and it's fun to discuss what you've learned, driving back from the classes." And for the most part, she says, that's all they discuss.

"I'd say that what we're doing is *doing* together, not being together," Suzanne says of her Tuesday-doubles friends. "It's mainly a tennis relationship, but we play together well. And I guess we all need to have a couple of playmates."

I agree.

My playmate is a shopping friend, a woman of marvelous taste, a woman who knows exactly *where* to buy *what*, and furthermore is a woman who always knows beyond a doubt what one ought to be buying. I don't have the time to keep up with what's new in eyeshadow, hemlines and shoes and whether the smock look is in or finished already. But since (oh, shame!) I care a lot about eyeshadows, hemlines and shoes, and since I don't *want* to wear smocks if the smock look is finished, I'm very glad to have a shopping friend.

3. **Historical friends.**   We all have a friend who knew us when . . . maybe way back in Miss Meltzer's second grade, when our family lived in that three-room flat in Brooklyn, when our dad was out of work for seven months, when our brother Allie got in that fight where they had to call the police, when our sister married the endodontist from Yonkers and when, the morning after we lost our virginity, she was the first, the only, friend we told.

The years have gone by and we've gone separate ways and we've little in common now, but we're still an intimate part of each other's past. And so whenever we go to Detroit we always go to visit this friend of our girlhood. Who knows how we looked before our teeth were straightened. Who knows how we talked before our voice got un-Brooklyned. Who knows what we ate before we learned about artichokes. And who, by her presence, puts us in touch with an earlier part of ourself, a part of ourself it's important never to lose.

"What this friend means to me and what I mean to her," says Grace, "is having a sister without sibling rivalry. We know the texture of each other's lives. She remembers my grandmother's cabbage soup. I remember the way her uncle played the piano. There's simply no other friend who remembers those things."

4. **Crossroads friends.**   Like historical friends, our crossroads friends are important for *what was*—for the friendship we shared at a crucial, now past time of life. A time, perhaps, when we roomed in college together; or worked as eager young singles in the Big City together; or went together, as my friend Elizabeth and I did, through pregnancy, birth and that scary first year of new motherhood.

Crossroads friends forge powerful links, links strong enough to endure with not much more contact than once-a-year letters at Christmas. And out of respect for those crossroads years, for those dramas and dreams we once shared, we will always be friends.

5. **Cross-generational friends.** Historical friends and crossroads friends seem to maintain a special kind of intimacy—dormant but always ready to be revived—and though we may rarely meet, whenever we do connect, it's personal and intense. Another kind of intimacy exists in the friendships that form across generations in what one woman calls her daughter-mother and her mother-daughter relationships.

Evelyn's friend is her mother's age—"but I share so much more than I ever could with my mother"—a woman she talks to of music, of books and of life. "What I get from her is the benefit of her experience. What she gets—and enjoys—from me is a youthful perspective. It's a pleasure for both of us."

I have in my own life a precious friend, a woman of 65 who has lived very hard, who is wise, who listens well; who has been where I am and can help me understand it; and who represents not only an ultimate ideal mother to me but also the person I'd like to be when I grow up.

In our daughter role we tend to do more than our share of self-revelation; in our mother role we tend to receive what's revealed. It's another kind of pleasure—playing wise mother to a questing younger person. It's another very lovely kind of friendship.

6. **Part-of-a-couple friends.** Some of the women we call our friends we never see alone—we see them as part of a couple at couples' parties. And though we share interests in many things and respect each other's views, we aren't moved to deepen the relationship. Whatever the reason, a lack of time or—and this is more likely—a lack of chemistry, our friendship remains in the context of a group. But the fact that our feeling on seeing each other is always, "I'm *so* glad she's here" and the fact that we spend half the evening talking together says that this too, in its own way, counts as a friendship.

(Other part-of-a-couple friends are the friends that came with the marriage, and some of these are friends we could live without. But sometimes, alas, she married our husband's best friend; and sometimes, alas, she *is* our husband's best friend. And so we find ourselves dealing with her, somewhat against our will, in a spirit of what I'll call *reluctant* friendship.)

7. **Men who are friends.** I wanted to write just of women friends, but the women I've talked to won't let me—they say I must mention man-woman friendships too. For these friendships can be just as close and as dear as those that we form with women. Listen to Lucy's description of one such friendship:

"We've found we have things to talk about that are different from what he talks about with my husband and different from what I talk about with his wife. So sometimes we call on the phone or meet for lunch. There are similar intellectual interests—we always pass on to each other the book that we love—but there's also something tender and caring too."

In a couple of crises, Lucy says, "he offered himself for talking and for helping. And when someone died in his family he wanted me there. The sexual, flirty part of our friendship is very small—but *some* just enough to make it fun and different." She thinks—and I agree—that the sexual part, though small, is always *some*, is always there when a man and a woman are friends.

It's only in the past few years that I've made friends with men, in the sense of a friendship that's *mine*, not just part of two couples. And achieving with them the ease and the trust I've found with women friends has value indeed. Under the dryer at home last week, putting on mascara and rouge, I comfortably sat and talked with a fellow named Peter. Peter, I finally decided, could handle the shock of me minus mascara under the dryer. Because we care for each other. Because we're friends.

There are medium friends, and pretty good friends, and very good friends indeed, and these friendships are defined by their level of intimacy. And what we'll reveal at each of these levels of intimacy is calibrated with care. We might tell a medium friend, for example, that yesterday we had a fight with our husband. And we might tell a pretty good friend that this fight with our husband made us so mad that we slept on the couch. And we might tell a very good friend that the reason we got so mad in that fight that we slept on the couch had something to do with that girl who works in his office. But it's only to our very best friends that we're willing to tell all, to tell what's going on with that girl in his office.

The best of friends, I still believe, totally love and support and trust each other, and bare to each other the secrets of their souls, and run—no questions asked—to help each other, and tell harsh truths to each other when they must be told.

But we needn't agree about everything (only 12-year-old girl friends agree about *everything*) to tolerate each other's point of view. To accept without judgment. To give and to take without ever keeping score. And to *be* there, as I am for them and as they are for me, to comfort our sorrows, to celebrate our joys.

Questions:

Judith Viorst describes convenience, special-interest, historical, and other kinds of friends. Select three of these kinds and consider people in your life now or in the past who exemplify one of each of these three kinds of friends. What reasoning and evidence might you use to develop the position that the person represents one form of friendship? Do you find that all of Viorst's kinds of friendship really constitute what you find or think friendship is? Or do you believe that one or some of her categories are closer to describing what are mere acquaintances? If the latter, then how does this change Viorst's definition for you?

V

Paired Definitions

Our coverage of definition concludes on a humorous and ironic note with two articles that have been brought together for your consideration and comparison. In her article, Judy Syfers Brady describes the "ideal" wife and in his, Kurt Fernsler describes the "ideal" husband. Brady's essay, which first appeared in "Ms." Magazine in 1971, has gained the status of a classic in feminist satire. Read her essay and then move on to Fernsler's.

WHY I WANT A WIFE

Judy Syfers Brady

When Judy Brady graduated from the University of Iowa in 1960, she wanted to continue her education and become a university teacher. Her male professors discouraged her from doing so. Although Brady describes herself as a "disenfranchised and fired housewife" rather than a writer, she has published articles on a number of topics including union organizing, the role of women in society, and abortion. "I Want a Wife," which has come to be regarded as a classic feminist satire, first appeared in Ms. magazine in 1971. In this essay, Brady describes the "ideal" wife and, with finely tuned irony, argues against the repressive marriages in which some women may find themselves.

I belong to that classification of people known as wives. I am a wife and, not altogether incidentally, I am a mother.

Not too long ago a male friend of mine appeared on the scene fresh from a recent divorce. He had one child, who is, of course, with his ex-wife. He is looking for another wife. As I thought about him while I was ironing one evening, it suddenly occurred to me that I, too, would like to have a wife. Why do I want a wife?

I would like to go back to school so that I can become economically independent, support myself, and, if need be, support those dependent upon me. I want a wife who will work and send me to school. And while I am going to school I want a wife to take care of my children. I want a wife to keep track of the children's doctor and dentist appointments. And to keep, track of mine, too. I want a wife to make sure my children eat properly and are kept clean. I want a wife who will wash the children's clothes and keep them mended. I want a wife who is a good nurturant attendant to my children, who arranges for their schooling, makes sure that they have an adequate social life with their peers, takes them to the park, the zoo, etc. I want a wife who takes care of the children when they are sick, a wife who arranges to be around when the children need special care, because, of course, I cannot miss classes at school. My wife must arrange to lose time at work and not lose the job. It may mean a small cut in my wife's income from time to time, but I guess I can tolerate that. Needless to say, my wife will arrange and pay for the care of the children while my wife is working.

I want a wife who will take care of *my* physical needs. I want a wife who will keep my house clean. A wife who will pick up after my children, a wife who will pick up after me. I want a wife who will keep my clothes clean, ironed, mended, replaced when need be, and who will see to it that my personal things are kept in their proper place so that I can find what I need the minute I need it. I want a wife who cooks the meals, a wife who is a *good* cook. I want a wife who will plan the menus, do the necessary grocery shopping, prepare the meals, serve them pleasantly, and then do the cleaning up while I do my studying. I want a wife who will care for me when I am sick and sympathize with my pain and loss of time from school. I want a wife to go along when our family takes a vacation so that someone can continue to care for me and my children when I need a rest and change of scene.

I want a wife who will not bother me with rambling complaints about a wife's duties. But I want a wife who will listen to me when I feel the need to explain a rather difficult point I have come across in my course of studies. And I want a wife who will type my papers for me when I have written them.

I want a wife who will take care of the details of my social life. When my wife and I are invited out by my friends, I want a wife who will take care of the babysitting arrangements. When I meet people at school that I like and want to entertain, I want a wife who will have the house clean, will prepare a special meal, serve it to me and my friends, and not interrupt when I talk about things that interest me and my friends. I want a wife who will have arranged that the children are fed and ready for bed before my guests arrive so that the children do not bother us. I want a wife who takes care of the needs of my guests so that they feel comfortable, who makes sure that they have an ashtray, that they are passed the hors d'oeuvres, that they are offered a second helping of the food, that their wine glasses are replenished when necessary, that their coffee is served to them as they like it. And I want a wife who knows that sometimes I need a night out by myself.

I want a wife who is sensitive to my sexual needs, a wife who makes love passionately and eagerly when I feel like it, a wife who makes sure that I am satisfied. And, of course, I want a wife who will not demand sexual attention when I am not in the mood for it. I want a wife who assumes the complete responsibility for birth control, because I do not want more children. I want a wife who will remain sexually faithful to me so that I do not have to clutter up my intellectual life with jealousies. And I want a wife who understands that *my* sexual needs may entail more than strict adherence to monogamy. I must, after all, be able to relate to people as fully as possible.

If, by chance, I find another person more suitable as a wife than the wife I already have, I want the liberty to replace my present wife with another one. Naturally, I will expect a fresh, new life; my wife will take the children and be solely responsible for them so that I am left free.

When I am through with school and have a job, I want my wife to quit working and remain at home so that my wife can more fully and completely take care of a wife's duties.

My God, who *wouldn't* want a wife?

WHY I WANT A HUSBAND

Kurt Fernsler

> *Kurt Fernsler (born in 1969) grew up in State College, Pennsylvania,
> and graduated in 1992 from Penn State with a degree in finance. He is
> planning a career in law. The following essay was written in 1988 for a
> class of fellow student writers, all of whom had read Judy Brady's essay
> "Why I Want a Wife."*

I am not a husband. I am, however, a male, and have a father who is a husband. I am also fortunate enough to know a great many men who are husbands and will probably become a husband myself someday.

I recently read Judy Syfers' essay "Why I Want a Wife" and decided a reply was in order. Though not the most qualified author for such an undertaking, I felt it my duty to make an effort. For I now realize that just as Judy Syfers wants a wife, I want a husband.

I want a husband who brings home the bacon. I mean really rakes in the bucks. After all, I certainly can't have anything less than the best. My husband must be driven to succeed; he must climb the corporate ladder quickly and efficiently. He must make every payroll and meet every deadline. Anything less would be completely unacceptable.

And I want a husband who bears the burden of being the wage earner without complaint. He must deal with the stresses of his job without bringing his problems home from the office so as not to upset me. I want a husband who deals patiently and lovingly with screaming, fighting kids even after a tough day. I want a husband who, for fairness's sake, does the dishes (even sometimes the wash) for me so that I can put my feet up after dinner. And, I want a husband who will leave the office during a busy day of work to check on a sick child while I'm out on the town shopping.

I want a husband who will gladly eat cold leftovers for a week while I am relaxing with a friend in sunny California. My husband will have to sit through boring PTA meetings and ice-cream socials after a rough day at work. My husband must, of course, be courteous and kind to meddling gossiping friends. (After all, I am entitled to my friends, too.) I want a husband who listens patiently to my panic about the oversudsing washing machine while he silently sweats about the thousands of dollars he just borrowed from the bank.

I want a husband who keeps the house and lawn looking beautiful in his spare time. He must be willing to spend his Saturday afternoons weeding my garden, and he must give up that tee time with the guys when I decide the grass is a little too long. I want one who makes sure the car is fixed (engines are so complicated and dirty!) and takes care of all the "little" chores around the house—raking leaves in the fall, shoveling snow in the winter, painting the house in spring. And I want one who will take out the garbage. When he's done with these chores, he can take the kids to the zoo or the park or the ballgame because these are things a father should share with his children.

I want a husband who gladly pays for his wife's shopping sprees without ever asking her where all the money goes. He will understand that women need to spend time with their friends. I want a husband who will watch the kids on vacation so my wife can shop and work on her tan. (He must accept the fact that after traveling so many miles, a shopping trip is the only way to wind down.)

And I want my husband to be completely receptive to my sexual needs. He must completely understand when I have a "headache." He will be sensitive to my problems and respect my private life. I want a husband who understands that I must have my freedom. He will be ready to accept the possibility that I may need to "find myself" and may walk out at any time. He will understand, of course, that I will take half of everything we own. He would keep the kids, however, because I would need to start a brand new life for myself.

I want a husband who will do all these things for me forever or until I decide we have enough money to retire, or until he has a heart attack and collapses in a heap. Yes, I want a husband.

How could anyone live without one?

Questions:

Satire can be a creative and memorable method by which to develop a definition. Try your own hand at writing a satiric argument on "What is a child and why I want to be one" from the perspective of an adult. Then reverse the assignment by composing a second satiric argument on "What is an adult and why I want to be one" from the perspective of a child. Remember to include explanation and examples in the way that our two authors do to elaborate on the primary qualities of the "adult" or "child." You may wish to model your arguments by the organizational means used to great effect by both Fernsler and Brady; namely, a repeating phrase at the beginning of the paragraphs in the body of your two essays.

UNIT FIVE

The Affirmative Argument

INTRODUCTION TO THE AFFIRMATIVE ARGUMENT

In your Pro/Pro papers, you will be developing two persuasive arguments for audiences who agree with your position. This may sound as if it is a waste of time. Why should anyone spend time arguing with an audience who already agrees with their position or trying to persuade a particular group to believe something they already do? If you look closely at essays, articles, editorials, or any other forms of persuasive writing, you will see that many, if not most, of them do appear to be written for an audience who agrees with the position being presented or one which is at most only mildly at odds with that position. Furthermore, if you think back on your own experiences in arguing a particular position on an issue, you will probably notice that there were few times where you were able to change someone's perspective on an issue completely.

So, to return to the question, why do we write to an audience who supports our position? The first, and most obvious reason, is to strengthen their belief in a particular position. Religious leaders, for example, regularly argue in favor of particular actions or behavior to groups who believe as they do. A second reason one might argue to an audience who is in fundamental agreement with one's position would be to modify that audience's stance in one particular area of the issue. For example, if you have a group of sociologists who believe that teenagers convicted of crimes should not be sent to prison but to rehabilitation programs, you might argue that teenagers committed of crimes should be sent to rehabilitation programs rather than jails, *except* for those who commit murder.

Nancy O. M. Dickson

I

Presenting the Affirmative Argument

The two arguments you construct will each need to argue for a position, not against one. The following arguments each argue for a particular idea, belief, or course of action.

FREUDIAN SLIP

Richard Cohen

Sigmund Freud wondered: What do women want? Richard Cohen also wonders: Why do women read and watch such dumb stuff?

I ask that question based not on the women I know, but on the magazines and television fare aimed at them. These are, almost without exception, so silly, so superficial, so about nothing—so dumb!!—that one can only conclude that the answer to Freud's famous question is this: Women, above all, want not to think.

What prompts this particular jeremiad is the recent decision by Bonnie Fuller, the new editor of *Glamour* magazine, to kill its monthly Washington political column and institute one devoted to . . . astrology. As you can imagine, the substitution of a crackpot astrology column for one dealing with such subjects as abortion, contraception, child care and other issues affecting women, produced a . . . well, actually, almost nothing—a peep of protest, not a full-throated roar of indignation. The original appointment of Fuller, after *Glamour's* owners, Advance Publications, sacked the magazine's well-regarded, longtime editor Ruth Whitney, did create something of a stir, but that, it seems, was about it.

You can imagine the response if something similar had happened at a classy men's magazine—*Esquire* or *GQ*, for instance. There would have been at least some yelling and screaming. You can imagine, too, what the reaction would have been if the editors of these two publications had been replaced, as Whitney was at *Glamour*, with someone like Fuller, who, *Brill's Content* magazine tells us, countenanced fabricated quotes, bogus bylines and facts concocted out of whole cloth when she edited *Cosmopolitan*. But so little is expected of women's magazines that not much fuss was made over Fuller and her astrology decision. All Fuller was doing, after all, was sinking the once well-regarded *Glamour* to the level of other women's magazines. It, like others in its field, is now wholly devoid of serious content.

Why is this? After all, even *Playboy*—check that: especially *Playboy*—has always contained first-class journalism and fiction. Sure, it has the naked ladies and the idiotic features about sex, but both the publisher and the readership feel it has to have something more. It is always possible—although not necessarily convincing—to maintain that you read *Playboy* for the articles.

No one could say that though, about *Vogue*. I have just perused the November issue and found nothing that, even for a nanosecond, would make you think. You might envy, you might covet, you might admire, but you would not pause to consider a political, ideological or cultural issue.

In contrast, the November issue of *GQ*—an equivalent publication of equivalent heft (486 pages)—has several articles that could, with just a little stretch, be called substantive. They include a profile of Philip Roth and a story on what makes a song a standard. There's a piece on a bitter-end secessionist in the South and another on bounty hunters. Okay, this is not exactly *Foreign Affairs*, but it ain't astrology either.

If mindless fare were limited to women's magazines, we would not have all that much cause for worry. But when you throw in daytime television—a succession of Montels, Maurys, Sallys, Rickis, Leezas and the ever-goopier Oprah—you have a prima facie case that the audience for these entertainments has the IQ of a turtle. Only one kind of human being watches daytime TV—women. There are the occasional unemployed or retired men, but the audience is overwhelmingly female. (Interestingly, Washington, where large numbers of women work, is a bad daytime TV town.) Would an audience made up largely of men watch such utter drivel? I don't know.

You could say the daytime TV audience is not typical of women in general. Granted. You could say—maybe argue is a better word—there is nothing especially elevated about sports, and men watch plenty of that. Granted. You could say many of the prime-time TV shows are aimed at young men, and these, by and large, are pretty stupid. Granted, granted, granted.

But when you combine daytime TV with women's magazines—when, in other words, you combine women who do not work with many women who do—you have to ask what in the world is going on? How come there is no female *Esquire*? How come *Cosmo* never rose to the quality of *Playboy*? How come, really, almost no one cares that Bonnie Fuller has replaced a political column of some use to women with an astrology column of no use to anyone?

The answer cannot be that women are dumber than men in an IQ sort of way. It has to be that they have different interests, different notions of what's important—relationships, for instance, and not yards-gained-rushing. But you cannot read women's magazines or watch daytime TV without concluding that the answer to Freud's famous question is given every day on television and every month on the newsstand. What do women want?

Really dumb stuff.

IF IT ONLY HAD A BRAIN

Maxim: *Mindless Entertainment for Men*

Peter Carlson

Maxim magazine isn't really edited by Homer Simpson. It just reads that way.

Actually, *Maxim* is edited by Mark Golin, who has not yet attained Homer's zen-like state of perfect mindlessness. But he's close. Here, from the editor's column in the December issue, is Golin's "Christmas Wish List":

1) *I wish Maserati would open a 99 cent store.*
2) *I wish we didn't have to blink (we'd all look a lot cooler).*
3) *I wish I could replace my right arm with a powerful flamethrower.*
4) *I wish the year 2000 computer glitch, known as the "millennium bug," were really a 900-foot-tall heavily armored insect that devoured cities.*

And so on. There are seven more but you get the idea.

Before Golin started running *Maxim*, he was an editor at *Cosmopolitan*. Apparently he learned two important lessons there:

1. Always put cleavage on the cover.

2. Dare to be dumb.

Maxim dares to be very dumb. It's a men's magazine for men who don't want to do too much heavy thinking. Or too much light thinking. Or any thinking at all. *Maxim* is a 100-percent thought-free magazine. Naturally, it's selling like crazy. Its circulation has gone up nearly 100,000 this year and now it's selling nearly half a million copies an issue, according to the Audit Bureau of Circulations. Its newsstand sales of more than 190,000 copies per issue are more than double those of *Esquire*, which is the grand old man of men's mags.

Maybe the success of *Maxim* says something about the current state of the American man. Or maybe it just says something about the current state of *Esquire*.

Maxim was born in England in 1995. The American edition premiered in the spring of 1997 and contained a manifesto called "Guy Pride," which summed up the *Maxim* philosophy: "Don't be ashamed of that fetid jockstrap and those toxic sweat socks. Leave that toilet seat up proudly! The time has come not only to live openly guy, but to embrace the whole guy lifestyle."

The guy lifestyle, according to *Maxim*, consisted of spitting, scratching, drinking beer, eating red meat, chasing "chicks," and making "that noise with your hand in your armpit."

At the time, that piece seemed like a deft bit of parody. In retrospect, it turns out to be a pretty straightforward summation on the *Maxim* worldview.

In the November issue, the magazine further codified its philosophy in a piece called "If Men Really Ruled the World," which listed the effects of a male takeover of the planet:

"Birth control would come in ale or lager."

"Instead of a beer belly, you'd get 'beer biceps.'"

"The victors in any athletic competition would get to kill and eat the losers."

"Anyone who didn't bow to peer pressure would be beaten senseless until they did."

And so on. And that seems as sophisticated as Oscar Wilde compared to most of the stuff in *Maxim*, which generally reads like it was written at a frat party.

The December issue is typical. There's advice on how to get rid of Christmas carolers: "Train a couple of attack dogs to go for the yule log, if you know what we mean." There's advice on how to steal your friend's girlfriend: "Use backhanded compliments, like: 'I really envy Joe's ability to make ends meet on his salary. Personally, I just don't think I could do it.'" And there's a piece alleging that women are particularly desperate for casual sex during the holiday season: "Women everywhere are looking to get their jingle-bell rocks off before ringing in the New Year."

And those are just the little fluffy stories. There are also some big important stories. For instance, "Men Are Pigs," which reveals that guys behave like other animals. Like gorillas, who enjoy loud belching. And eagles, who steal food from other animals. And lions, who make the females do all the work.

For decades, men's magazines have operated under a well-known but unwritten rule: *If We Print High-Class Articles, Then We Can Show Naked Women Without Being Considered Cheesy.* Under this rule, *Esquire* had the Vargas girl pinup and also short stories by Hemingway. And *Playboy* had its Playmates and also essays by Norman Mailer. *Maxim* has circumvented this rule by not printing pictures of naked women. Instead, it prints pictures of women—generally second-string actresses—who are clad in low-cut outfits and shot from above. This is a stroke of genius that allows Maxim to operate under its own rule: *If We Don't Show Nipples, Then We Don't Have to Run Those High-Class Articles.*

But maybe I'm being too hard on *Maxim*, which is an occasionally amusing magazine with no pretensions to be anything else. And it does have its uses. For instance, if you buy *Maxim* at an airport newsstand before boarding a flight from Washington to Los Angeles, it will keep you entertained until somewhere over West Virginia. Also, it can serve as a temporary transition publication for 13-year-old boys who have outgrown *Mad* but are not quite ready for real magazines.

The problem isn't *Maxim* itself, it's *Maxim's* success, which will no doubt encourage other men's mags to dumb themselves down. That's scary. If men's magazines get much dumber they'll be almost as dumb as most women's magazines. And, as Golin learned at *Cosmo*, that's pretty dumb.

Questions:

1. Are both authors writing to the same audience?
2. What assumptions do both authors make about their audience(s)?

THE DEATH PENALTY IS A STEP BACK

Coretta Scott King

Coretta Scott King is the wife of slain civil rights leader Martin Luther King, Jr.

When Steven Judy was executed in Indiana [in 1981] America took another step backwards towards legitimizing murder as a way of dealing with evil in our society.

Although Judy was convicted of four of the most horrible and brutal murders imaginable, and his case is probably the worst in recent memory for opponents of the death penalty, we still have to face the real issue squarely: Can we expect a decent society if the state is allowed to kill its own people?

In recent years, an increase of violence in America, both individual and political, has prompted a backlash of public opinion on capital punishment. But however much we abhor violence, legally sanctioned executions are no deterrent and are, in fact, immoral and unconstitutional.

Although I have suffered the loss of two family members by assassination, I remain firmly and unequivocally opposed to the death penalty for those convicted of capital offenses.

An evil deed is not redeemed by an evil deed of retaliation. Justice is never advanced in the taking of a human life.

Morality is never upheld by legalized murder. Morality apart, there are a number of practical reasons which form a powerful argument against capital punishment.

First, capital punishment makes irrevocable any possible miscarriage of justice. Time and again we have witnessed the specter of mistakenly convicted people being put to death in the name of American criminal justice. To those who say that, after all, this doesn't occur too often, I can only reply that if it happens just once, that is too often. And it has occurred many times.

Second, the death penalty reflects an unwarranted assumption that the wrongdoer is beyond rehabilitation. Perhaps some individuals cannot be rehabilitated; but who shall make that determination? Is any amount of academic training sufficient to entitle one person to judge another incapable of rehabilitation?

Third, the death penalty is inequitable. Approximately half of the 711 persons now on death row are black. From 1930 through 1968, 53.5 percent of those executed were black Americans, all too many of whom were represented by court-appointed attorneys and convicted after hasty trials.

The argument that this may be an accurate reflection of guilt, and homicide trends, instead of a racist application of laws lacks credibility in light of a recent Florida survey which showed that persons convicted of killing whites were four times more likely to receive a death sentence than those convicted of killing blacks.

Proponents of capital punishment often cite a "deterrent effect" as the main benefit of the death penalty. Not only is there no hard evidence that murdering murderers will deter other potential killers, but even the "logic" of this argument defies comprehension.

Numerous studies show that the majority of homicides committed in this country are the acts of victim's relatives, friends and acquaintances in the "heat of passion."

What this strongly suggests is that rational consideration of future consequences are seldom a part of the killer's attitude at the time he commits a crime.

The only way to break the chain of violent reaction is to practice nonviolence as individuals and collectively through our laws and institutions.

THE PENALTY OF DEATH

H. L. Mencken

> *H. L. Menken, who lived in Baltimore, Maryland and wrote for the Bal-timore Sun, was noted for his acerbic wit. This essay is taken from a col-lection of his writings called* A Menken Chrestomathy *(a chrestomathy is a collection of literary passages or excerpts used to study literature or a language, from a Greek word* krestomatheia *which means "useful learning").*

Of the arguments against capital punishment that issue from uplifters, two are commonly heard most often, to wit:

1. That hanging a man (or frying him or gassing him) is a dreadful business, degrading to those who have to do it and revolting to those who have to witness it.

2. That it is useless, for it does not deter others from the same crime.

The first of these arguments, it seems to me, is plainly too weak to need serious refutation. All it says, in brief, is that the work of the hangman is unpleasant. Granted. But suppose it is? It may be quite necessary to society for all that. There are, indeed, many other jobs that are unpleasant, and yet no one thinks of abolishing them—that of the plumber, that of the soldier, that of the garbage-man, that of the priest hearing confessions, that of the sand-hog, and so on. Moreover, what evidence is there that any actual hangman complains of his work? I have heard none. On the contrary, I have known many who delighted in their ancient art, and practiced it proudly.

In the second argument of the abolitionists there is rather more force, but even here, I believe, the ground under them is shaky. Their fundamental error consists in assuming that the whole aim of punishing criminals is to deter other (potential) criminals—that we hang or electrocute A simply in order to so alarm B that he will not kill C. This, I believe, is an assumption which confuses a part with the whole. Deterrence, obviously, is *one* of the aims of punishment, but it is surely not the only one. On the contrary, there are at least a half dozen, and some are probably quite as important. At least one of them, practically considered is *more* important. Commonly, it is described as revenge, but revenge is really not the word for it. I borrow a better term from the late Aristotle: *katharsis*. *Katharsis*, so used, means a salubrious discharge of emotions, a healthy letting off of steam. A school-boy, disliking his teacher, deposits a tack upon the pedagogical chair; the teacher jumps and the boy laughs. This is *katharsis*. What I contend is that one of the prime objects of all judicial punishments is to afford the same grateful relief *(a)* to the immediate victims of the criminal punished, and *(b)* to the general body of moral and timorous men.

These persons, and particularly the first group, are concerned only indirectly with deterring other criminals. The thing they crave primarily is the satisfaction of seeing the criminal actually before them suffer as he made them suffer. What they want is the peace of mind that goes with the feeling that accounts are squared. Until they get that satisfaction they are in a state of emotional tension, and hence unhappy. The instant they get it they are comfortable. I do not argue that this yearning is noble; I simply argue that it is almost universal among human beings. In the face of injuries that are unimportant and can be borne without damage it may yield to higher impulses; that is to say, it may yield to what is called Christian charity. But when the injury is serious Christianity is adjourned, and even saints reach for their sidearms. It is plainly asking too much of human nature to expect it to conquer so natural an impulse. A keeps a store and has a bookkeeper, B. B steals $700, employs it in playing at dice or bingo, and is cleaned out. What is A to do? Let B go? If he does so he will be unable to sleep at night. The sense of injury, of injustice, of frustration will haunt him like pruritus. So he turns B over to the police, and they hustle B to prison. Thereafter A can sleep. More, he has pleasant dreams. He pictures B chained to the wall of a dungeon a hundred feet underground, devoured by rats and scorpions. It is so agreeable that it makes him forget his $700. He has got his *katharsis*.

The same thing precisely takes place on a larger scale when there is a crime which destroys a whole community's sense of security. Every law-abiding citizen feels menaced and frustrated until the criminals have been struck down—until the communal capacity to get even with them, and more than even, has been dramatically demonstrated. Here, manifestly, the business of deterring others is no more than an afterthought. The main thing is to destroy the concrete scoundrels whose act has alarmed everyone, and thus made everyone unhappy. Until they are brought to book that unhappiness continues; when the law has been executed upon them there is a sigh of relief. In other words, there is *katharsis*.

I know of no public demand for the death penalty for ordinary crimes, even for ordinary homicides. Its infliction would shock all men of normal decency of feeling. But for crimes involving the deliberate and inexcusable taking of human life, by men openly defiant of all civilized order—for such crimes it seems, to nine men out of ten, a just and proper punishment. Any lesser penalty leaves them feeling that the criminal has got the better of society—that he is free to add insult to injury by laughing. That feeling can be dissipated only by a recourse to *katharsis*, the invention of the aforesaid Aristotle. It is more effectively and economically achieved, as human nature now is, by wafting the criminal to realms of bliss.

The real objection to capital punishment doesn't lie against the actual extermination of the condemned, but against our brutal American habit of putting it off so long. After all, every one of us must die soon or late, and a murderer, it must be assumed, is one who makes that sad fact the cornerstone of his metaphysic. But it is one thing to die, and quite another thing to lie for long months and even years under the shadow of death. No sane man would choose such a finish. All of us, despite the Prayer Book, long for a swift and unexpected end. Unhappily, a murderer, under the irrational American system, is tortured for what, to him, must seem a whole series of eternities. For months on end he sits in prison while his lawyers carry on their idiotic buffoonery with writs, injunctions, mandamuses, and appeals. In order to get his money (or that of his friends) they have to feed him with hope. Now and then, by the imbecility of a judge or some trick of juridic science, they actually justify it. But let us say that, his money all gone, they finally throw up their hands. Their client is now ready for the rope or the chair. But he must still wait for months before it fetches him.

That wait, I believe, is horribly cruel. I have seen more than one man sitting in the death-house, and I don't want to see any more. Worse, it is wholly useless. Why should he wait at all? Why not hang him the day after the last court dissipates his last hope? Why torture him as not even cannibals would torture their victims? The common answer is that he must have time to make his peace with God. But how long does that take? It may be accomplished, I believe, in two hours quite as comfortably as in two years. There are, indeed, no temporal limitations upon God. He could forgive a whole herd of murderers in a millionth of a second. More, it has been done.

Questions:

1. What assumptions do these authors make about their audience?
2. Which argument do you find more persuasive? Why?
3. On what points do the two authors agree?
4. Can you summarize King's argument in one sentence? Menken's?

WHAT OUR EDUCATION SYSTEM NEEDS IS MORE F'S

Carl Singleton

> *Carl Singleton wrote this essay for the* Chronicle of Higher Education
> *in response to recommendations made earlier for improving the quality
> of American education.*

I suggest that instituting merit raises, getting back to basics, marrying the university to industry, and the other recommendations will not achieve measurable success [in restoring quality to American education] until something even more basic is returned to practice. The immediate need for our educational system from prekindergarten through post-Ph.D. is not more money or better teaching but simply a widespread giving of F's.

Before hastily dismissing the idea as banal and simplistic, think for a moment about the implications of a massive dispensing of failing grades. It would dramatically, emphatically, and immediately force into the open every major issue related to the inadequacies of American education.

Let me make it clear that I recommend giving those F's—by the dozens, hundreds, thousands, even millions—only to students who haven't learned the required material. The basic problem of our educational system is the common practice of giving credit where none has been earned, a practice that has resulted in the sundry faults delineated by all the reports and studies over recent years. Illiteracy among high-school graduates is growing because those students have been passed rather than flunked; we have low-quality teaching because of low-quality teachers who never should have been certified in the first place; college students have to take basic reading, writing, and mathematics courses because they never learned those skills in classrooms from which they never should have been granted egress.

School systems have contributed to massive ignorance by issuing unearned passing grades over a period of some 20 years. At first there was tolerance of students who did not fully measure up (giving D's to students who should have received firm F's); then our grading system continued to deteriorate (D's became C's, and B became the average grade); finally we arrived at total accommodation (come to class and get your C's, laugh at my jokes and take home B's).

Higher salaries, more stringent certification procedures, getting back to basics will have little or no effect on the problem of quality education unless and until we insist, as a profession, on giving F's whenever students fail to master the material.

Sending students home with final grades of F would force most parents to deal with the realities of their children's failure while it is happening and when it is yet possible to do something about it (less time on TV, and more time on homework, perhaps?). As long as it is the practice of teachers to pass students who should not be passed, the responsibility will not go home to the parents, where, I hope, it belongs. (I am tempted to make an analogy to then Gov. Lester Maddox's statement some years ago about prison conditions in Georgia—"We'll get a better grade of prisons when we get a better grade of prisoners"—but I shall refrain.)

Giving an F where it is deserved would force concerned parents to get themselves away from the TV set, too, and take an active part in their children's education. I realize, of course, that some parents would not help; some cannot help. However, Johnny does not deserve to pass just because Daddy doesn't care or is ignorant. Johnny should pass only when and if he knows the required material.

Giving an F whenever and wherever it is the only appropriate grade would force principals, school boards, and voters to come to terms with cost as a factor in improving our educational system. As the numbers of students at various levels were increased by those not being passed, more money would have to be spent to accommodate them. We could not be accommodating them in the old sense of passing them on, but by keeping them at one level until they did in time, one way or another, learn the material.

Insisting on respecting the line between passing and failing would also require us to demand as much of ourselves as of our students. As every teacher knows, a failed student can be the product of a failed teacher.

Teaching methods, classroom presentations, and testing procedures would have to be of a very high standard—we could not, after all, conscionably give F's if we have to go home at night thinking it might somehow be our own fault.

The results of giving an F where it is deserved would be immediately evident. There would be no illiterate college graduates next spring—none. The same would be true of high-school graduates, and consequently next year's college freshmen—*all* of them—would be able to read.

I don't claim that giving F's will solve all of the problems, but I do argue that unless and until we start failing those students who should be failed, other suggested solutions will make little progress toward improving education. Students in our schools and colleges should be permitted to pass only after they have fully met established standards; borderline cases should be retained.

The single most important requirement for solving the problems of education in America today is the big fat F, written decisively in red ink millions of times in schools and colleges across the country.

Questions:

1. What values does Singleton share with his audience?
2. On what points does Singleton disagree with his audience?
3. What do you see as the function of grades?

II

Writing to a Sympathetic Audience

WHAT'S HAPPENED TO DISNEY FILMS?

John Evans

This essay originally appeared in The Dallas/Fort Worth Heritage *in August 1995.*

Many of today's over-30 adults who grew up on a diet of Disney movies are now responsible, God-honoring parents. They want their children to experience the same magic in films and videos that they once enjoyed.

Does the name "Disney" still mean the same in the '90s that it did in the '60s? Not at all. Disney is now a huge conglomerate with such diverse subsidiaries as Miramax Films, Hollywood Pictures, and Touchstone Pictures. The films they produce range from the violent, degrading *Pulp Fiction*, a Miramax film, to the delightful *Beauty and the Beast*, a Walt Disney Co. film. In between these two extremes are a myriad of movies of varying degrees of decency and offensiveness.

Listed below are descriptions which illustrate the undesirable content included in some Walt Disney Pictures films intended for young children. These comments are based on reviews from the *Preview* Family Movie and TV Guide.

The Little Mermaid (1989), G-rated animated film. While Disney's villains in the past have simply been mean and nasty, Ursula, the wicked sea witch, is downright evil. Her bizarre appearance and morbid undersea abode exude images of witchcraft, and some scenes are likely to frighten small children. Also, offensive, sexually suggestive dialogue is uncalled for. In one scene the evil Ursula intimates that the mermaid will have to "let her body do her talking." In romantic song, Ariel sings to Eric, "You know you want to do it." Even more disturbing, however, is the picture on the video box that includes a very obvious phallic symbol.

Aladdin (1992), G-rated animated film. The panther head entrance to the cave and a volcanic eruption are violent, jolting, and intense. The Genie transforms the evil Jofar into a sorcerer who violently manipulates others. Jofar changes into a giant snake to fight Aladdin. Again, the evil characters are more than scary—they attack. Also, the video tape includes some suggestive dialogue whispered in the background during a balcony scene between Aladdin and Jasmine. The words, "Take off your—" can be heard, implying that the muffled word is "clothes."

Lion King (1994), G-rated animated film. New Age and occultic concepts appear to be introduced when it's said that the father lion is living on in the son. Also, a remark is made that dead kings are looking down on the young lion. These can be interpreted literally as the Hindu concept of the universality of the soul. Also, when the young lion talks to his dead father, this violates the biblical admonition against communicating with the spirits of the dead.

Lion King also includes intense violence, including a graphic stampede and clawing and biting among animals. This continues the trend to show hand-to-hand combat that inflicts severe injuries.

Pocahontas (1995), G-rated animated film. This brand new feature film favorably depicts Indian animism, the belief that every natural object, such as rocks and trees, have spirits. Also, it portrays communication with spirits of the dead as acceptable. "The producers give an exaggerated picture of the white colonists as greedy, bloodthirsty monsters who just want to rid the land of 'those savages.'"

The Walt Disney Pictures company continues to produce Disney's G-rated films as well as its more family oriented movies, such as *Iron Will, Angels in the Outfield, White Fang,* and the *Mighty Ducks* series. However, several years ago, the Disney organization decided to produce more "mature" films and established two wholly owned companies to produce them, Hollywood Pictures and Touchstone Pictures. Also, a few years ago, Disney acquired Miramax Films, which distributes some very offensive films, most of them produced in foreign countries.

A few examples of the most offensive films these companies have produced or distributed are given below.

Pulp Fiction (1994-Miramax Films). Disgusting R-rated adult film which contains over 320 obscenities and profanities, ongoing graphic and gratuitous violence, a homosexual rape, and much bizarre behavior.

Color of Night (1994-Hollywood Pictures). Gruesome R-rated murder mystery with bloody killings, stabbings, an impaling, and choking. Also, a sexual affair with graphic sexual content and nudity, and over 100 obscenities and profanities.

Priest (1995-Miramax Films). This controversial R-rated film sympathetically portrays a homosexual priest and depicts other Catholic priests as disreputable characters. Contains scenes of graphic homosexual lovemaking. Catholics nation-wide protested the film.

Who Framed Roger Rabbit? (1988-Touchstone Pictures). Suggestive, violent PG-rated cartoon film in which some characters are boiled in toxic waste and flattened by a steam roller. Also, features an implied extramarital affair, crude language, sexually suggestive humor, and a voluptuous, seductive female character.

For parents who want to select only wholesome, decent entertainment for their families, the *Preview* Family Movie and TV Guide publishes reviews of all current films twice a month. The reviews contain information on the desirable elements in a film as well as a detailed description of any offensive material.

WE'RE GOOD REPUBLICANS—AND PRO-CHOICE

Beverly G. Hudnut and William H. Hudnut III

An open letter to the Republican National Committee:

Last year, during the 18th week of Beverly's pregnancy, we discovered through testing that our baby suffered from grave defects that would have prevented him from becoming a healthy human being. Anencephaly was just one problem. Ultrasound and, later, an autopsy revealed several more.

After talking with our families, physicians and pastors, we decided to terminate the pregnancy. It was a heart-wrenching decision, because we wanted our baby very badly and already loved him dearly. But we felt that our decision was the only good one to make, grounded as it was in sound professional advice, the love of family and friends, and our faith.

At the time, Bill was in his 16th year as Republican Mayor of Indianapolis. So ours was a public decision as well as a private one. We issued a news release, and tried to be upfront with the press. The outpouring of love and support from all over the country—mostly from people who had struggled with the same decision—was heartwarming.

We would have been terribly upset if an outside force, namely government, had prevented us from following the dictates of our conscience in this matter. Granted, our case represents a small fraction of the total number of abortions performed in the U.S., but nonetheless we feel constrained to ask: Why should political parties, our party in particular, stake out a position on abortion? Why borrow trouble on a matter on which people are so seriously divided?

It seems to us that under traditional minimalist Republican policy, government would choose *not* to interfere with a woman's right to make her own decision about whether or not to bear a child. We consider ourselves to be good members of the Republican team. It has been fairly easy to keep quiet about the abortion issue in the past and vote for candidates in spite of their position on abortion. It was perhaps easy because we felt protected by the *Roe v. Wade* decision. Following the same logic, it is now easy to speak up publicly because our party leaders are encouraging the Supreme Court to reverse *Roe v. Wade*.

If the Court takes steps this year to dilute laws determining whether or not a woman has control over her choice about bearing a child, we fear for our party in this year's election and those in the future. Pro-choice Republicans can no longer afford to keep their opinions to themselves. There are many of us with different political beliefs who find ourselves in the middle. Our voices are not being heard, primarily because we have kept quiet, and no forum of discussion has existed to date to learn from one another. Surely we are mature enough as a country to be able to talk civilly about abortion without yelling or screaming or trying to force our viewpoint on others.

When Beverly applied to testify at Tuesday's party platform meeting in Salt Lake City, she was told that the Republican National Committee had already selected its speakers on "both sides" of the abortion issue. The response perplexed us, because this complex subject has more sides than two. How about a third side? Granted, we are pro-choice, but why not simply leave abortion out of the platform, which has opposed abortion in recent years. As soon as a party or politician or citizen takes a stand on abortion, an "us against them" situation is set in place, leaving little room for dialogue or diversity of opinion.

In his book, *Life Itself,* Roger Rosenblatt wrote that we have to "learn to live on 'uncommon ground' in the matter of abortion; that we must not only accept but embrace a state of tension that requires a tolerance of ambivalent feelings, respect for different values and sensibilities, and no small amount of compassion." We call on our party leadership to take a stand on that "uncommon ground" by not taking a stand on abortion.

BAN THE THINGS. BAN THEM ALL.

Molly Ivins

Guns. Everywhere guns.

Let me start this discussion by pointing out that I am not anti-gun. I'm pro-knife. Consider the merits of the knife.

In the first place, you have to catch up with someone to stab him. A general sub- stitution of knives for guns would promote physical fitness. We'd turn into a whole nation of great runners. Plus, knives don't ricochet. And people are seldom killed while cleaning their knives.

As a civil libertarian, I of course support the Second Amendment. And I believe it means exactly what it says: "A well-regulated militia being necessary to the security of a free state, the right of the people to keep and bear arms shall not be infringed." Fourteen-year-old boys are not part of a well-regulated militia. Members of wacky religious cults are not part of a well-regulated militia. Permitting unregulated citizens to have guns is destroying the security of this free state.

I am intrigued by the arguments of those who claim to follow the judicial doc- trine of original intent. How do they know it was the dearest wish of Thomas Jeffer- son's heart that teenage drug dealers should cruise the cities of this nation perforating their fellow citizens with assault rifles? Channeling?

There is more hooey spread about the Second Amendment. It says quite clearly that guns are for those who form part of a well-regulated militia, i.e., the armed forces including the National Guard. The reasons for keeping them away from everyone else get clearer by the day.

The comparison most often used is that of the automobile, another lethal object that is regularly used to wreak great carnage. Obviously, this society is full of people who haven't got enough common sense to use an automobile properly. But we haven't outlawed cars yet.

We do, however, license them and their owners, restrict their use to presumably sane and sober adults and keep track of who sells them to whom. At a minimum, we should do the same with guns.

In truth, there is no rational argument for guns in this society. This is no longer a frontier nation in which people hunt their own food. It is a crowded, overwhelm- ingly urban country in which letting people have access to guns is a continuing dis- aster. Those who want guns—whether for target shooting, hunting or potting rattlesnakes (get a hoe)—should be subject to the same restrictions placed on gun owners in England—a nation in which liberty has survived nicely without an armed populace.

The argument that "guns don't kill people" is patent nonsense. Anyone who has ever worked in a cop shop knows how many family arguments end in murder because there was a gun in the house. Did the gun kill someone? No. But if there had been no gun, no one would have died. At least not without a good footrace first. Guns do kill. Unlike cars, that is all they do.

Michael Crichton makes an interesting argument about technology in his thriller *Jurassic Park*. He points out that power without discipline is making this society into a wreckage. By the time someone who studies the martial arts becomes a master—literally able to kill with bare hands—that person has also undergone years of training and discipline. But any fool can pick up a gun and kill with it.

"A well-regulated militia" surely implies both long training and long discipline. That is the least, the very least, that should be required of those who are permitted to have guns, because a gun is literally the power to kill. For years, I used to enjoy taunting my gun-nut friends about their psycho-sexual hangups—always in a spirit of good cheer, you understand. But letting the noisy minority in the National Rifle Association force us to allow this carnage to continue is just plain insane.

I do think gun nuts have a power hangup. I don't know what is missing in their psyches that they need to feel they have the power to kill. But no sane society would allow this to continue.

Ban the damn things. Ban them all.

You want protection? Get a dog.

Questions:

1. Who are the audiences these three authors address?
2. The Hudnuts have written to a specific audience. Is there a wider audience implied?

III

Figures of Speech

A GIFT OF OPPRESSION

Leonard Pitts, Jr.

Leonard Pitts, Jr. is a columnist for the Chicago Tribune.

This is an open letter to young black America. People are asking me about you again. They're writing and calling, challenging me to explain why you sometimes call each other "nigger," then profess anger and hurt when a white person uses the same word.

They think you're hypocritical. They think you're hypersensitive. They think you should be more like the Italian guy who'll let a friend get away with the word "wop" or the Irish person who, in the spirit of good fun, now and then tolerates being called a "mick."

They think you should emulate those people in other ways, too: Stop whining about the names you are called and the mistreatment you have received. Life here has been no picnic for them, either. They worked, they educated themselves, they moved ahead and assimilated. Why can't you?

But you aren't Irish or Italian, are you? You're African. Skin the color of creamless coffee. Or pecan shell. Or sandy shore. Skin that makes you stand out in a crowd of Europeans like "a fly in the buttermilk," as the old folks used to say.

That's why your forebears and mine were chosen to bear the burden of slavery—the fact that it was beyond their ability to run off and blend in. And there you have the defining difference, the thing that makes our experience unique. With the possible exception of the original tenants of this land, no group of Americans—not Irish, Italian, Chinese, woman nor gay—ever suffered on these shores as we did.

Ten million to 20 million kidnapped from the bosom of home. Half again that many left dead by the horrors of the Middle Passage. Centuries of enslavement, rape, torture, disenfranchisement, theft, poverty, ignorance, murder and hate. And then someone asks in well-meaning innocence why we can't be more like the Irish.

Makes me want to holler.

That's why you call yourself "nigger" sometimes, I know.

Oppression long ago taught us how to build a mansion from a stack of debris, weave a symphony from a moan of pain. Look at the record. Given hog entrails, we made chit'lins. Given agony, we invented the blues. Given the bruising hardness of city streets, we created cool.

And given "nigger," a word white men meant as an emblem of our stupidity, meanness and filth, we made a multipurpose word useful in the expression of everything from anger and humor to sarcasm and fraternity. We made it our word. And the whole weight of history bars white people from using it the way we do—or even understanding it the way we do.

But here's my problem: Unlike chit'lins, unlike cool and unlike the blues, this gift of oppression always took from us more than it gave. Meaning that if there's a certain sense of in-group smugness in greeting your brother as a "nigger," there is also, unspoken between the consonants, an admission that the white man was right when he said we were lower and lesser.

That word is drenched with four centuries of blood and tears. It hates us, even when it issues from our own lips.

And it is time we got beyond self-loathing.

I know what "Action News" says about you. I know how police act like you're a crime waiting to happen. I know the advice the crack man gives, know the terrible things family and friends sometimes say because they don't know better and they don't know you.

Love yourself anyway. Love yourself past the hateful words and the hurtful lies. Love yourself over the empty pockets of poverty and the bare walls of spirit. Love yourself through the narrowness of days and the meanness of nights.

Love yourself with a fierceness and an urgency, and I promise that it will lead you up to this truth: You are the flower of 400 years. You are the dream a slave once had.

And there is no such thing as a nigger.

There never was.

STATEMENT ON THE ASSASSINATION OF MARTIN LUTHER KING, JR.

Robert F. Kennedy

Robert F. Kennedy delivered this speech in Indianapolis, Indiana on April 4, 1968, following the death of civil rights leader Dr. Martin Luther King, Jr.

I have bad news for you, for all of our fellow citizens, and people who love peace all over the world, and that is that Martin Luther King was shot and killed tonight.

Martin Luther King dedicated his life to love and to justice for his fellow human beings, and he died because of that effort.

In this difficult day, in this difficult time for the United States, it is perhaps well to ask what kind of a nation we are and what direction we want to move in. For those of you who are black—considering the evidence there evidently is that there were white people who were responsible—you can be filled with bitterness, with hatred, and a desire for revenge. We can move in that direction as a country, in great polarization—black people amongst black, white people amongst white, filled with hatred toward one another.

Or we can make an effort, as Martin Luther King did, to understand and to comprehend, and to replace that violence, that stain of bloodshed that has spread across our land, with an effort to understand with compassion and love.

For those of you who are black and are tempted to be filled with hatred and distrust at the injustice of such an act, against all white people, I can only say that I feel in my own heart the same kind of feeling. I had a member of my family killed, but he was killed by a white man. But we have to make an effort in the United States, we have to make an effort to understand, to go beyond these rather difficult times.

My favorite poet was Aeschylus. He wrote: "In our sleep, pain which cannot forget falls drop by drop upon the heart until, in our own despair, against our will, comes wisdom through the awful grace of God."

What we need in the United States is not division; what we need in the United States is not hatred; what we need in the United States is not violence or lawlessness; but love and wisdom, and compassion toward one another, and a feeling of justice toward those who still suffer within our country, whether they be white or they be black.

So I shall ask you tonight to return home, to say a prayer for the family of Martin Luther King, that's true, but more importantly to say a prayer for our own country, which all of us love—a prayer for understanding and that compassion of which I spoke.

We can do well in this country. We will have difficult times; we've had difficult times in the past; we will have difficult times in the future. It is not the end of violence; it is not the end of lawlessness; it is not the end of disorder.

But the vast majority of white people and the vast majority of black people in this country want to live together, want to improve the quality of our life, and want justice for all human beings who abide in our land.

Let us dedicate ourselves to what the Greeks wrote so many years ago: to tame the savageness of man and make gentle the life of this world.

Let us dedicate ourselves to that, and say a prayer for our country and for our people.

INAUGURAL ADDRESS

President John F. Kennedy

> *John F. Kennedy delivered this speech on Friday, January 10, 1961 at his inauguration as the thirty-second president of the United States.*

As Actually Delivered

Vice President Johnson, Mr. Speaker, Mr. Chief Justice, President Eisenhower, Vice President Nixon, President Truman, Reverend Clergy, Fellow Citizens:

We observe today not a victory of party but a celebration of freedom—symbolizing an end as well as a beginning—signifying renewal as well as change. For I have sworn before you and Almighty God the same solemn oath our forebears prescribed nearly a century and three quarters ago.

The world is very different now. For man holds in his mortal hands the power to abolish all forms of human poverty and all forms of human life. And yet the same revolutionary beliefs for which our forebears fought are still at issue around the globe—the belief that the rights of man come not from the generosity of the state but from the hand of God.

We dare not forget today that we are the heirs of that first revolution. Let the word go forth from this time and place, to friend and foe alike, that the torch has been passed to a new generation of Americans—born in this century, tempered by war, disciplined by a hard and bitter peace, proud of our ancient heritage—and unwilling to witness or permit the slow undoing of those human rights to which this nation has always been committed, and to which we are committed today at home and around the world.

Let every nation know, whether it wishes us well or ill, that we shall pay any price, bear any burden, meet any hardship, support any friend, oppose any foe to assure the survival and the success of liberty.

This much we pledge—and more.

To those old allies whose cultural and spiritual origins we share, we pledge the loyalty of faithful friends. United, there is little we cannot do in a host of cooperative ventures. Divided, there is little we can do—for we dare not meet a powerful challenge at odds and split asunder.

To those new states whom we welcome to the ranks of the free, we pledge our word that one form of colonial control shall not have passed away merely to be replaced by a far more iron tyranny. We shall not always expect to find them supporting our view. But we shall always hope to find them strongly supporting their own freedom—and to remember that, in the past, those who foolishly sought power by riding the back of the tiger ended up inside.

To those peoples in the huts and villages of half the globe struggling to break the bonds of mass misery, we pledge our best efforts to help them help themselves, for whatever period is required—not because the communists may be doing it, not because we seek their votes, but because it is right. If a free society cannot help the many who are poor, it can not save the few who are rich.

To our sister republics south of our border, we offer a special pledge—to convert our good words into good deeds—in a new alliance for progress—to assist free men and free governments in casting off the chains of poverty. But this peaceful revolution of hope cannot become the prey of hostile powers. Let all our neighbors know that we shall join with them to oppose aggression or subversion anywhere in the Americas. And let every other power know that this Hemisphere intends to remain the master of its own house.

To that world assembly of sovereign states, the United Nations, our last best hope in an age where the instruments of war have far outpaced the instruments of peace, we renew our pledge of support—to prevent it from becoming merely a forum for invective—to strengthen its shield of the new and the weak—and to enlarge the area in which its writ may run.

Finally, to those nations who would make themselves our adversary, we offer not a pledge but a request: that both sides begin anew the quest for peace, before the dark powers of destruction unleashed by science engulf all humanity in planned or accidental self-destruction.

We dare not tempt them with weakness. For only when our arms are sufficient beyond doubt can we be certain beyond doubt that they will never be employed.

But neither can two great and powerful groups of nations take comfort from our present course—both sides overburdened by the cost of modern weapons, both rightly alarmed by the steady spread of the deadly atom, yet both racing to alter that uncertain balance of terror that stays the hand of mankind's final war.

So let us begin anew—remembering on both sides that civility is not a sign of weakness, and sincerity is always subject to proof. Let us never negotiate out of fear. But let us never fear to negotiate.

Let both sides explore what problems unite us instead of belaboring those problems which divide us.

Let both sides, for the first time, formulate serious and precise proposals for the inspection and control of arms—and bring the absolute power to destroy other nations under the absolute control of all nations.

Let both sides seek to invoke the wonders of ancient instead of its terrors. Together let us explore the stars, conquer the deserts, eradicate disease, tap the ocean depths and encourage the arts and commerce.

Let both sides unite to heed in all corners of the earth the command of Isaiah— to "undo the heavy burdens . . . (and) let the oppressed go free."

And if a beach-head of cooperation may push back the jungle of suspicion, let both sides join in creating a new endeavor, not a new balance of power, but a new world of law, where the strong are just and the weak secure and the peace preserved.

All this will not be finished in the first one hundred days. Nor will it be finished in the first one thousand days, nor in the life of this Administration, nor even perhaps in our lifetime on this planet. But let us begin.

In your hands, my fellow citizens, more than mine, will rest the final success or failure of our course. Since this country was founded, each generation of Americans has been summoned to give testimony to its national loyalty. The graves of young Americans who answered the call to service surround the globe.

Now the trumpet summons us again—not as a call to bear arms, though arms we need—not as a call to battle, though embattled we are—but a call to bear the burden of a long twilight struggle, year in and year out, "rejoicing in hope, patient in tribulation"—a struggle against the common enemies of man: tyranny, poverty, disease and war itself.

Can we forge against those enemies a grand and global alliance, North and South, East and West, that can assure a more fruitful life for all mankind? Will you join in that historic effort?

In the long history of the world, only a few generations have been granted the role of defending freedom in its hour of maximum danger. I do not shrink from this responsibility—I welcome it. I do not believe that any of us would exchange places with any other people or any other generation. The energy, the faith, the devotion which we bring to this endeavor will light our country and all who serve it—and the glow from that fire can truly light the world.

And so, my fellow Americans: ask not what your country can do for you—ask what you can do for your country.

My fellow citizens of the world: ask not what America will do for you, but what together we can do for the freedom of man.

Finally, whether you are citizens of America or citizens of the world, ask of us here the same high standards of strength and sacrifice which we ask of you. With a good conscience our only sure reward, with history the final judge of our deeds, let us go forth to lead the land we love, asking His blessing and His help, but knowing that here on earth God's work must truly be our own.

IV

Parody, Marked Style, and Satire

LESSON ON MARKED STYLES

English 101

Keely McCarthy

This very short exercise helps you understand what the term "marked styles" means.

1. Read the following:

    Too Many Daves

    Did I ever tell you that Mrs. McCave
    Had twenty-three sons and she named them all Dave?

    Well she did. And that wasn't a smart thing to do.
    You see, when she wants one and calls out, "Yoo-Hoo!
    Come into the house, Dave!" she doesn't get *one*.
    All twenty-three Daves of hers come on the run!

    This makes things quite difficult at the McCaves'
    As you can imagine, with so many Daves.
    And often she wishes that, when they were born,
    She had named one of them Bodkin Van Horn
    And one of them Hoos-Foos. And one of them Snimm.
    And one of them Hot-Shot. And one Sunny Jim.

And one of them Shadrack. And one of them Blinkey.
And one of them Stuffy. And one of them Stinkey.
Another one Putt-Putt. Another one Moon Face.
Another one Marvin O'Gravel Balloon Face.
And one of them Ziggy. And one Soggy Muff.
One Buffalo Bill. And one Biffalo Buff.
And one of them Sneepy. And one Weepy Weed.
And one Paris Garters. And one Harris Tweed.
And one of them Sir Michael Carmichael Zutt.
And one of them Oliver Boliver Butt.
And one of them Zanzibar Buck-Buck McFate . . .
But she didn't do it. And now it's too late.

2. Who is the author? (Dr. Seuss, of course!)

3. What "marks" Seuss's style?

BODY RITUAL AMONG THE NACIREMA

Horace Miner

The anthropologist has become so familiar with the diversity of ways in which different peoples behave in similar situations that he is not apt to be surprised by even the most exotic customs. In fact, if all of the logically possible combinations of behavior have not been found somewhere in the world, he is apt to suspect that they must be present in some yet undescribed tribe. This point has, in fact, been expressed with respect to clan organization by Murdock (1949: 71). In this light, the magical beliefs and practices of the Nacirema present such unusual aspects that it seems desirable to describe them as an example of the extremes to which human behavior can go.

Professor Linton first brought the ritual of the Nacirema to the attention of anthropologists twenty years ago (1936: 326), but the culture of this people is still very poorly understood. They are a North American group living in the territory between the Canadian Cree, the Yaqui and Tarahumare of Mexico, and the Carib and Arawak of the Antilles. Little is known of their origin, although tradition states that they came from the east. According to Nacirema mythology, their nation was originated by a culture hero, Notgnihsaw, who is otherwise known for two great feats of strength—the throwing of a piece of wampum across the river Pa-To-Mac and the chopping down of a cherry tree in which the Spirit of Truth resided.

Nacirema culture is characterized by a highly developed market economy which has evolved in a rich natural habitat. While much of the people's time is devoted to economic pursuits, a large part of these labors and a considerable portion of the day are spent in ritual activity. The focus of this activity is the human body, the appearance and health of which loom as a dominant concern in the ethos of the people. While such a concern is certainly not unusual, its ceremonial aspects and associated philosophy are unique.

The fundamental belief underlying the whole system appears to be that the human body is ugly and that its natural tendency is to debility and disease. Incarcerated in such a body, man's only hope is to avert these characteristics through the use of the powerful influences of ritual and ceremony. Every household has one or more shrines devoted to this purpose. The more powerful individuals in the society have several shrines in their houses and, in fact, the opulence of a house is often referred to in terms of the number of such ritual centers it possesses. Most houses are of wattle and daub construction, but the shrine rooms of the more wealthy are waited with stone. Poorer families imitate the rich by applying pottery plaques to their shrine walls.

While each family has at least one such shrine, the rituals associated with it are not family ceremonies but are private and secret. The rites are normally only discussed with children, and then only during the period when they are being initiated into these mysteries. I was able, however, to establish sufficient rapport with the natives to examine these shrines and to have the rituals described to me.

The focal point of the shrine is a box or chest which is built into the wall. In this chest are kept the many charms and magical potions without which no native believes he could live. These preparations are secured from a variety of specialized practitioners. The most powerful of these are the medicine men, whose assistance must be rewarded with substantial gifts. However, the medicine men do not provide the curative potions for their clients, but decide what the ingredients should be and then write them down in an ancient and secret language. This writing is understood only by the medicine men and the herbalists who, for another gift, provide the required charm.

The charm is not disposed of after it has served its purpose, but is placed in the charm-box of the household shrine. As these magical materials are specific for certain ills, and the real or imagined maladies of the people are many, the charm-box is usually full to overflowing. The magical packets are so numerous that people forget what their purposes were and fear to use them again. While the natives are very vague on this point, we can only assume that the idea in retaining all the old magical materials is that their presence in the charm-box, before which the body rituals are conducted, will in some way protect the worshipper.

Beneath the charm-box is a small font. Each day every member of the family, in succession, enters the shrine room, bows his head before the charm-box, mingles different sorts of holy water in the font, and proceeds with a brief rite of ablution. The holy waters are secured from the Water Temple of the community, where the priests conduct elaborate ceremonies to make the liquid ritually pure.

In the hierarchy of magical practitioners, and below the medicine men in prestige, are specialists whose designation is best translated "holy-mouth-men." The Nacirema have an almost pathological horror of and fascination with the mouth, the condition of which is believed to have a supernatural influence on all social relationships. Were it not for the rituals of the mouth, they believe that their teeth would fall out, their gums bleed, their jaws shrink, their friends desert them, and their lovers reject them. They also believe that a strong relationship exists between oral and moral characteristics. For example, there is a ritual ablution of the mouth for children which is supposed to improve their moral fiber.

The daily body ritual performed by everyone includes a mouth-rite. Despite the fact that these people are so punctilious about care of the mouth, this rite involves a practice which strikes the uninitiated stranger as revolting. It was reported to me that the ritual consists of inserting a small bundle of hog hairs into the mouth, along with certain magical powders, and then moving the bundle in a highly formalized series of gestures.

In addition to the private mouth-rite, the people seek out a holy-mouth-man once or twice a year. These practitioners have an impressive set of paraphernalia, consisting of a variety of augers, awls, probes, and prods. The use of these objects in the exorcism of the evils of the mouth involves almost unbelievable ritual torture of the client. The holy-mouth-man opens the client's mouth and, using the above mentioned tools, enlarges any holes which decay may have created in the teeth. Magical materials are put into these holes. If there are no naturally occurring holes in the teeth, large sections of one or more teeth are gouged out so that the supernatural substance can be applied. In the client's view, the purpose of these ministrations is to arrest decay and to draw friends. The extremely sacred and traditional character of the rite is evident in the fact that the natives return to the holy-mouth-men year after year, despite the fact that their teeth continue to decay.

It is to be hoped that, when a thorough study of the Nacirema is made, there will be careful inquiry into the personality structures of these people. One has but to watch the gleam in the eye of a holy-mouth-man, as he jabs an awl into an exposed nerve, to suspect that a certain amount of sadism is involved. If this can be established, a very interesting pattern emerges, for most of the population shows definite masochistic tendencies. It was to these that Professor Linton referred in discussing a distinctive part of the daily body ritual which is performed only by men. This part of the rite involves scraping and lacerating the surface of the face with a sharp instrument. Special women's rites are performed only four times during each lunar month, but what they lack in frequency is made up in barbarity. As part of this ceremony, women bake their heads in small ovens for about an hour. The theoretically interesting point is that what seems to be a preponderantly masochistic people have developed sadistic specialists.

The medicine men have an imposing temple, or *latipso*, in every community of any size. The more elaborate ceremonies required to treat very sick patients can only be performed at this temple. These ceremonies involve not only the thaumaturge but a permanent group of vestal maidens who move sedately about the temple chambers in distinctive costume and headdress.

The *latipso* ceremonies are so harsh that it is phenomenal that a fair proportion of the really sick natives who enter the temple ever recover. Small children whose indoctrination is still incomplete have been known to resist attempts to take them to the temple because "that is where you go to die." Despite this fact, sick adults are not only willing but eager to undergo the protracted ritual purification, if they can afford to do so. No matter how ill the supplicant or how grave the emergency, the guardians of many temples will not admit a client if he cannot give a rich gift to the custodian. Even after one has gained admission and survived the ceremonies, the guardians will not permit the neophyte to leave until he makes still another gift.

The supplicant entering the Temple is first stripped of all his or her clothes. In every-day life the Nacirema avoids exposure of his body and its natural functions. Bathing and excretory acts are performed only in the secrecy of the household shrine, where they are ritualized as part of the body-rites. Psychological shock results from the fact that body secrecy is suddenly lost upon entry into the *latipso*. A man, whose own wife has never seen him in an excretory act, suddenly finds himself naked and assisted by a vestal maiden while he performs his natural functions into a sacred vessel. This sort of ceremonial treatment is necessitated by the fact that the excreta are used by a diviner to ascertain: the course and nature of the client's sickness. Female clients, on the other hand, find their naked bodies are subjected to the scrutiny, manipulation and prodding of the medicine man.

Few supplicants in the temple are well enough to do anything but lie on their hard beds. The daily ceremonies, like the rites of the holy-mouth-men, involve discomfort and torture. With ritual precision, the vestals awaken their miserable charges each dawn and roll them about on their beds of pain while performing ablutions, in the formal movements of which the maidens are highly trained. At other times they insert magic wands in the supplicant's mouth or force him to eat substances which are supposed to be healing. From time to time the medicine men come to their clients and jab magically treated needles into their flesh. The fact that these temple ceremonies may not cure, and may even kill the neophyte, in no way decreases the people's faith in the medicine men.

There remains one other kind of practitioner, known as a "listener." This witch-doctor has the power to exorcise the devils that lodge in the heads of people who have been bewitched. The Nacirema believe that parents bewitch their own children. Mothers are particularly suspected of putting a curse on children while teaching them the secret body rituals. The counter-magic of the witch-doctor is unusual in its lack of ritual. The patient simply tells the "listener" all his troubles and fears, beginning with the earliest difficulties he can remember. The memory displayed by the Nacirema in these exorcism sessions is truly remarkable. It is not uncommon for the patient to bemoan the rejection he felt upon being weaned as a babe, and a few individuals even see their troubles going back to the traumatic effects of their own birth.

In conclusion, mention must be made of certain practices which have their base in native esthetics but which depend upon the pervasive aversion to the natural body and its functions. There are ritual fasts to make fat people thin and ceremonial feasts to make thin people fat. Still other rites are used to make women's breasts larger if they are small, and smaller if they are large. General dissatisfaction with breast shape is symbolized in the fact that the ideal form is virtually outside the range of human variation. A few women afflicted with almost inhuman hypermammary development are so idolized that they make a handsome living by simply going from village to village and permitting the natives to stare at them for a fee.

Reference has already been made to the fact that excretory functions are ritualized, routinized, and relegated to secrecy. Natural reproductive functions are similarly distorted. Intercourse is taboo as a topic and scheduled as an act. Efforts are made to avoid pregnancy by the use of magical materials or by limiting intercourse to certain phases of the moon. Conception is actually very infrequent. When pregnant, women dress so as to hide their condition. Parturition takes place in secret, without friends or relatives to assist, and the majority of women do not nurse their infants.

Our review of the ritual life of the Nacirema has certainly shown them to be magic-ridden people. It is hard to understand how they have managed to exist so long under the burdens which they have imposed upon themselves. But even such exotic customs as these take on real meaning when they are viewed with the insight provided by Malinowski when he wrote (1948: 70):

> Looking from far and above, from our high places of safety in the developed civilization, it is easy to see all the crudity and irrelevance of magic. But without its power and guidance early man could not have mastered his practical difficulties as he has done, nor could man have advanced to the higher stages of civilization.

References Cited

Linton, Ralph. (1936). *The Study of Man.* New York: D. Appleton Century Co.

Malinowski, Bronislaw. (1948). *Magic, Science, and Religion.* Glencoe: The Free Press.

Murdock, George P. (1949). *Social Structure.* New York: The Macmillan Co.

A MODEST PROPOSAL

Jonathan Swift

Jonathan Swift (1667–1745) was a prolific Irish author, best known for his scathing political essays.

It is a melancholy object to those who walk through this great town or travel in the country, when they see the streets, the roads, and cabin doors, crowded with beggars of the female sex, followed by three, four, or six children, all in rags and importuning every passenger for an alms. These mothers, instead of being able to work for their honest livelihood, are forced to employ all their time in strolling to beg sustenance for their helpless infants, who, as they grow up, either turn thieves for want of work, or leave their dear native country to fight for the Pretender in Spain, or sell themselves to the Barbados.[1]

I think it is agreed by all parties that this prodigious number of children in the arms, or on the backs, or at the heels of their mothers, and frequently of their fathers, is in the present deplorable state of the kingdom a very great additional grievance; and therefore whoever could find out a fair, cheap, and easy method of making these children sound, useful members of the commonwealth would deserve so well of the public as to have his statue set up for a preserver of the nation.

But my intention is very far from being confined to provide only for the children of professed beggars; it is of a much greater extent, and shall take in the whole number of infants at a certain age who are born of parents in effect as little able to support them as those who demand our charity in the streets.

As to my own part, having turned my thoughts for many years upon this important subject, and maturely weighed the several schemes of other projectors, I have always found them grossly mistaken in their computation. It is true, a child just dropped from its dam may be supported by her milk for a solar year, with little other nourishment; at most not above the value of two shillings, which the mother may certainly get, or the value in scraps, by her lawful occupation of begging; and it is exactly at one year that I propose to provide for them in such a manner as instead of being a charge upon their parents or the parish, or wanting food and raiment for the rest of their lives, they shall on the contrary contribute to the feeding, and partly to the clothing, of many thousands.

There is likewise another great advantage in my scheme, that it will prevent those voluntary abortions, and that horrid practice of women murdering their bastard children, alas, too frequent among us, sacrificing the poor innocent babes, I doubt, more to avoid the expense than the shame, which would move tears and pity in the most savage and inhuman breast.

The number of souls in this kingdom being usually reckoned one million and a half, of these I calculate there may be about two hundred thousand couples whose wives are breeders; from which number I subtract thirty thousand couples who are able to maintain their own children, although I apprehend there cannot be so many under the present distress of the kingdom; but this being granted, there will remain an hundred and seventy thousand breeders. I again subtract fifty thousand for those women who miscarry, or whose children die by accident or disease within the year. There only remain an hundred and twenty thousand children of poor parents annually born. The question therefore is, how this number shall be reared and provided for, which, as I have already said, under the present situation of affairs, is utterly impossible by all the methods hitherto proposed. For we can neither employ them in handicraft or agriculture; we neither build houses (I mean in the country) nor cultivate land. They can very seldom pick up a livelihood by stealing till they arrive at six years old, except where they are of towardly parts; although I confess they learn the rudiments much earlier, during which time they can however be looked upon only as probationers, as I have been informed by a principal gentleman in the county of Cavan, who protested to me that he never knew above one or two instances under the age of six, even in a part of the kingdom so renowned for the quickest proficiency in that art.

I am assured by our merchants that a boy or a girl before twelve years old is no salable commodity; and even when they come to this age they will not yield above three pounds, or three pounds and half a crown at most on the Exchange; which cannot turn to account either to the parents or the kingdom, the charge of nutriment and rags having been at least four times that value.

I shall now therefore humbly propose my own thoughts, which I hope will not be liable to the least objection.

I have been assured by a very knowing American of my acquaintance in London, that a young healthy child well nursed is at a year old a most delicious, nourishing, and wholesome food, whether stewed, roasted, baked, or boiled; and I make no doubt that it will equally serve in a fricassee or a ragout.

I do therefore humbly offer it to public consideration that of the hundred and twenty thousand children, already computed, twenty thousand may be reserved for breed, whereof only one fourth part to be males, which is more than we allow to sheep, black cattle, or swine; and my reason is that these children are seldom the fruits of marriage, a circumstance not much regarded by our savages, therefore one male will be sufficient to serve four females. That the remaining hundred thousand may at a year old be offered in sale to the persons of quality and fortune through the kingdom, always advising the mother to let them suck plentifully in the last month, so as to render them plump and fat for a good table. A child will make two dishes at an entertainment for friends; and when the family dines alone, the fore or hind quarter will make a reasonable dish, and seasoned with a little pepper or salt will be very good boiled on the fourth day, especially in winter.

I have reckoned upon a medium that a child just born will weigh twelve pounds, and in a solar year if tolerably nursed increaseth to twenty-eight pounds.

I grant this food will be somewhat dear, and therefore very proper for landlords, who, as they have already devoured most of the parents, seem to have the best title to the children.

Infant's flesh will be in season throughout the year, but more plentiful in March, and a little before and after. For we are told by a grave author, an eminent French physician,[2] that fish being a prolific diet, there are more children born in Roman

Catholic countries about nine months after Lent than at any other season; therefore, reckoning a year after Lent, the markets will be more glutted than usual, because the number of popish infants is at least three to one in this kingdom; and therefore it will have one other collateral advantage, by lessening the number of Papists among us.

I have already computed the charge of nursing a beggar's child (in which list I reckon all cottagers, laborers, and four-fifths of the farmers) to be about two shillings per annum, rags included; and I believe no gentleman would repine to give ten shillings for the carcass of a good fat child, which as I have said, will make four dishes of excellent nutritive meat, when he hath only some particular friend or his own family to dine with him. Thus the squire will learn to be a good landlord, and grow popular among the tenants; the mother will have eight shillings net profit, and be fit for work till she produces another child.

Those who are more thrifty (as I must confess the times require) may flay the carcass; the skin of which artificially dressed will make admirable gloves for ladies, and summer boots for fine gentlemen.

As to our city of Dublin, shambles may be appointed for this purpose in the most convenient parts of it, and butchers we may be assured will not be wanting; although I rather recommend buying the children alive, and dressing them hot from the knife as we do roasting pigs.

A very worthy person, a true lover of his country, and whose virtues highly esteem, was lately pleased in discoursing on this matter to offer a refinement upon my scheme. He said that many gentlemen of his kingdom having of late destroyed their deer, he conceived that the want of venison might be well supplied by the bodies of young lads and maidens, not exceeding fourteen years of age nor under twelve, so great a number of both sexes in every country being now ready to starve for want of work and service vice; and these to be disposed of by their parents, if alive, or otherwise their nearest relations. But with due deference to so excellent a friend and deserving a patriot, I cannot be altogether in his sentiments; for as to the males, my American acquaintance assured me from frequent experience that their flesh was generally tough and lean, like that of our schoolboys, by continual exercise, and their taste disagreeable; and to fatten them would not answer the charge. Then as to the females, it would, I think with humble submission, be a loss to the public, because they soon would become breeders themselves; and besides, it is not improbable that some scrupulous people might be apt to censure such a practice (although indeed very unjustly) as a little bordering upon cruelty; which, I confess, hath always been with me the strongest objection against any project, how well soever intended.

But in order to justify my friend, he confessed that this expedient was put into his head by the famous Psalmanazar,[3] a native of the island Formosa, who came from thence to London about twenty years ago, and in conversation told my friend that in his country when any young person happened to be put to death, the executioner sold the carcass to persons of quality as a prime dainty; and that in his time the body of a plump girl of fifteen, who was crucified for an attempt to poison the emperor, was sold to his Imperial Majesty's prime minister of state, and other great mandarins of the court, in joints from the gibbet, at four hundred crowns. Neither indeed can I deny that if the same use were made of several plump young girls in this town, who without one single groat to their fortunes cannot stir abroad without a chair, and appear at the playhouse and assemblies in foreign fineries which they never will pay for, the kingdom would not be the worse.

Some persons of a desponding spirit are in great concern about that vast number of poor people who are aged, diseased, or maimed, and I have been desired to employ my thoughts what course may be taken to ease the nation of so grievous an encumbrance. But I am not in the least pain upon that matter, because it is very well known that they are every day dying and rotting by cold and famine, and filth and vermin, as fast as can be reasonably expected. And as to the younger laborers, they are now in almost as hopeful a condition. They cannot get work, and consequently pine away for want of nourishment to a degree that if any time they are accidentally hired to common labor, they have not strength to perform it; and thus the country and themselves are happily delivered from the evils to come.

I have too long digressed, and therefore shall return to my subject. I think the advantages by the proposal which I have made are obvious and many, as well as of the highest importance.

For first, as I have already observed, it would greatly lessen the number of Papists, with whom we are yearly overrun, being the principal breeders of the nation as well as our most dangerous enemies; and who stay at home on purpose to deliver the kingdom to the Pretender, hoping to take their advantage by the absence of so many good Protestants, who have chosen rather to leave their country than to stay at home and pay tithes against their conscience to an Episcopal curate.

Secondly, the poorer tenants will have something valuable of their own, which by law may be made liable to distress, and help to pay their landlord's rent, their corn and cattle being already seized and money a thing unknown.

Thirdly, whereas the maintenance of an hundred thousand children, from two years old and upwards, cannot be computed at less than ten shillings a piece per annum, the nation's stock will be thereby increased fifty thousand pounds per annum, besides the profit of a new dish introduced to the tables of all gentlemen of fortune in the kingdom who have any refinement in taste. And the money will circulate among ourselves, the goods being entirely of our own growth and manufacture.

Fourthly, the constant breeders, besides the gain of eight shillings sterling per annum by the sale of their children, will be rid of the charge of maintaining them after the first year.

Fifthly, this food would likewise bring great custom to taverns, where the vintners will certainly be so prudent as to procure the best receipts for dressing it to perfection, and consequently have their houses frequented by all the fine gentlemen, who justly value themselves upon their knowledge in good eating; and a skillful cook, who understands how to oblige his guests, will contrive to make it as expensive as they please.

Sixthly, this would be a great inducement to marriage, which all wise nations have either encouraged by rewards or enforced by laws and penalties. It would increase the care and tenderness of mothers toward their children, when they were sure of a settlement for life to the poor babes, provided in some sort by the public, to their annual profit instead of expense. We should see an honest emulation among the married women, which of them could bring the fattest child to the market. Men would become as fond of their wives during the time of their pregnancy as they are now of their mares in foal, their cows in calf, or sows when they are ready to farrow; nor offer to beat or kick them (as is too frequent a practice) for fear of a miscarriage.

Many other advantages might be enumerated. For instance, the addition of some thousand carcasses in our exportation of barreled beef, the propagation of swine's flesh, and improvements in the art of making good bacon, so much wanted among us by the great destruction of pigs, too frequent at our tables, which are no way comparable in taste or magnificence to a well-grown, fat, yearling child, which roasted whole will make a considerable figure at a lord mayor's feast or any other public entertainment. But this and many others I omit, being studious of brevity.

Supposing that one thousand families in this city would be constant customers for infants' flesh, besides others who might have it at merry meetings, particularly weddings and christenings, I compute that Dublin would take off annually about twenty thousand carcasses, and the rest of the kingdom (where probably they will be sold somewhat cheaper) the remaining eighty thousand.

I can think of no one objection that will possibly be raised against this proposal, unless it should be urged that the number of people will be thereby much lessened in the kingdom. This I freely own, and it was indeed one principal design in offering it to the world. I desire the reader will observe, that I calculate my remedy for this one individual kingdom of Ireland and for no other that ever was, is, or I think ever can be upon earth. Therefore let no man talk to me of other expedients: of taxing our absentees at five shillings a pound: of using neither clothes nor household furniture except what is of our own growth and manufacture: of utterly rejecting the materials and instruments that promote foreign luxury: of curing the expensiveness of pride, vanity, idleness, and gaming in our women: of introducing a vein of parsimony, prudence, and temperance: of learning to love our country, in the want of which we differ even from Laplanders and the inhabitants of Topinamboo: of quitting our animosities and factions, nor acting any longer like the Jews, who were murdering one another at the very moment their city was taken: of being a little cautious not to sell our country and conscience for nothing: of teaching landlords to have at least one degree of mercy toward their tenants: lastly, of putting a spirit of honesty, industry, and skill into our shopkeepers; who, if a resolution could now be taken to buy only our native goods, would immediately unite to cheat and exact upon us in the price, the measure, and the goodness, nor could ever yet be brought to make one fair proposal of just dealing, though often and earnestly invited to it.

Therefore I repeat, let no man talk to me of these and the like expedients, till he hath at least some glimpse of hope that there will ever be some hearty and sincere attempt to put them in practice.

But as to myself, having been wearied out for many years with offering vain, idle, visionary thoughts, and at length utterly despairing of success. I fortunately fell upon this proposal, which, as it is wholly new, so it hath something solid and real, of no expense and little trouble, full in our own power, and whereby we can incur no danger in disobliging England. For this kind of commodity will not bear exportation, the flesh being of too tender a consistence to admit a long continuance in salt, although perhaps I could name a country which would be glad to eat up our whole nation without it.

After all, I am not so violently bent upon my own opinion as to reject any offer proposed by wise men, which shall be found equally innocent, cheap, easy, and effectual. But before something of that kind shall be advanced in contradiction to my scheme, and offering a better, I desire the author or authors will be pleased maturely to consider two points. First, as things now stand, how they will be able to find food and raiment for an hundred thousand useless mouths and backs. And secondly, there being a round million of creatures in human figure throughout this kingdom, whose sole subsistence put into a common stock would leave them in debt two millions of pounds sterling, adding those who are beggars by profession to the bulk of farmers, cottagers, and laborers, with their wives and children who are beggars in effect; I desire those politicians who dislike my overture, and may perhaps be so bold to attempt an answer, that they will first ask the parents of these mortals whether they would not at this day think it a great happiness to have been sold for food at a year old in this manner I prescribe, and thereby have avoided such a perpetual scene of misfortunes as they have since gone through by the oppression of landlords, the impossibility of paying rent without money or trade, the want of common sustenance, with neither house nor clothes to cover them from the inclemencies of the weather, and the most inevitable prospect of entailing the like or greater miseries upon their breed forever.

I profess, in the sincerity of my heart, that I have not the least personal interest in endeavoring to promote this necessary work, having no other motive than the public good of my country, by advancing our trade, providing for infants, relieving the poor, and giving some pleasure to the rich. I have no children by which I can propose to get a single penny; the youngest being nine years old, and my wife past childbearing.

Notes

1. The Pretender was James Stuart, the Catholic son of James II. Exiled in Spain, he sought to gain the throne his father had lost to the Protestant rulers William and Mary in 1688. Attempting to escape from destitution, many Irish people went to Barbados and other colonies as indentured servants.

2. François Rabelais (1494?–1533) was the author of *Garganna and Pantagroel*, a five-volume said to be much admired by Swift.

3. George Psalmanazar (?1679–1763) published an imaginary description of Formosa and became well known in English society.

MYSTIQUE AND MISTAKES

Abigail Trafford

Abigail Trafford is editor of and regular columnist for the Health Section of The Washington Post.

Evel Knievel and "Easy Rider," the smell of leather and thirst for freedom. Elvis Presley and King Hussein, the suntanned look, the feel of metal. Hell's Angels and James Dean—the biker mystique of noise, youth, sweat and . . .

Brains splattering on the pavement.

For all the rough glamour of riding a motorcycle, suffering a head injury is a major risk if you crash and you're not wearing a helmet. Decades of research have shown that helmets protect riders from serious head injuries.

Yet a number of bikers are enraged that anyone would tell them they have to wear helmets. Their opposition is based not on medical grounds but the principle of individual rights and personal freedom.

House Speaker Newt Gingrich explained it best when, according to news reports, he promised a crowd of 1,500 bandanna-and-leather bikers at the recent Republican Convention that the GOP would oppose laws that require riders to wear helmets. "This party's about freedom. It's about your opportunity to go out and work your heart out and enjoy yourself, lead the kind of life you want," he said.

This captures the essence of the debate on many behavioral health issues, whether it's smoking in office buildings, having unprotected sex, playing Little League baseball or riding a motorcycle without a helmet. In arguments from family rooms to city hall, individual freedom is pitted against intrusive rules. One side argues for the right of the individual to make choices about personal behavior—even foolish ones like smoking or not wearing a helmet. The other side calls for a government or parental role in influencing individual behaviors that present a burden to the society at large.

To emergency room physicians and highway safety experts, the medical case for motorcycle helmet use is overwhelming. To insist on feeling the wind through your hair in the name of individual rights is just "dumb and dumber," says Arthur L. Kellermann, director of the Emory University Center for Injury Control in Atlanta. "It requires a suspension of reality to make this kind of argument."

The reality, he says, is that without strong helmet laws, riders suffer more deaths and serious head injuries. According to estimates by the National Highway Traffic Safety Administration, an unhelmeted rider who has an accident is 40 percent more likely to suffer a fatal head injury and 15 percent more likely to incur nonfatal brain damage. Only about 50 percent of riders wear helmets voluntarily. But in states where a helmet law has been enacted, helmet use approaches 100 percent. As Allan Williams, senior vice president for research at the Insurance Institute for Highway Safety says: "Helmets are very effective. The evidence is very clear. It's common sense."

A study of motorcycle crashes in Nebraska concluded that the reinstitution of the state's helmet law in 1989 had resulted in fewer "fatalities and severe head injuries," according to a report in the Annals of Emergency Medicine. The percentage of serious brain damage among injured riders was "much lower among helmeted motorcy-clists (5 percent) than among unhelmeted cyclists (14 percent)," concluded physicians at the University of Nebraska Medical Center.

In California, fatal crashes decreased by more than 35 percent after a 1992 helmet law was enacted, the *Journal of the American Medical Association* reported.

"Our results point uniformly to the effectiveness of unrestricted motorcycle hel-met uses laws [with] . . . decreases in motorcycle fatalities . . . head injuries and head injury severity," concluded researchers at the Southern California Injury Prevention Research Center at UCLA.

To be sure, most people who ride motorcycles do not have crashes and motorcy-cle deaths have been declining since 1980. The 2,135 fatalities reported in 1995 accounted for 5 percent of all motor vehicle deaths.

Still, the Easy Rider life puts you on the edge. It's 20 times riskier to ride on a motorcycle than in a car. Most bikers are young and male. The consequences of a long-term head injury can be devastating.

It gets down to personal choices. Motorcycle mystique has great appeal. My god-son started down the Harley culture road by racing dirt bikes in a cornfield in Potomac. But by age 25 he made a pact with a friend to swear off the steel beast. Too many friends in too many accidents, often caused by drivers in cars, he explains. "Sure it's one of the highest highs in the world . . . an adrenaline rush-a-rama. It's tremen-dous freedom. But anybody's mistake and you're dead."

A significant part of a person's health status is determined by behavior. For those who want to smoke, or drink to excess, or take drugs, or ride a motorcycle without a helmet, it's easy to embrace the principle of individual rights. The question of per-sonal responsibility is more difficult to answer.

In the case of motorcycle injuries, it's usually the tax-paying public that has to pick up the pieces, because many bikers have no private funds to take care of themselves if they are injured. In the Nebraska study, more than 40 percent of injured motorcyclists lacked health insurance or received Medicaid or Medicare. More than 45 percent of motorcyclists treated at Massachusetts General Hospital had no insurance.

That's one reason society has an interest in setting standards for personal behav-ior. Ultimately society pays the bill. But as every student of human nature knows, when it comes to risky behaviors that make people feel good, it's hard to make peo-ple just say no.

UNIT SIX

Putting It All Together

WHERE *IS* UNIT SIX, ANYWAY?

If you are sitting in your room, Unit Six may be all around you. And the fact that you are reading this page guarantees that at least part of Unit Six is at your disposal.

Unit Six, then, is comprised of two kinds of readings:

1. Your own research — the twenty or more articles you've read while researching your Linked Assignments.

2. All the other articles you've read this semester.

Too often, students get bogged down by the end of the semester, and forget just how much they have already learned. Unit Six is about putting it all together, and you certainly don't need to read any *more* in order to do that!

Now is a good time for you to revisit the articles you've read during the semester, and to think about how the concepts you've learned apply to your own readings, research, and writing.

Ask yourself some questions:

1. What are my **goals** in the final position paper? How have I chosen to argue? (You might look back to Diane Cyr's piece on Alan Dershowitz — are you arguing to win?)

2. How can I use the **tactics of praise** I practiced while writing my encomium? How can they help me to present my point of view? (Is it important that some idea or person seem praiseworthy to your audience members?)

3. Who is my **audience**? What choices — about language, for example — am I going to make based on what I know about them? (Take a look at the articles in Unit One by Truth, Jordan, "Gallagher," and Saige.)

4. With what **schemas** is my audience familiar? How can I complicate or add to what they already know? To what they don't know? (Re-read Unit One essays by Barry, Alter, Buckley, and Clifford-Gonzalez.)

5. How can I build a strong **ethos**? (Remember that you can build what at first seem like limitations into a stronger ethos — see Wallace, "Give Children the Vote.")

6. How can I use **pathos** to strengthen my argument? How can I present pathos in balance with the other appeals? (Revisit Dickerson's "Who Shot Johnny?" and the speech from *Patton*.)

7. How can **logical appeals** help people to see that problems exist? (See Wiesenfeld's "Making the Grade," for example.)

8. How can I use the **common topics?**

9. How can I convince my readers that I have a firm grasp of the issues within the debate I'm working on? What do they need to be taught about it? How can I **map it out** for them? Can my mapping out be part of my argument? (Look again at Hancock and Kalb, Weiss, and Shipley in Unit Three.)

10. What terms can I — and what terms *must* I — **define**? How will defining (or redefining) these terms help my audience see new angles in my debate? (See Naylor, Pitts, Allport, Brady, Fernsler, and Allison in Unit Four.)

11. How can I use my knowledge of how an **affirmative argument** works to help me write to a hostile audience? What different strategies can I employ? (Look back at articles by the Hudnuts, Evans, and Ivins in Unit Five — how would they fare with a hostile audience?)

12. How can I use my understanding of the affirmative arguments within the debate to help me come up with points to **concede** or **refute**? Use your Pro/Pro essays to help you see some possibilities. Think, too, about how your opponents might refute *your* argument. Anticipate their objections, and try to respond to them.

13. What **lines of argument** and **figures of speech** can I use?

14. Should I use **parody** at all? How might my audience respond if I do? (Return to Miner and Swift in Unit Five, and to Barry and Buckley in Unit One — what kinds of audiences were they writing to?)

15. Will I take a **bridged position**? How can I use my Pro/Pro essays and my "What Are the Issues?" paper to help me locate possible points at which bridging is possible?

16. How will I use the **parts of a full argument**? How have other writers done so? (Try an analysis of King's "Letter from Birmingham Jail.")

Perhaps the best way to prepare to hand in your Final Position Paper is to imagine it as the object of a rhetorical analysis essay. If you had to write a rhetorical analysis of your own work, how would it rate? Would you be able to make and defend a convincing argument that your paper is persuasive to its intended audience?

Finally, think a bit more about the title of this text: *Perspectives.* Now it's your turn to make others see from your own perspective. How can you get them to see it most clearly? How can you help them look at it the right way? Remember, your job is to take a confusing subject — rather like the figure on the cover — and to make it seem suddenly clear, from your own perspective.

APPENDIX

Arguments in Advertising

INTRODUCTION

Although we do not always think of them as such, advertisements are, in fact, arguments. Ads generally seek to persuade viewers/listeners to take some sort of action. Most often, advertisers want their audience to purchase some object or service. Other, more "political" types of advertising often request that viewers change their beliefs. All of that is, of course, a great amount of work to do in a fairly limited amount of space or time.

In order to be effective, as with other persuasive writing, ads must target a specific audience. It would hardly do, for example, to market a costly luxury automobile to the average sixteen-year-old. Professional advertisers take great pains to research potential markets for the products they promote, and they use their knowledge of their audience to present those products in the best light possible. Advertisers who do not, you will discover in the essays that begin this section, sometimes make mistakes that can cost them large portions of their share of a market.

Like others who seek to persuade, advertisers use a number of rhetorical tools to influence potential consumers. The ads contained in this unit complement your other reading in the sense that they illustrate a number of the tactics of persuasion you will study throughout English 101.

Tricia Slusser

MORE GREENERY, LESS GARAGE

Michael Arlen

The following is part of a conversation that took place as the advertising firm NW Ayers worked on the AT&T commercial campaign, "Reach Out and Touch Someone." In the mid-seventies, Michael Arlen followed the firm as they worked on the campaign, and used several of the conversations he recorded to recreate the narrative of the making of a television commercial. He published that narrative in his 1979 book, Thirty Seconds, *which is where the material contained in this excerpt originally appeared.*

Early in May, Steve Horn returns from Florida, muttering about bad weather in the Sunshine State, various delays, and a recalcitrant child actor, and asks the Ayer people to come by for a meeting at five in the afternoon. Once again, the group assembles in Horn's basement conference room, whose oak table is once again laden with Perrier, soft drinks, fruit, and cheese. Horn, with his gray silk scarf around his neck, sits at the head of the table, eating grapes. Linda, as usual, is on his left, with a large accordion folder beside her that contains the files on various shooting locations: the files are ordinary manila folders whose inside surfaces are covered with Polaroid snapshots of locations—mainly interiors—with numerical information penciled in about light and exposure angles.

At the moment, a suburban-house folder is being passed around for consideration as one of the locations for the yoga vignette.

Steve says: "I like this house. It's a little upscale, but it photographs very well."

Gaston says: "We could do the white yoga here."

Linda says: "Wouldn't the black yoga be better?"

Jerry says: "I'm not sure it reads black."

Steve says: "Don't worry. We can fix the downstairs room like a black girl's apartment, whatever that is. You know, give it a condominium look."

Gaston is meanwhile looking through another house folder. "There's a nicer house here," he says.

Linda says: "That's the Zacharia house. We've used that a lot. I know it almost as well as I know my own house."

Jerry says: "We have a black scene, but I don't know if this looks like a black house, either."

Steve says: "Let's take a look. I like this house, too. This room here has a very nice quality of light."

Gaston says: "I think we could do the white yoga here."

Jerry says: "It's a good house, but it's awfully up-scale."

Steve says: "You know what I could do in this house? I could do the kid tap dancing."

Linda says: "I thought we were going to do the tap dancing in the Lawrence house."

Steve says: "Well, that's a good one, too, but I like this one better. It says tap dancing to me."

Gaston and Jerry have been looking at still another folder, and now they pass it to Linda.

Linda says: "I know *this* house as well as I know my own house."

Steve says: "You say that about every house."

Linda says: "That's not true. Just this one and maybe a couple of others. This one is a real dirty, low-down house, but we can make it look young again."

Steve says: "We could put some frills around, right?"

Linda says: "We could clean it up."

Jerry says: "Where do we need a young house?"

Steve says: "I'd like a young house for the toothless kid, but I don't think this is it."

Gaston passes him another folder. "What about this for white yoga?"

Steve looks at it in silence for a moment. Then: "You know, I could make it rain there."

"I don't think we're utilizing rain."

"Visually, it's one of the best things. We could do something very nice in soft focus."

Steve says: "But I can utilize it here. I love rain."

Jerry says: "Not too soft."

Steve says: "I mean normal soft focus."

Linda says: "You don't want to make it look too period."

Steve says: "I wasn't talking about period, I was talking about soft focus. Normal soft focus, nothing special."

Gaston says: "Maybe we should talk about the backstage vignette."

Steve says: "Let's use the Beacon Theatre."

Linda says: "I think we used it on the Rhonda Fleming shot."

Alayne produces a folder from a pile in front of her and gives it to Steve.

Steve opens it and examines the pictures with an increasingly perplexed expression. "Hell, this isn't the Beacon, this is the Lotos Club."

Linda says: "I like the Lotos Club. Remember? We used it for Paine Webber."

Steve says: "But it's not a theater."

Now Alayne hands him the Beacon folder and takes back the Lotos Club.

"Here we are," he says. "This is old-timey as hell."

Jerry says: "Maybe we should go with it."

Linda says: "We were hoping for the City Center, but there's a ballet there."

Gaston says: "Does it bother you to go back to the same location?"

Steve says: "Nobody knows if you go back. Besides, I hardly ever shoot wide angle."

Now the group turns to a discussion of race-track locations for the jockey vignette. In the course of the past ten days, Ray Guarino, Steve Horn's location scout, has been checking on race tracks within a hundred miles of New York and has brought back at least fifty different Polaroid views. But as soon as Jerry and Gaston start looking at them it is apparent that something is wrong.

Jerry says: "The problem I'm having with these locations is that they don't say race track to me, they say garage."

Ray says: "I Polaroided every track and paddock in the area."

Steve says: "I agree about this bunch, but I think we could use that area out at Roosevelt Raceway."

Gaston says: "If this is Roosevelt I'm looking at, it has an awful lot of concrete. It looks like a car-racing place."

Steve says: "A while ago, we shot a race-track thing for 7Up in California. We brought in all sorts of trees and grass to make it look right."

Jerry says: "I don't see how we can make Roosevelt look right."

Gaston says: "I'd say we need more greenery, less garage."

Ray says: "I think they're all like that. I checked out every track in the area."

Steve says: "Maybe we should check farther away. Maybe we should even cheat a little—you know, go for the greenery and prop the track effect."

Finally, there is a discussion of locations for the rodeo vignette, which Ray has been scouting in what might seem unlikely areas of New Jersey and Pennsylvania. The generally favored location is in New Jersey, but it apparently presents a difficulty.

Gaston says: "I think we have a phone problem."

Steve says: "What kind of a phone problem?"

Gaston says: "Well, this is a phone-company ad. We have to have a phone there somewhere."

Steve says: "Well, we can just put one in, like we do everywhere else."

Linda says: "The point is, you can't just put a phone *anywhere* in a rodeo corral."

Steve says: "Well, I didn't mean we'd put it *anywhere*. We could stick a phone on one of the posts."

Linda says: "What's a phone doing on a post?"

Jerry says: I don't think the phone problem is going to be so hard to solve. I think our main problem is getting a place that says rodeo."

Steve says: "Yes, we have to be careful it doesn't say farm."

Jerry says: "Something rustic and rundown."

Steve says: "Definitely not farm."

Gaston says: "So where do we put the phone?"

Jerry says: "The phone problem isn't major. Trust me."

Questions:

1. What are the advertisers' main concerns, as they are suggested in Arlen's piece?

2. Name a few of the locations where the advertisers plan to film the ads. What are your schemas regarding these types of places? How are the advertisers planning to create their commercials in such a way as to play on those schemas? Why might they want to?

3. Notice, particularly, the discussion about "black yoga" and "white yoga." Here the production team is attempting to find locations to

shoot their commercial that "read" Black or White. What sorts of con-cerns and opinions do they express on the matter? Keeping in mind that this conversation took place approximately twenty years ago, do you find that those types of concerns have changed in today's advertis-ing? Do advertisers today still strive to make a location "read" Black or White (or Asian, Latino, etc.)? If so, how do they do that today?

ARE YOU SELLING TO ME?

Bernice Kanner

> *Bernice Kanner writes on marketing issues for* Working Woman *magazine, where this article originally appeared. In it, Kanner comments on some of the changes in strategies of advertising to a multicultural audience that have taken place over the past decade.*

In a memorable McDonald's commercial, a father prods his baby to say "daddy." Nothing works until the resourceful dad shakes a bag of McDonald's fries before the happy toddler, who obliges by cheerfully uttering "papa." Americans liked the TV spot. Hispanics got it: In Spanish, the word for *dad* and *fries* is the same.

Either way, the ad was a hit. Anglos "responded to the magic of the relationship," says Luis Messianu, chief creative officer at del Rivero Messianu Advertising in Coral Gables, Florida, which created the spot. "Hispanics can tell it was conceived by one of their own." The McDonald's ad and others like it, including the hot "¡Yo quiero Taco Bell!" campaign, featuring a Spanish-speaking Chihuahua, are part of a new wave in multicultural marketing. They develop a strong connection with ethnic consumers by their use of familiar words and images.

Time was, if you were a marketer looking to grab a piece of the ethnic pie, you more than likely tried to reach minority consumers simply by translating English-language commercials verbatim or by substituting African-American, Hispanic, or Asian actors for whites in mainstream scripts. Sometimes the method worked, but it also produced some spectacular flops. Perhaps the most famous foreign-language gaffe was committed by the marketers of the Chevrolet Nova—the car's name literally means "doesn't go" in Spanish. More recently, Frank Perdue's "It takes a tough man to make a tender chicken" slogan became a mandate for a "hard," or sexually excited, man in Spanish, says Lisa Skriloff, president of Multicultural Marketing Resources in New York. When translated into Chinese, Pepsi's "Come alive" ads declared, "Wake up your dead ancestors." And KFC's "Finger-lickin' good" slogan turned into "Eat your fingers off."

Money Talks

Marketers are much more careful these days about avoiding embarrassing slip-ups. The incentive has been a flurry of new data. Demographics alone point to the perils of ignoring ethnic markets: According to Census Bureau data released last fall, there are 34.5 million African-Americans, who represent 12.7 percent of the U.S. population, and 30.7 million Hispanics, who represent 11.3 percent. By 2005, the bureau predicts, those numbers will mushroom to more than 36 million in each group. Add in Asian-Americans, and the ethnic trio currently makes up more than a quarter of the U.S. population.

It is estimated that minorities will grow to nearly one-third of the population by 2010 and almost one-half by 2050, says Vanguard Communications, a New York-based agency that specializes in multicultural marketing. In key markets such as New

York, Miami, and Los Angeles, they're already more than half. A study by ad agency Stedman Graham & Partners pegs the buying power of the African-American market at $450 billion and the Latino market at $380 billion, a 150 percent increase since 1973. A study by the University of Georgia's Selig Center for Economic Growth predicts that black purchasing power will reach $533 billion in 1999, a 73 percent jump from $308 billion in 1990. Compare that with a forecast increase of 57 percent for Americans overall. With stats like these, mainstream marketers are falling all over themselves to reach ethnic consumers. "Mature brands are looking for new audiences to grow their market shares," says Esther Novak, the Peruvian-born president of Vanguard Communications. And for the first time, they're getting solid support from the companies that track consumer spending. Notes Novak, "ACNielsen and Information Resources, which used to just track just general market media, have substantiated the buying clout of these markets." Thanks to the newly available data on ethnic spending habits and media outlets, she adds, "strategies and tactics are becoming much more sophisticated."

Fewer Faux Pas

Advertisers are showing their multicultural marketing know-how in different ways. While some are taking the cross-cultural route, with ads that appeal to both ethnic groups and mainstream consumers (the McDonald's "papa" ad is a good example), others are hypertargeting ethnic markets. Instead of treating the Latino audience as one homogenous group, for example, advertisers are dexterously slicing the market into niches based on differences in language, sex, religion, age, and country of origin. In 1997, various TV commercials for Budweiser featured a Spaniard, a Puerto Rican, an Argentinean, a Cuban, and a Mexican.

New York-based Kang & Lee Advertising has created ads for AT&T that target particular Asian audiences. To reach Vietnamese-American consumers unable to visit their homeland, the agency used nostalgic images of instruments, games, and festivities in its ads. To address Japanese customers stationed in the U.S. for several years, it used holiday reminders to encourage calls home, instead of written greetings.

Some ads are reaching out to certain groups by reflecting cultural norms. For Asians, *family* connotes not just parents and children but also grandparents, aunts, and uncles. So ads aimed at this group often teem with multiple generations, says Bill Imada, chief executive officer of Imada Wong Communications Group, an ethnic marketing firm based in Los Angeles.

Fewer advertisers are making the previously common mistake of using words and images that turn off the very consumers they're supposed to entice. The image of a man in a sombrero snoozing under a tree may have been acceptable to most Anglos, but Mexican-Americans took umbrage when an AT&T ad featured this scene, which could be interpreted as portraying the man as lazy. Likewise, although the promise of "four times the savings" might be a carrot for the general public, the Cantonese word for *four* sounds like the word for *death*, warns Eliot Kang of Kang & Lee Advertising.

Marketers are also reaching out with campaigns that put products directly into the hands of targeted consumers. Revlon distributes free baskets of hair products at gospel conventions and is a major sponsor of the Stellar Awards, the Grammys of black gospel. Coors Brewing Co. has sponsored a concert tour and sweepstakes in honor of Black Music Month.

Minorities can't always be reached via mainstream media. Doug Alligood, senior vice president of special markets at BBDO Worldwide, has tracked black TV viewing habits for 11 years and found that, when it comes to TV, American blacks and whites may as well be living on separate planets. "None of the top 10 network shows among black households overlap with the top 10 among total U.S. households this year," says Alligood. "The most popular shows for blacks weren't even among the 90 most popular shows for all households." This split continues an 11-year trend.

Fortunately, finding multicultural media outlets has never been easier. There's been a virtual explosion in minority media, from cable TV channels to ethnic Yellow Pages. Abbott Wool Media Marketing puts the current number of print and TV media outlets devoted to blacks at 1,479; Hispanics, 1,174; and Asian-Americans, 608.

To respond to this marketing juggernaut, the American Association of Advertising Agencies launched the Hispanic Advertising Committee in 1997 and recently kicked off the first O'Toole Multicultural Advertising Award competition. The Association of National Advertisers created the Multicultural Marketing Committee, and the Advertising Research Foundation formed the Ethnic Research Council. Individual ad agencies are homing in on multicultural consumers by setting up special units or strategic alliances with minority-owned firms. Chicago-based Leo Burnett recently established Vigilante, a black-run agency, to reach inner-city audiences. True North Communications, the parent of Foote, Cone & Belding Worldwide and Bozell Worldwide, launched a multicultural marketing unit called New America Strategies Group.

"The decade of multicultural marketing was predicted to be the '80s, but it turned out to be the '90s," says Novak. "There were misperceptions about these markets. But that barrier has finally broken down."

Questions:

1. What sorts of changes does Kanner point to as evidence that advertisrs are more aware of their multicultural audience?

2. Do you agree with Kanner's findings? Why or why not? (Point to other specific examples that support your opinion.)

3. What do you think of advertisers' attempts to reflect a more diverse public? Does it indicate a new awareness and acceptance that will hopefully become part of all consumers' consciousness? Or do you find it to be exploitative, with little hope that more representation in commercials will have a positive impact on, for example, US race relations?

BEAUTY . . . AND THE BEAST OF ADVERTISING

Jean Kilbourne

The following article originally appeared as part of a series on images of women and men in the media printed in Media & Values *in 1989. Its author, Jean Kilbourne, is an award-winning filmmaker and lecturer, whose work often focuses on advertising and gender stereotypes in the media.*

"You're a Halston woman from the very beginning," the advertisement proclaims. The model stares provocatively at the viewer, her long blonde hair waving around her face, her bare chest partially covered by two curved bottles that give the illusion of breasts and a cleavage.

The average American is accustomed to blue-eyed blondes seductively touting a variety of products. In this case, however, the blonde is about five years old.

Advertising is an over $100 billion a year industry and affects all of us throughout our lives. We are each exposed to over 2,000 ads a day, constituting perhaps the most powerful educational force in society. The average adult will spend one and one-half years of his/her life watching television commercials. But the ads sell a great deal more than products. They sell values, images and concepts of success and worth, love and sexuality, popularity and normalcy. They tell us who we are and who we should be. Sometimes they sell addictions.

Advertising's foundation and economic lifeblood is the mass media, and the primary purpose of the mass media is to deliver an audience to advertisers, just as the primary purpose of television programs is to deliver an audience for commercials.

Adolescents are particularly vulnerable, however, because they are new and inexperienced consumers and are the prime targets of many advertisements. They are in the process of learning their values and roles and developing their self-concepts. Most teenagers are sensitive to peer pressure and find it difficult to resist or even question the dominant cultural messages perpetuated and reinforced by the media. Mass communication has made possible a kind of nationally distributed peer pressure that erodes private and individual values and standards.

But what does society, and especially teenagers, learn from the advertising messages that proliferate in the mass media? On the most obvious level they learn the stereotypes. Advertising creates a mythical, WASP-oriented world in which no one is ever ugly, overweight, poor, struggling or disabled either physically or mentally (unless you count the housewives who talk to little men in toilet bowls, animated germs in drains or muscle-bound giants clad in white clothing). And it is a world in which people talk only about products.

Housewives or Sex Objects

The aspect of advertising most in need of analysis and change is the portrayal of women. Scientific studies and the most casual viewing yield the same conclusion: Women are shown almost exclusively as housewives or sex objects.

The housewife, pathologically obsessed by cleanliness and lemonfresh scents, debates cleaning products with herself and worries about her husband's "ring around the collar."

The sex object is a mannequin, a shell. Conventional beauty is her only attribute. She has no lines or wrinkles (which would indicate she had the bad taste and poor judgment to grow older), no scars or blemishes—indeed, she has no pores. She is thin, generally tall and long-legged, and, above all, she is young. All "beautiful" women in advertisements (including minority women), regardless of product or audience, conform to this norm. Women are constantly exhorted to emulate this ideal, to feel ashamed and guilty if they fail, and to feel that their desirability and lovability are contingent upon physical perfection.

Creating Artificiality

The image is artificial and can only be achieved artificially (even the "natural look" requires much preparation and expense). Beauty is something that comes from without; more than one million dollars is spent every hour on cosmetics. Desperate to conform to an ideal and impossible standard, many women go to great lengths to manipulate and change their faces and bodies. A woman is conditioned to view her face as a mask and her body as an object, as *things* separate from and more important than her real self, constantly in need of alteration, improvement, and disguise. She is made to feel dissatisfied with and ashamed of herself, whether she tries to achieve "the look" or not. Objectified constantly by others, she learns to objectify herself. (It is interesting to note that one in five college-age women has an eating disorder.)

"When *Glamour* magazine surveyed its readers in 1984, 75 percent felt too heavy and only 15 percent felt just right. Nearly half of those who were actually underweight reported feeling too fat and wanting to diet. Among a sample of college women, 40 percent felt overweight when only 12 percent actually were too heavy," according to Rita Freedman in her book *Beauty Bound.*

There is evidence that this preoccupation with weight begins at ever-earlier ages for women. According to a recent article in *New Age Journal,* "even grade-school girls are succumbing to sticklike standards of beauty enforced by a relentless parade of waspwaisted fashion models, movie stars and pop idols." A study by a University of California professor showed that nearly 80 percent of fourth-grade girls in the Bay Area are watching their weight.

A recent *Wall Street Journal* survey of students in four Chicago-area schools found that more than half the fourth-grade girls were dieting and three-quarters felt they were overweight. One student said, "We don't expect boys to be that handsome. We take them as they are." Another added, "But boys expect girls to be perfect and beautiful. And skinny."

Dr. Steven Levenkron, author of *The Best Little Girl in the World,* the story of an anorexic, says his blood pressure soars every time he opens a magazine and finds an ad for women's fashions. "If I had my way," he said, "every one of them would have to carry a line saying, 'Caution: This model may be hazardous to your health.'"

Women are also dismembered in commercials, their bodies separated into parts in need of change or improvement. If a woman has "acceptable" breasts, then she must also be sure that her legs are worth watching, her hips slim, her feet sexy, and that her buttocks look nude under her clothes ("like I'm not wearin' nothin'"). This image is difficult and costly to achieve and impossible to maintain (unless you buy the product)—no one is flawless and everyone ages. Growing older is the great taboo. Women are encouraged to remain little girls ("because innocence is sexier than you think"), to be passive and dependent, never to mature. The contradictory message— "sensual, but not too far from innocence"—places women in a double bind; somehow we are supposed to be both sexy and virginal, experienced and naive, seductive and chaste. The disparagement of maturity is, of course, insulting and frustrating to adult women, and the implication that little girls are seductive is dangerous to real children.

Influencing Sexual Attitudes

Young people also learn a great deal about sexual attitudes from the media and from advertising in particular. Advertising's approach to sex is pornographic; it reduces people to objects and de-emphasizes human contact and individuality. This reduction of sexuality to a dirty joke and of people to object is the real obscenity of the culture. Although the sexual sell, overt and subliminal, is at a fevered pitch in most commercials, there is at the same time a notable absence of sex as an important and profound human activity.

There have been some changes in the images of women. Indeed, a "new woman" has emerged in commercials in recent years. She is generally presented as super-woman, who manages to do all the work at home and on the job (with the help of a product, of course, not of her husband or children or friends), or as the liberated woman, who owes her independence and self-esteem to the products she uses. These new images do not represent any real progress but rather create a myth of progress, an illusion that reduces complex sociopolitical problems to mundane personal ones.

Advertising images do not cause these problems, but they contribute to them by creating a climate in which the marketing of women's bodies—the sexual sell and dismemberment, distorted body image ideal and children as sex objects—is seen as acceptable.

This is the real tragedy, that many women internalize these stereotypes and learn their "limitations," thus establishing a self-fulfilling prophecy. If one accepts these mythical and degrading images, to some extent one actualizes them. By remaining unaware of the profound seriousness of the ubiquitous influence, the redundant message and the subliminal impact of advertisements, we ignore one of the most powerful "educational" forces in the culture—one that greatly affects our self-images, our ability to relate to each other, and effectively destroys any awareness and action that might help to change that climate.

Questions:

1. Who is the "new woman," and what does Kilbourne find to be so offensive about her? Do you agree?

2. How significant do you believe media images are to our perceptions of ourselves?

3. How successful are ads that attempt to sell products by portraying sexist images of women? Can you name a few of these ads? How do these ads attempt to persuade their audience to buy the advertised product? Who is the audience for each ad? Do any of the sexist ads target women?

4. Are there ads that portray men in a negative, sexist light? How do those ads function, and for whom are they being produced?

WHY ARE YOU BUYING YOUR FOOD FROM A TOBACCO COMPANY?

Did you know that every product pictured here is owned by Philip Morris, the world's largest cigarette company? Chances are you've been helping to promote Marlboro cigarettes without even knowing it. Now is your opportunity to withdraw that support by personally boycotting these products. It's sort of like giving money to a health organization that is working to find a cure for cancer — but in this case, you're taking money from a corporation that causes it. So next time you're at the supermarket — try it. You'll like it.

Introducing Philip Morris' newest partner — Starbucks Coffee. On September 28, 1998 Kraft Foods and Starbucks Coffee announced a licensing agreement, "to accelerate growth of the Starbucks brand into the grocery channel across the United States — the first phase of a broader domestic and global partnership."

Reproduce this ad in your publication. Call 1-800-663-1243.

This advertisement appeared in *Adbusters,* a magazine which bills itself as a "Journal of the Mental Environment." Articles in this publication investigate the advertising industry and deconstruct ads, revealing trends such as race and gender bias within them.

Background Music.

Romantic Whispers.

Flirtatious Laughter.

Machine Gun Fire.

NPR®

takes you there.

Listen to National Public Radio's® *All Things Considered*® and let us take you from the everyday to the unreal. From the politically astute to the criminally insane. Stay tuned to NPR and discover news that intrigues, music that enchants and talk that challenges. Go to where the sound shapes the story. And change the way you experience everything.

WETA
FM 90.9

The Nation's Station,
The Community's Voice

www.weta.org

Craig Cutler 1997

The above ad was included in the "Sunday Magazine" section of *The Washington Post.*

This is a copy of a promotional brochure which invites men to participate in the program it describes.

Who is the New Warrior?

1 MEN HAVE BEEN WARRIORS since the beginning of time and every man has his warrior side. But social forces pressure many to repress this part of themselves. They unconsciously substitute a distorted shadow for the healthy warrior energy so essential to sustaining individual and communal balance.

2 The New Warrior is a man who has confronted this destructive "shadow" form and has achieved hard-won ownership of the highly focused, aggressive energy that empowers and shapes the inner masculine self. Sustained by this new energy, the New Warrior is at once tough and loving, wild and gentle, fierce and tolerant. He lives passionately and compassionately, because he has learned to live his mission with integrity, and without apology.

What happens in the training?

3 THE NEW WARRIOR TRAINING ADVENTURE is a process of initiation and self-examination that is crucial to the development of a healthy and mature male self. It is the "hero's journey" of classical literature and myth—the process of moving away from the comforting embrace of the mother's feminine energy and safely into the masculine kingdom. It is a journey of the soul during which men confront their dependence on women, their mistrust of other men and their need to be special.

> "The truth is, I was afraid of this training. Even though I've written about men and worked with men for many years, the fact is—as I discovered on the Weekend—I didn't really trust men. I'm glad I overcame my fear. This was the most powerful training I've ever done, and the changes it started in me have been both deep and positive."
>
> Mark Gerzon, author of "A Choice of Heroes"

Who runs the training?

4 THE NEW WARRIOR NETWORK, a national not-for-profit corporation, has assembled a highly motivated, experienced staff to lead the training programs. Most staff members are volunteers, and because all have experienced the initiation process themselves, they have a compelling sense of male initiation and authentic self-examination.

5 In the final analysis, however, you run your own training through the responses and decisions you make along your journey. The staff serve as your guides and mentors, but you choose your own level of commitment, and you decide how far you will explore the inner terrain of your life, to discover the treasures and obstacles buried within your self.

How do I register?

6 YOU WILL FIND AN ENROLLMENT FORM enclosed with this brochure. Only you can decide if you are ready to participate in the New Warrior Training Adventure. Because training sessions are booked far in advance, it may take some time before you are admitted.

Who comes to the training?

7 DURING YOUR TRAINING you will stand shoulder to shoulder with an immensely rich mix of masculinity, with occupations and ages as wide as masculinity itself. Whether they're corporate executives or high school students, all come to share a common understanding that their lives as men can be empowered with greater focus and direction, and that this personal initiation into manhood is crucial to their full development as men.

Am I ready?

8 WE DO NOT RECOMMEND this training for every man. We urge you not to apply to this program without serious forethought, and not to enroll simply at the urging of a spouse or friend.

9 To participate in this training, you must be in reasonably good physical condition and willing to face the prospect of transformative change in your life. You must be highly committed to your life, and ready to participate fully in all training activities, many of which encourage you to take a hard look at yourself, your deepest fears, your wounds from the past, and the specific ways in which your life is not working for you. We choose to work only with men who are ready and willing to do this initiatory work with us.

What happens after the training?

10 SEVERAL DAYS AFTER you have completed your initiation into manhood, you are welcomed back into the community of your families, friends and fellow Warriors at a graduation ceremony. There, you will join a small voluntary team called an Integration Group, which will help you integrate the training into your life. These Integration Groups have proven as valuable as the training itself, so we urge each graduate to join one.

What will I get out of this?

"Previous cultures throughout history always intended authentic masculine initiation. But their vision and their cultural context of the world was necessarily limited. Since the first earthrise photograph from outer space, we have entered a new mythological era. For the first time in human history, we have before us the possibility of authentic masculine initiation—an initiation into the global brotherhood."

Dr. Robert Moore, Coauthor of "King, Warrior, Magician, Lover"

"New Warrior training is an authentic initiation into the cauldron of mature masculinity. I recommend it highly to deeply committed men. The NW staff are loving, generous, and deep-intentioned men who will evoke the very best within you."

Forrest Craver, Convener of the North American Confederation of Men's Councils

"The New Warrior Training Adventure is the finest experience I've ever had in all my years of men's work. I support it one hundred percent, and I know in my heart that it is critical to our lives, our longevity, our brotherhood, and our health."

Asa Baber, Men's Columnist for *Playboy* magazine

"In 1983, I wrote The Secrets that Men Keep. After experiencing the New Warrior Training I'm rewriting that book. It's the most important men's work occurring in the U.S., and perhaps in the world, today."

Dr. Ken Druck, psychologist, consultant, author

New Warrior Training Center, Director, Phone & Address

For training dates, write or call a center near you.

Tuition—$550 covers complete training, including room and board.

Deposit—$100 (non-refundable) reserves your space. Payment plans and some scholarships are available. Make checks payable, and clip and mail the Enrollment Form below, to the Training Center of your choice.

Visa and Mastercard accepted at most Centers.

This ad appeared in *Girlfriends,* a nationally-circulated magazine dedicated to lesbian interests including entertainment, politics and culture.

Subaru cars and sport utility vehicles come in all shapes and sizes. But one thing doesn't change. Each one features our popular full-time All-Wheel Drive for maximum traction and performance. From the comfort and versatility of the new Forester, to the ruggedness of the Outback, to the get-up-and-go of the 2.5 GT, we think you'll find the right match for your lifestyle. To test drive one of our family of cars, stop by your nearest Subaru dealer, call **1-800-WANT-AWD** or visit our website at **www.subaru.com**.

Subaru supports the community as the proud founding sponsor of the Rainbow Endowment. The **Rainbow** benefits community health, civil rights and cultural interests. For more information or to apply, call 1-800-99-RAINBOW.

SUBARU

The Beauty of All-Wheel Drive.

This ad for Adelphi University has appeared in numerous magazines.

HARVARD.
THE ADELPHI
OF
MASSACHUSETTS.

Believe it or not, Harvard actually lives up to this
reputation.

Its academic mission is every bit as lofty as
Adelphi's: to develop the whole man and the whole
woman; to expose students to liberal learning, the
2500-year tradition of Western Civilization; to prepare
you for life, not just to occupy your mind for the
years between high school and post-pubescence.

Its location in Cambridge, just across the river
from Boston, may not promise the Museum of
Modern Art, Lincoln Center, Broadway, or the United
Nations. But it holds its own against Adelphi's cam-
pus, which is less than an hour from New York City.

And don't overlook Harvard's extracurriculars:
its century-old clubs and organizations are the stuff
of legend, along the lines of the Adelphi athletic
department. No less than three Adelphi Panther
teams currently hold rankings in the national
top ten.

For more information about Harvard, the
Adelphi of Massachusetts, call (617) 495-1551.

For a brochure and video about Adelphi, the
Adelphi of New York, call (516) 663-1100. You'll also
receive a free "Harvard, the Adelphi of Massachusetts" t-shirt. But hurry. As they say in advertising,
supplies are limited.

ADELPHI UNIVERSITY

Garden City, New York 11530. (516) 663-1100. For application materials and a video, write or call.

Submission Credits

UNIT ONE: INTRODUCTION TO RHETORIC

I. What Is Rhetoric?
    Genius at Work: How to Argue
        Diane Cyr
            SUBMITTED BY KEELY MCCARTHY

    Ain't I a Woman?
        Sojourner Truth
            SUBMITTED BY MATTHEW ELLIOT

    Nobody Mean More to Me Than You and the Future Life of Willie Jordan
        June Jordan
            SUBMITTED BY ADRIANNE JOHNSTON DIMARCO

II. Audience and Schema
    NYU Application Essay
        "Hugh Gallagher"
            SUBMITTED BY ALLISON BROVEY WARNER

    Mega Buys
        Franklin Saige
            SUBMITTED BY TRICIA SLUSSER

    All Ivana All the Time
        Peter Carlson
            SUBMITTED BY PATRICIA A. LISSNER

    Class Action
        Dave Barry
            SUBMITTED BY MATTHEW ELLIOT

Henry V IV.iii. 18–67
William Shakespeare
SUBMITTED BY NELS PEARSON

Excerpt from "Patton"
SUBMITTED BY STEPHEN E. SEVERN

Letter from Birmingham Jail
Martin Luther King, Jr.
SUBMITTED BY DINA L. LONGHITANO AND KATE DOBSON

III. Paired Selections for Rhetorical Analysis
They Can Be a Couple, But Not Married
Jeff Jacoby
SUBMITTED BY KEELY MCCARTHY

Gay "Marriage" Obfuscation
Thomas Sowell
SUBMITTED BY KEELY MCCARTHY

Should Same-Sex Couples Be Permitted to Marry?
Anna Quindlen
SUBMITTED BY DINA L. LONGHITANO

Why I Changed My Mind
Sidney Callahan
SUBMITTED BY DINA L. LONGHITANO

Ice-T: Is the Issue Social Responsibility...
Michael Kinsley
SUBMITTED BY DINA L. LONGHITANO AND ADRIANNE JOHNSTON DIMARCO

. . . Or Is It Creative Freedom?
Barbara Ehrenreich
SUBMITTED BY DINA L. LONGHITANO AND ADRIANNE JOHNSTON DIMARCO

IV. Longer Pairs for Rhetorical Analysis
Making the Grade
Kurt Wiesenfeld
SUBMITTED BY ADRIANNE JOHNSTON DIMARCO

A Liberating Curriculum
Roberta F. Borkat
SUBMITTED BY ADRIANNE JOHNSTON DIMARCO

UNIT THREE: MAPPING A DEBATE

I. Overview Articles

II. Identifying Positions in Opinion Pieces

UNIT FIVE: THE AFFIRMATIVE ARGUMENT